The Reasonable Person

Jeutner argues that the reasonable person is, at heart, an empathetic perspective-taking device, by tracing the standard of the reasonable person across time, legal fields and countries. Beginning with a review of imaginary legal figures in the legal systems of ancient Egypt, Greece and Rome, the book explains why the common law's reasonable person emerged amid British industrialisation under the influence of Scottish Enlightenment thinking. Following the figure into colonial courts, onto battlefields and into self-driving cars, the book contends that the reasonable person invites judges, jury members, and lawyers to take another person's perspective when assessing their own or another person's conduct. The perspective of another is taken by means of empathy, by feeling what others might feel in a particular situation. Thus construed, the figure of the reasonable person can help us make more accurate judgments in a diverse world.

Valentin Jeutner is Associate Professor at the Faculty of Law, Lund University and Senior Retained Lecturer, Pembroke College, Oxford. He has also been admitted to the bar of New York State. Jeutner encountered the reasonable person when studying law at Oxford and Cambridge, United Kingdom and Georgetown, United States. Previous publications include *Irresolvable Norm Conflicts in International Law* (2017) and *[L]ex machina* (2020).

Law in Context

Since 1970, the Law in Context series has been at the forefront of a movement to broaden the study of law. The series is a vehicle for the publication of innovative monographs and texts that treat law and legal phenomena critically in their cultural, social, political, technological, environmental and economic contexts. A contextual approach involves treating legal subjects broadly, using materials from other humanities and social sciences, and from any other discipline that helps to explain the operation in practice of the particular legal field or legal phenomena under investigation. It is intended that this orientation is at once more stimulating and more revealing than the bare exposition of legal rules. The series includes original research monographs, coursebooks and textbooks that foreground contextual approaches and methods. The series includes and welcomes books on the study of law in all its contexts, including domestic legal systems, European and international law, transnational and global legal processes, and comparative law.

Books in the Series

Acosta: *The National versus the Foreigner in South America: 200 Years of Migration and Citizenship Law*
Alaattinoğlu: *Grievance Formation, Rights and Remedies*
Ali: *Modern Challenges to Islamic Law*
Alyagon Darr: *Plausible Crime Stories: The Legal History of Sexual Offences in Mandate Palestine*
Anderson, Schum & Twining: *Analysis of Evidence, 2nd Edition*
Ashworth: *Sentencing and Criminal Justice, 6th Edition*
Barton & Douglas: *Law and Parenthood*
Baxi, McCrudden & Paliwala: *Law's Ethical, Global and Theoretical Contexts: Essays in Honour of William Twining*
Beecher-Monas: *Evaluating Scientific Evidence: An Interdisciplinary Framework for Intellectual Due Process*
Bell: *French Legal Cultures*
Bercusson: *European Labour Law, 2nd Edition*

Birkinshaw: *European Public Law*
Birkinshaw: *Freedom of Information: The Law, the Practice and the Ideal, 4th Edition*
Blick: *Electrified Democracy: The Internet and the United Kingdom Parliament in History*
Broderick & Ferri: *International and European Disability Law and Policy: Text, Cases and Materials*
Brownsword & Goodwin: *Law and the Technologies of the Twenty-First Century: Text and Materials*
Cane & Goudkamp: *Atiyah's Accidents, Compensation and the Law, 9th Edition*
Clarke: *Principles of Property Law*
Clarke & Kohler: *Property Law: Commentary and Materials*
Collins: *The Law of Contract, 4th Edition*
Collins, Ewing & McColgan: *Labour Law, 2nd Edition*
Cowan: *Housing Law and Policy*
Cranston: *Making Commercial Law Through Practice 1830–1970*
Cranston: *Legal Foundations of the Welfare State*
Darian-Smith: *Laws and Societies in Global Contexts: Contemporary Approaches*
Dauvergne: *Making People Illegal: What Globalisation Means for Immigration and Law*
David: *Kinship, Law and Politics: An Anatomy of Belonging*
Davies: *Perspectives on Labour Law, 2nd Edition*
Dembour: *Who Believes in Human Rights?: Reflections on the European Convention*
de Sousa Santos: *Toward a New Legal Common Sense: Law, Globalization, and Emancipation*
Diduck: *Law's Families*
Douglas-Scott: *Brexit, Union, and Disunion: The Evolution of British Constitutional Unsettlement*
Dowdle: *Transnational Law: A Framework for Analysis*
Dupret: *Positive Law from the Muslim World: Jurisprudence, History, Practices*
Emon: *Jurisdictional Exceptionalisms: Islamic Law, International Law, and Parental Child Abduction*
Estella: *Legal Foundations of EU Economic Governance*
Fortin: *Children's Rights and the Developing Law, 3rd Edition*
Garnsey: *The Justice of Visual Art: Creative State-Building in Times of Political Transition*
Garton, Probert & Bean: *Moffat's Trusts Law: Text and Materials, 7th Edition*
Ghai & Woodman: *Practising Self-Government: A Comparative Study of Autonomous Regions*
Glover-Thomas: *Reconstructing Mental Health Law and Policy*
Gobert & Punch: *Rethinking Corporate Crime*
Goldman: *Globalisation and the Western Legal Tradition: Recurring Patterns of Law and Authority*
Haack: *Evidence Matters: Science, Proof, and Truth in the Law*
Harlow & Rawlings: *Law and Administration, 4th Edition*
Harris: *An Introduction to Law, 8th Edition*
Harris, Campbell & Halson: *Remedies in Contract and Tort, 2nd Edition*
Harvey: *Seeking Asylum in the UK: Problems and Prospects*
Herring: *Law and the Relational Self*
Hervey & McHale: *European Union Health Law: Themes and Implications*

Hervey & McHale: *Health Law and the European Union*
Holder & Lee: *Environmental Protection, Law and Policy: Text and Materials, 2nd Edition*
Jackson & Summers: *The Internationalisation of Criminal Evidence: Beyond the Common Law and Civil Law Traditions*
Kostakopoulou: *The Future Governance of Citizenship*
Kreiczer-Levy: *Destabilized Property: Property Law in the Sharing Economy*
Kubal: *Immigration and Refugee Law in Russia: Socio-Legal Perspectives*
Lewis: *Choice and the Legal Order: Rising above Politics*
Likosky: *Law, Infrastructure and Human Rights*
Likosky: *Transnational Legal Processes: Globalisation and Power Disparities*
Lixinski: *Legalized Identities: Cultural Heritage Law and the Shaping of Transitional Justice*
Loughnan: *Self, Others and the State: Relations of Criminal Responsibility*
Lunney: *A History of Australian Tort Law 1901-1945: England's Obedient Servant?*
Maughan & Webb: *Lawyering Skills and the Legal Process, 2nd Edition*
McGaughey: *Principles of Enterprise Law*
McGlynn: *Families and the European Union: Law, Politics and Pluralism*
Mertens: *A Philosophical Introduction to Human Rights*
Miller: *An Introduction to German Law and Legal Culture: Text and Materials*
Moffat: *Trusts Law: Text and Materials*
Monti: *EC Competition Law*
Morgan: *Contract Law Minimalism: A Formalist Restatement of Commercial Contract Law*
Morgan & Yeung: *An Introduction to Law and Regulation: Text and Materials*
Nash: *British Islam and English Law: A Classical Pluralist Perspective Ng, Political Censorship in British Hong Kong: Freedom of Expression and the Law (1842–1997)*
Nicola &Davies: *EU Law Stories: Contextual and Critical Histories of European Jurisprudence*
Norrie: *Crime, Reason and History: A Critical Introduction to Criminal Law, 3rd Edition*
O'Dair: *Legal Ethics: Text and Materials*
Oliver: *Common Values and the Public–Private Divide*
Oliver & Drewry: *The Law and Parliament*
Palmer & Roberts: *Dispute Processes: ADR and the Primary Forms of Decision-Making, 1st Edition*
Palmer & Roberts: *Dispute Processes: ADR and the Primary Forms of Decision-Making, 3rd Edition*
Picciotto: *International Business Taxation*
Pieraccini: *Regulating the Sea: A Socio-Legal Analysis of English Marine Protected Areas*
Probert: *The Changing Legal Regulation of Cohabitation, 1600-2010: From Fornicators to Family, 1600-2010*
Radi: *Rules and Practices of International Investment Law and Arbitration*
Reed: *Internet Law: Text and Materials*
Richardson: *Law, Process and Custody*
Roberts & Palmer: *Dispute Processes: ADR and the Primary Forms of Decision-Making, 2nd Edition*
Rowbottom: *Democracy Distorted: Wealth, Influence and Democratic Politics*
Sauter: *Public Services in EU Law*

Scott & Black: *Cranston's Consumers and the Law*
Seneviratne: *Ombudsmen: Public Services and Administrative Justice*
Seppänen: *Ideological Conflict and the Rule of Law in Contemporary China: Useful Paradoxes*
Siems: *Comparative Law, 3rd Edition*
Stapleton: *Product Liability*
Stewart: *Gender, Law and Justice in a Global Market*
Tamanaha: *Law as a Means to an End: Threat to the Rule of Law*
Taylor: *Fortin's Children's Rights and the Developing Law, 4th Edition*
Tuori: *Properties of Law: Modern Law and After*
Turpin & Tomkins: *British Government and the Constitution: Text and Materials, 7th Edition*
Twining: *General Jurisprudence: Understanding Law from a Global Perspective*
Twining: *Globalisation and Legal Theory*
Twining: *Human Rights, Southern Voices: Francis Deng, Abdullahi An-Na'im, Yash Ghai and Upendra Baxi*
Twining: *Jurist in Context: A Memoir*
Twining: *Karl Llewellyn and the Realist Movement, 2nd Edition*
Twining: *Rethinking Evidence: Exploratory Essays, 2nd Edition*
Twining & Miers: *How to Do Things with Rules, 5th Edition*
Wan: *Film and Constitutional Controversy: Visualizing Hong Kong Identity in the Age of 'One Country, Two Systems'*
Ward: *A Critical Introduction to European Law, 3rd Edition*
Ward: *Law, Text, Terror*
Ward: *Shakespeare and Legal Imagination*
Watt: *The Making Sense of Politics, Media, and Law: Rhetorical Performance as Invention, Creation, Production*
Wells & Quick: *Lacey, Wells and Quick: Reconstructing Criminal Law: Text and Materials, 4th Edition*
Woodhead: *Caring for Cultural Heritage: An Integrated Approach to Legal and Ethical Initiatives in the United Kingdom*
Young: *Turpin and Tomkins' British Government and the Constitution: Text and Materials, 8th Edition*
Zander: *Cases and Materials on the English Legal System, 10th Edition*
Zander: *The Law-Making Process, 6th Edition*

International Journal of Law in Context: A Global Forum for Interdisciplinary Legal Studies

The *International Journal of Law in Context* is the companion journal to the Law in Context book series. It provides a forum for interdisciplinary legal studies and offers intellectual space for ground-breaking critical research. It publishes contextual work about law and its relationship with other disciplines including but not limited to science, literature, humanities, philosophy, sociology, psychology, ethics, history and geography. More information about the journal and how to submit an article can be found at http://journals.cambridge.org/ijc.

The Reasonable Person

A Legal Biography

VALENTIN JEUTNER
Lund University

CAMBRIDGE
UNIVERSITY PRESS

CAMBRIDGE
UNIVERSITY PRESS

Shaftesbury Road, Cambridge CB2 8EA, United Kingdom

One Liberty Plaza, 20th Floor, New York, NY 10006, USA

477 Williamstown Road, Port Melbourne, VIC 3207, Australia

314–321, 3rd Floor, Plot 3, Splendor Forum, Jasola District Centre, New Delhi – 110025, India

103 Penang Road, #05-06/07, Visioncrest Commercial, Singapore 238467

Cambridge University Press is part of Cambridge University Press & Assessment, a department of the University of Cambridge.

We share the University's mission to contribute to society through the pursuit of education, learning and research at the highest international levels of excellence.

www.cambridge.org
Information on this title: www.cambridge.org/9781009445627

DOI: 10.1017/9781009445672

First published 2024

A catalogue record for this publication is available from the British Library

A Cataloging-in-Publication data record for this book is available from the Library of Congress

ISBN 978-1-009-44562-7 Hardback

Till Tova

Contents

Acknowledgements

Throughout my years as a law student, I often wondered where the reasonable person may have come from, what this figure might look like, whether it is a distinctly English character and, of course, what role exactly it was meant to play in the theatre of law. When I began teaching law, the plan emerged to take the reasonable person seriously as a person by writing a biography about this character. After initial reservations, but maybe entirely predictably, I soon began to harbour for the reasonable person that particular affection that, Sigmund Freud says, so often characterises the relationship between biographers and their chosen subject. As I argue in the book, I genuinely believe that this figure has the potential to play a meaningful role in helping people understand (and judge) each other better and more accurately.

Several people and institutions have accompanied and encouraged me while I was writing this biography. At Cambridge University Press, I thank Tobias Ginsberg, Marianne Nield and Gemma Smith. I wish to thank Maks Del Mar for helping me to improve the framing of the project in its early stages and for including the book in this series. I am grateful to three anonymous reviewers for their feedback and helpful suggestions. I thank Manuela Tecusan for copy-editing the manuscript so diligently and for her assistance with questions concerning not only the English language but also Greek and Latin. The Ragnar Söderberg Foundation funded my position in Lund and the research visits to Harvard Law School and Münster University that gave me the time to complete the book.

I thank the participants of seminars in Aix-en-Provence, Berlin, Bonn, Cambridge, Edinburgh, Los Angeles, Lund, New York, Oslo and Tehran for their questions and comments. I thank my colleagues in Lund and Oxford for the many conversations over the years about empathy and reasonableness. Discussions of the book project with Marina Aksenova, Janina Barkholdt, Moa de Lucia Dahlbeck, James Manwaring, Gregor Noll, Dana Schmalz, Andreas Televantos and Matthew Windsor enriched my thinking. Alma Bergqvist's research assistance helped prepare the manuscript for publication. Pippa Rogerson helped me track down the portrait of Chapter 2's fellow Caian, Edward Hall Alderson, in the Lord Colyton Hall. Naphtali Ukamwa helped me access several Nigerian law reports discussed in Chapter 4. The comments of Carola Lingaas and Nobuo Hayashi greatly improved Chapter 5. A version of that chapter also appears in Carola and Nobuo's edited collection *Honest Errors? Combat Decision Autonomy 75 Years after Hostage* (TMC Asser Press 2023). Tereza Plačková assisted me with questions on the Czech language related to Chapter 6. I thank Benjamin J. Spagnolo, Christian Neumeier, Jørn Jacobsen, Katie A. Johnston and Léa Steinacker for taking the time to review the entire manuscript. Their critical observations significantly improved the text.

I thank my family in Germany and Sweden for their support and inspiration. My most important conversation partner and critic has been Tova Bennet. I thank her for being a constant source of encouragement and for our countless discussions on reasonableness, perspective taking and empathy. They inform every part of the book. The end of my work on this manuscript coincided with the arrival of Otis. I have shared with him my thoughts on empathetic perspective taking and I look forward to the day when he will share his point of view with me. May he grow up in a world in which people remember that the reasonable person is always someone else.

Table of Cases

England and Wales

Federation of Rhodesia and Nyasaland

United States of America

Israel

Other Jurisdictions

Table of Legislation

United Kingdom

Other Jurisdictions

International Conventions

Introduction

This is the story of law's reasonable person. The reasonable person is no ordinary person and their story is no ordinary story: it has many beginnings and no end. For as long as the reasonable person has existed, they led a double life, as both an unpretentious but powerful legal standard and as the common law's most legendary but also most controversial character. As a legal standard, the concept of the reasonable person is ubiquitous. In the United Kingdom alone, lawmakers have referred to it in more than 250 statutes and judges have enlisted its help in more than 10,000 cases. Beyond the United Kingdom, the reasonable person can be found in systems influenced by the common law across the globe, for instance in Australia, Canada, Nigeria, India, South Africa and the United States. In these jurisdictions, the reasonable person features in virtually all areas of law. In contract law, judges determine the meaning of particular clauses by considering how a reasonable person would interpret them. In criminal law, judges and juries test whether a defendant engages in lawful self-defence by asking whether a reasonable person would have responded to an attack in the same way as the defendant did. In tort law, the reasonable person helps judges and juries to distinguish negligent from diligent conduct by providing an answer to the question whether a defendant's behaviour fell below the standard of care that one could expect from a reasonable person. In administrative law, asking whether a reasonable person could have reached the same conclusion as a public authority facilitates the review of administrative decisions.

Apart from judges and jurors, lawyers, too, advise their clients on the legal consequences of their actions by referring to the reasonable person. Legal academics cite the standard when evaluating legal provisions or when proposing reforms. For law students, getting a sense of what the reasonable person may or may not do is one of the most important parts of learning how to think like a lawyer. Often forgotten among those who invoke the reasonable person are ordinary members of the public who seek to identify the legality of a given action by wondering whether what they plan to do is something a reasonable person would do. Admittedly, this habit may be particularly well pronounced among persons trained in the art of law. But, as we shall soon see, one of the appeals of the reasonable person concept is that it aims to make legal standards more relatable to legal laypersons. The story of the reasonable person is addressed to all these groups: judges, jurors, lawmakers, lawyers, legal academics, law students and members of the general public. All of them – all of us – apply the standard. All of them – all of us – are judged by it. All of them – and all of us – benefit from knowing the story of the reasonable person and from an accurate understanding of the features of the reasonable person's perspective.

The exact features of the perspective of the reasonable person are notoriously difficult to define. Some think that this perspective is that of the judge or jurors in a particular case. Others argue that it reflects the views of society as a whole. Still others maintain that the reasonable person's perspective should be that of the accused in a particular case, or that of the original parties to a contract. The different episodes of the reasonable person's story presented in the following chapters show that each of these three interpretations has been favoured at one time or another. In light of the reasonable person's biography, I will argue, however, that the most important aspect of the reasonable person's perspective is that it is the perspective of another. Whoever it is, wherever it lives, whatever it looks like, the reasonable person figure is not you. This is its most important characteristic. Regrettably, the various chapters of this biography will show that those who apply the concept frequently depart from the rationale behind it by focusing unduly on the features rather than the perspective of the reasonable person. This is in no small part due to the fact that, apart from its existence as a legal concept, the reasonable person has gradually acquired the status of the common law's most legendary character.

The precise origins of the reasonable person, like those of any legend, are uncertain, its identity is a matter of intense speculation, and its deeds form the subject matter of songs and poems. With respect to the concept's history, those who search for its time and place of birth have been likened to palaeontologists hunting for a 'living fossil'.[1] Some led this hunt to the conclusion that the reasonable person is a distinctly English creation of distinctly English judges. Proposed 'fathers' include Sir William Jones (1746–94), Baron Alderson (1787–1857),[2] Lord Bowen (1835–94)[3] and Lord Atkin (1867–1944).[4] As I will show in Chapter 1, others trace the concept to the legal traditions of ancient Rome[5] or ancient Greece[6] or to

[1] M.J. De Vinne, 'The Reasonable Person as a Living Fossil Evolution' (2010) 37 Litigation 15, 15.

[2] P.H. Winfield, 'The History of Negligence in the Law of Torts' (1926) 42 Law Quarterly Review 184, 185.

[3] *McQuire v Western Morning News Co Ltd* [1903] 2 KB 100 (Court of Appeal) 109 (Collins MR).

[4] *Stewart v Nisbet* [2012] HCJAC 167; 2013 SCL 209 (High Court of Justiciary (Scotland)) 223.

[5] L. Hoffmann, 'Anthropomorphic Justice: The Reasonable Man and His Friends' (2010) 29 The Law Teacher 127, 128.

[6] L. Zwiffelhoffer, *Die Figur des Durchschnittssmenschen im Verwaltungsrecht* (Mohr Siebeck 2020) 42–5.

the Bible.[7] Still others argue that the concept is a part of any legal system and that the concept's time and place have always been and will always be the same as the law's time and place.

The mystery related to the concept's origin also extends to the identity of the reasonable person. The terms prudent, skilful, careful, fair-minded, typical, diligent or well-informed capture the more ordinary attributes ascribed to this figure. Less common are identity markers that seek to define the person's characteristics in quite extraordinary detail, by situating the figure on specific means of public transport or in specific places and by focusing on specific habits. In Chapter 3 it will emerge, for instance, that the reasonable person is associated with a passenger, placed variously on the Clapham omnibus, on Glasgow's Sauchiehall Street tram,[8] on the Ipoh omnibus in Malaysia,[9] on the Molue bus of Lagos,[10] in a Venetian gondola,[11] on the Brussels tram,[12] on Sydney's Bondi tram,[13] on Hong Kong's Shaukiwan tram,[14] on the Paris metro,[15] or on Melbourne's Bourke Street tram.[16] Most recently, the reasonable person has even been spotted 'on the Boris bus with their Oyster card'.[17] As for habits, it has been claimed that the reasonable person never reads a newspaper while walking along a street[18] but, when it does read a newspaper, it is *The Guardian*.[19] The English variant of the reasonable person wears a 'bowler hat and umbrella, sitting neither too far forward nor too far back'.[20] Its American counterpart, while not being 'some totally humorless drudge',[21] 'takes the magazine at home, and in the evening pushes the lawn mower in

[7] *Stewart v Nisbet* [2012] HCJAC 167; 2013 SCL 209 (n 4) 223. See also De Vinne (n 1), 15.

[8] *George Mackie Thompson Bryceland (aka Nelson)* [2006] HCJAC 38; 2006 SCCR 291 (High Court of Justiciary (Scotland)) 300 (Editorial Comment).

[9] B. Brown, 'The "Ordinary Man" in Provocation: Anglo-Saxon Attitudes and "Unreasonable Non-Englishmen"' (1964) 13 The International and Comparative Law Quarterly 203, 220.

[10] *Sola Kuti v Vanguard Media Ltd* [1991] 2 CCHCJ 185 (High Court of Lagos State) 204 (Onalaja J).

[11] *Nursaw v Dansk Jersey Eksport* [2009] ILPr 19 (Queen's Bench Division, District Registry (Bristol)) 271 (Judge Havelock-Allan QC).

[12] Ibid.

[13] *Papatonakis v Australian Telecommunications Commission* [1985] HCA 3; 156 CLR 7; 57 ALR 1 (High Court of Australia) [36] (Deane J).

[14] *Ng Chiu Mui et al v Securities and Futures Commission* (Applications 7-9 of 2007) (Securities and Futures Appeals Tribunal (Hong Kong)) [95].

[15] *R (on the application of Drax Power Ltd) v HM Treasury* [2016] EWHC 228 (Admin) (Queen's Bench Division) [106] (Jay J).

[16] *Re Sortirios Pandos and Commonwealth of Australia* [1991] AATA 18 (Administrative Appeals Tribunal of Australia) [88].

[17] *Owens v Owens* [2017] EWCA Civ 182 (Court of Appeal) [41] (Sir James Munby P).

[18] W. Pengilley, *Advertising and the Trade Practices Act* (CCH Australia 1981) 10–12. Quoted by S. Kapnoullas and B. Clarke, 'The Legal Regulation of Comparative Advertising: Old Game, New Rules' (1995) 11 Queensland University of Technology Law Journal 7, 13–14.

[19] *Stewart v Nisbet* [2012] HCJAC 167; 2013 SCL 209 (n 4), 223.

[20] Hoffmann (n 5), 127.

[21] *Patrick v Superior Court of Los Angeles County* 27 CalRptr2d 883 [1994] Court of Appeal, Fourth District, Division 3 G013978 887.

his shirt sleeves'.[22] More generally, the figure has been described as 'meager and murky',[23] the 'hot fudge sundae of indeterminacy',[24] 'curious',[25] 'illusive'[26] or 'ephemeral'.[27] Some of the reasonable person's attributes are so uncertain that observers have framed them as questions. They ask, for example, whether the reasonable person has obsessive–compulsive disorder.[28] Is the reasonable person a racist,[29] a glue sniffer,[30] an erotomaniac,[31] a hipster?[32] Does the reasonable person believe in a god and, if so, which one(s)?[33] While some claim that the reasonable person has friends[34] and even siblings,[35] others wonder whether such a person is not an automaton rather than a human being.[36]

These questions are also taken up in songs,[37] poems,[38] a cartoon,[39] fictional cases,[40] and even a full-length movie.[41] A 1926 ballad entitled 'The Lament of the Reasonable Man'[42] written from the perspective of the reasonable person begins by noting:

[22] *Hall v Brooklands Auto Racing Club* [1933] 1 KB 205 (Court of Appeal) 224. Greer LJ attributed this phrase to an unspecified American author. Stern has recently suggested that the author in question could be the US short-story writer O. Henry (1862–1910); see S. Stern, 'From Clapham to Salina: Locating the Reasonable Man' (2023) Law & Literature 1, 16–17. A short story by O. Henry contains the following passage: 'an ordinary man out of the city directory that subscribes for magazines and pushes the lawn-mower in his shirt-sleeves of evenings': O. Henry, 'The Atavism of John Tom Little Bear' (1903) IX *Everybody's Magazine* 57, 60.

[23] B. Sheppard, 'The Reasonableness Machine' (2021) 62 Boston College Law Review 2259, 2265.

[24] Ibid. [25] De Vinne (n 1), 15.

[26] I.J. Cosgrove, 'The Illusive Reasonable Person: Can Neuroscience Help the Mentally Disabled' (2015) 91 Notre Dame Law Review 421.

[27] De Vinne (n 1), 15.

[28] L. Jewel, 'Does the Reasonable Man Have Obsessive Compulsive Disorder?' (2019) 54 Wake Forest Law Review 1049.

[29] S.P. Garvey, 'Self-Defense and the Mistaken Racist' (2008) 11 New Criminal Law Review 119, 125.

[30] A. Norrie, 'From Criminal Law to Legal Theory: The Mysterious Case of the Reasonable Glue Sniffer' (2002) 65 The Modern Law Review 538.

[31] Ibid., 539.

[32] A.E. Jackson and J.S. del Ceno, 'Privacy, Participation and the City', in N.M. Davidson and G. Tewari (eds), *Global Perspectives in Urban Law: The Legal Power of Cities* (Routledge 2019) 37.

[33] W.J. Vallar, 'Can the Reasonable Person Be Religious? Accommodation and the Common Law' (2021) 107 Virginia Law Review 189.

[34] Hoffmann (n 5).

[35] C. Dent, 'The Reasonable Man, His Nineteenth-Century Siblings, and Their Legacy' (2017) 44 Journal of Law and Society 406.

[36] Pengilley (n 18), 10–12.

[37] Law School Outline Songs, 'Duty of Reasonable Care', https://soundcloud.com/onel-8/duty-of-reasonable-care.

[38] W. Heighington, 'The Lament of the Reasonable Man' (1926) 4 Canadian Bar Review 644.

[39] A. Saunders, 'Clapham, Please', https://www.cartoonstock.com/cartoonists/alansaunders.

[40] A.P. Herbert, 'Fardell v. Potts', in his *Uncommon Law* (Methuen 1948).

[41] *A Reasonable Man* (dir. G. Hood, Pandora Cinema 1999).

[42] Heighington (n 38). See also E.J. Eberle and B. Grossfeld, 'Law and Poetry' (2006) 11 Roger Williams University Law Review 353, 399.

Oh pity me, whose life is spent
Creating legal precedent –
Whatever I may choose to do
The Court will hold it proper to
In all the circumstances.

The poem concludes by cautioning lawyers against their hope of ever finding the reasonable person:

But to the many who would find
This marvel of all human kind
I really must remove the doubt –
Confessing now to fraud throughout –
I never have existed.

The poem, written by a Canadian lawyer, is just one example of the particular kind of interest that the figure attracts from members of the legal profession. On other occasions, lawyers have issued health reports,[43] expressed an interest in meeting the reasonable person,[44] and even put this character on trial.[45] All the same, as the attempt to take the reasonable person to court intimates, lawyers tend to view it with critical eyes. It is not unusual, of course, for legendary characters to invite controversy. But in the case of the reasonable person it is particularly difficult to find positive descriptions. One of the few exceptions is an English lawyer's introduction of the reasonable person as a 'delightful character'[46] in a lecture delivered before Japanese students at the English Law School in Tokyo, on 22 June 1889. Exceptions like this lecture apart, negative accounts predominate. The character has been called a 'condescending joke',[47] 'the enemy of legal certainty',[48] a 'mythic Cheshire-Cat',[49] and the weed that grows in 'the garden of the common law'.[50] It has been characterised as a 'notorious'[51] and 'odious' creature,[52] lurking in law's 'nooks

[43] O.M. Reynolds, Jr, 'The Reasonable Man of Negligence Law: A Health Report on the Odious Creature' (1970) 23 Oklahoma Law Review 410, 410.

[44] L.J. Carlsgaard, 'Reasonable Person and I' (2016) 27 Hastings Women's Law Journal 165, 165.

[45] H. O'Reilly, 'The Trial of the Reasonable Man' (*Trinity College Law Review (TCLR) | Trinity College Dublin*, 22 November 2017), https://trinitycollegelawreview.org/the-trial-of-the-reasonable-man.

[46] F.T. Piggott, 'The Reasonable Man at Common Law' (1889) 14 Law Magazine and Law Review 314, 318.

[47] M. Saltman, *The Demise of the Reasonable Man: A Cross-Cultural Study of a Legal Concept* (Transaction Publishers 1991) 143.

[48] J. Gardner, 'The Many Faces of the Reasonable Person' (2015) Law Quarterly Review 563, 582.

[49] *Patrick v Superior Court of Los Angeles County* (n 21), 887.

[50] S. Stern, 'R v Jones (1703)', in P. Handler, H. Mares and I. Williams (eds), *Landmark Cases in Criminal Law* (Hart 2017) 59.

[51] R.K.L. Collins, 'Language, History and the Legal Process: A Profile of the Reasonable Man' (1976) 8 Rutgers Camden Law Journal 311, 312.

[52] Reynolds (n 43), 410.

and crannies'[53] or 'in the statutory undergrowth'.[54] It has been associated with various monsters from Greek mythology such as the Lernaean Hydra, a gigantic water snake with nine heads,[55] and – with the explicit approval of the US Supreme Court[56] – the Chimaera, a fire-breathing hybrid creature.[57] It is true that the reasonable person figure has also been compared to Greek heroes, but only negatively: it has been said to lack the courage of Achilles, the strength of Hercules or the wisdom of Ulysses.[58]

In light of the character's negative reputation, it is not surprising that its demise has been a subject of speculation for almost as long as it has existed. Some observers expect the character to 'outlive' a system that has raised it to great fame,[59] or believe that it 'is now so embedded and pervasive in the common law that its removal is well nigh unthinkable'.[60] Others have issued requiems[61] or announced its death.[62] Still others acknowledge that the reasonable person could still be alive, but in their view the time has come to bid it farewell[63] and let it rest in peace.[64]

These eccentric accounts and colourful portrayals of the legendary and mysterious reasonable person tell us very little about the legal function of the corresponding concept. But they do tell us that the common lawyer's relationship with the reasonable person is a complicated one. This is understandable. As a lawyer's account of the reasonable person as 'Law's Ghost God' indicates,[65] this concept exercises awesome powers across all areas of law. It is applied in thousands of court rooms all around the world on a daily basis. Against this background, one commentator has even gone as far as to argue that the reasonable person 'has had a greater impact on the Anglo-American

[53] D. Mellinkoff, 'Reasonable Man', in D. Mellinkoff (ed), *Mellinkoff's Dictionary of American Legal Usage* (Wipf and Stock Publishers 1992) 540.

[54] *R v Philip Rowland* [2003] EWCA Crim 3636, 2003 WL 23014759 (Court of Appeal) 41 (Potter LJ).

[55] M. Vitiello, 'Defining the Reasonable Person in the Criminal Law: Fighting the Lernean Hydra Symposium: Who Is the Reasonable Person' (2010) 14 Lewis & Clark Law Review 1435.

[56] *William Pinkus, dba 'Rosslyn News Company' and 'Kamera' v United States* 436 US 293 (1978) (United States Supreme Court) [22] (Burger CJ).

[57] S.E. Sobeloff, 'Insanity and the Criminal Law: From McNaghten to Durham, and Beyond' (1955) 41 American Bar Association Journal 793, 796.

[58] D.M. Walker, *The Oxford Companion to Law* (Clarendon 1980) 1038, 228.

[59] Reynolds (n 43), 430. See also De Vinne (n 1), 20.

[60] Stern (n 22), 5.

[61] D.S. Greer, 'Requiem for the Reasonable Man' (1967) 18 Northern Ireland Legal Quarterly 437.

[62] B.R. Clarke, *The Death of the Reasonable Man* (Faculty of Business, Swinburne Institute of Technology 1990).

[63] R.T. Austin, 'Better Off with the Reasonable Man Dead, or the Reasonable Man Did the Darndest Things' 1992 Brigham Young University Law Review 479, 492.

[64] Hoffmann (n 5), 141.

[65] L. Duhaime, 'The Reasonable Man: The Law's Ghost God' (Duhaime.org - Learn Law, 26 April 2014), https://web.archive.org/web/20170409075430/http://www.duhaime.org/LegalResources/TortPersonalInjury/LawArticle-1378/The-Reasonable-Man–Laws-Ghost-God.aspx. See also G. Shajobi-Ibikunle, 'The Concept of a Reasonable Man in Tort Law: A Need for a Paradigm Shift?' (2018) 2 Kampala International University Law Journal 267, 268.

system of jurisprudence than most of the renowned jurists of the last three centuries'.[66] And yet the function of this figure, its history and its rationale remain little understood. This is problematic, because limited understanding of a concept leads to its misapplication and makes it difficult for that concept to realise its full potential. And the reasonable person's potential is enormous: I will argue that the concept of the reasonable person is particularly well equipped to facilitate the process of making fair judgments in contemporary heterogenous societies, provided that the concept is accurately understood.

This is why this biography attempts to tell for the first time the reasonable person's story from the beginning of time until today. The potential irony of dedicating a biography to a concept whose fetishization I just lamented does not escape me. There is the risk that a legal biography of the reasonable person exacerbates tendencies to approach this figure as a caricature painted in lurid colours. But my intention is to contrast these tendencies with an approach that accepts the reasonable person as an imaginary character instead of seeing its fictional nature as a reason to ridicule it. I want to take the reasonable person seriously and treat its imaginary nature as an invitation to serious reflection about the way in which judges, juries, lawyers and humans at large make decisions. As the subsequent chapters will show, the reasonable person's humanity – the fact that, although a concept, it is not an abstract idea but an *embodied* perspective – is crucial. For this reason, it is fitting to tell the reasonable person's story in a manner that resembles a biography.

To claim that a concept such as the reasonable person has a biography means claiming that it has a life. The fact that a concept has a life implies that it has a past, a present, a future – that it has a time. It also implies that this life unfolds somewhere – that it has a place. Since no life is lived in isolation, life also means social context or environment. To write a concept's biography means to consider its time, place, social context, how it shapes them and how it is shaped by them. While these aspects could also be considered in the course of writing a conceptual history or the history of an idea, the biography format complicates the time, place and social context of the reasonable person by studying them through the perspective of a particular character.[67] It complicates these three dimensions, because approaching them through the perspective of a character acknowledges the contingent nature of the

[66] Collins (n 51), 312.

[67] As Stefan Zweig notes, historical material becomes accessible through the 'synthetically connective perspective' of a human being, as opposed to a 'cold presentation' of facts by a scientific expert. See S. Zweig, 'Geschichte als Dichterin', in his *Die schlaflose Welt: Aufsätze und Vorträge aus den Jahren 1909–1941* (K. Beck ed., S Fischer 1983) 263. Similarly, Samuel Johnson speaks of the 'kindred images to which we readily conform our minds' and that 'are, above all other writings, to be found in the narratives of the lives of particular persons': S. Johnson, 'The Dignity and Usefulness of Biography (13 October 1750)', *The Rambler*, vol. 2 (J. Payne 1752) 208.

concept itself: it is what it is (or became, or was), but it could have been different. Not only could it have been different, but it is – or at least appears to be – different to different people, in different times and places – just like a human character. Framing the study of the reasonable person as a biography rather than as a systematic, coherent, streamlined, authoritative account of how the concept emerged and functions allows me to account for, and capture, its complexity and, at times, contradictory nature while I am still able to relate it to a unifying core.

Of course, one can speak only to a limited extent of the unifying core that the protagonist of any biography represents. Just as the 'us' of yesterday is not identical with the 'us' of tomorrow, the reasonable person concept, whose life span exceeds that of any human, also changes. The categorical function of the reasonable person as a legal device that engenders perspective taking remains the same, but the insights, the results that this process yields, change considerably. I argue that there is an essence that connects all these figures, but that the particular manifestation of the concept of the reasonable person is always intimately linked to its context.

In conformity with the customary structure of biographies, the book's chapters are roughly arranged in chronological order. The story begins at the beginning, in ancient Egypt. I then go on to discuss the concept's further development in ancient Greece and in ancient Rome (Chapter 1). The objective of this first chapter is to communicate that the common law's reasonable person continues an ancient tradition of judging others by reference to paradigmatic persons. The objective is also to show that the reasonable person is one distinct type of paradigmatic person. Other types have existed in the past. The common law's construction of the reasonable person is not a necessary one but one contingent upon specific social, political, legal and economic factors.

Chapter 2 considers what social, political, legal and economic factors shaped the emergence of the common law's reasonable person in nineteenth-century England. The chapter's main objective is to show how the convergence between the Scottish branch of the sentimental Enlightenment and the social, political and economic changes brought about by the industrial revolution triggered the emergence of the modern reasonable person in the common law. The chapter also introduces the main thesis of this book: the reasonable person concept invites judges to take the perspective of another through empathy.

The application of the concept in English legal practice up until the mid-twentieth century is discussed in Chapter 3. In relation to the frequent associations with the man on the Clapham omnibus, this chapter problematises the masculinity of the reasonable person figure, the normative versus empirical nature of the corresponding concept, and the extent to which the standard was meant to be relatable to members of the public.

Chapter 4 begins on the eve of the nineteenth century and follows the reasonable person from England into the British colonial courts of Africa.

Based on an in-depth analysis of available case law, this chapter shows that some colonial courts identified the reasonable person with an Englishman, and hence used the standard to discriminate against members of the local population. The chapter then contrasts these cases with decisions in which judges invoked the standard empathetically, in a manner that allowed them to understand a specific case and a specific defendant better.

Picking up the thread at the point in time where Chapters 3 and 4 left off, Chapter 5 details the concept's operation in international law, and specifically in the international law of armed conflict. It becomes apparent that the standard's modus operandi in international law suffers from the same problems as its domestic counterparts, while its application is particularly challenging in the empathy-deprived setting of war and armed conflict.

Reaching the present and looking into the future, Chapter 6 discusses to what extent the reasonable person concept can accommodate new kinds of legal actors and be applied to them – actors such as AI-empowered entities, which continue to appear in the wake of the ongoing digital revolution. This chapter also considers whether big data allows for the individualisation of law in a manner that would dispense with the need for a reasonable person standard.

The Conclusion offers a restatement of the function of the reasonable person. Importantly, it also engages with numerous critiques of empathy by addressing head-on the problems related to a presupposed homogeneity of humanity, the limits of empathizing beyond the familiar, the subjectivity and biases that empathy can introduce into judging, and the relativity of the answers it yields. Some of these concerns pertain to judging in general (as opposed to being specific to the reasonable person concept). Others are less pressing in a legal environment (as opposed to that of moral philosophy, for instance), since legal judgments are situated within a net of precedent and legal norms. But there is no doubt that empathy, like any relational act, is inherently problematic. It must be applied carefully. An important aim of the biography of the reasonable person is to help the concept realise its potential while keeping in check the risks associated with it.

The selection of episodes from the reasonable person's life aims to provide a representative but necessarily incomplete overview of the concept's different functions and invocations. Additional chapters could have focused, for instance, on the reasonable person at work, the incorporated reasonable person or the reasonable person as a public body. However, to the extent that these chapters raise questions of analytical importance, the reader will find that many of these questions are addressed in connection with the six chapters presented here. To the extent that these unwritten chapters illustrate yet more instances where the standard was applied, it would be futile to strive for a complete account of all the reasonable person's various appearances. They are simply too numerous. An additional chapter I could have included would have explored the distinction between reasonable persons and those deemed unreasonable or a-reasonable. The reasons for not including it are partly the same as the two provided above.[68] A third reason is, however, that I have taken the decision not to address the notion of reasonableness and, by implication, of unreasonableness.

While much of the academic commentary on the reasonable person focuses on the meaning of the concept of 'reasonableness', I argue that the attribute of reasonableness is just that: an attribute. Explicit judicial discussions of this attribute and how it might differ, for instance, from 'ordinary', 'prudent', 'diligent', 'fair-minded' or 'officious' are rare. This suggests that these terms, including 'reasonable', are not legal terms of art but placeholders for behaviour that would be considered justified under the circumstances.[69] Thus construed, the reasonable person concept enables those who apply it to evaluate a given legal actor's conduct in light of the circumstances of a particular case with reference to the applicable law and with reference to whatever a person who applies the standard 'takes to be the ordinary standard of justification that would apply to the situation'.[70] The 'ordinary standard of justification' necessarily differs across different times, situations and places.[71] In some settings, the standard might be particularly high (e.g. when a medical practitioner's conduct is at issue) or exclusive (e.g. when the reference group includes only male property owners); in others it might be less sophisticated (e.g. when considering whether an ordinary person would have been offended by a defendant's words) or egalitarian in nature (e.g. when the reference group includes all members of society). Importantly – and this sets the reasonable person standard apart from non-anthropomorphised standards – the assessment of a given person or situation is carried out not (only) by reference to particular norms but by reference to the perspective of another person. Thus I argue that the most significant feature of the reasonable person is not the attribute of 'reasonableness' but that the concept refers to the perspective of another.

The decision to focus on 'person' rather than 'reasonableness' does not mean that the biography omits the problematic aspects related to reasonableness, for instance the standard's equation with normality, masculinity, ordinariness, whiteness and the corresponding exclusionary potential of the concept. All these aspects are addressed in connection with the biography's discussion of the consequences of a judge's failure to engage in an act of

[68] Questions related to the distinction between reasonableness and unreasonableness and, more specifically, to the challenges of assessing the behaviour of persons with atypical frames of reference are discussed in the witchcraft cases of Chapter 4. For a discussion of 'atypical' mental states as a legal term of art, see T. Bennet, *Straffansvar vid atypiska sinnestillstånd* (Norstedts Juridik 2020).

[69] Accordingly, John Gardner construes the reasonable person as a 'justified person': Gardner (n 48), 565. See also J. Gardner, 'The Mysterious Case of the Reasonable Person' (2001) 51 The University of Toronto Law Journal 273; J. Baker, *Introduction to English Legal History* (5th ed., Oxford University Press 2019) 441–2; Dent (n 35), 408.

[70] Gardner (n 48), 572. [71] Ibid., 567.

empathetic perspective taking when applying the reasonable person concept. Refraining from engaging with the notion of reasonableness thus does not, and is explicitly not meant to, avoid addressing the numerous problematic aspects of the reasonable person. Leaving reasonableness aside, however, does avoid being side-tracked into debates concerning reason, reasonableness and rationality that distract from the reasonable person's most important characteristic: that its perspective is always that of someone else.

I have also taken the decision to discuss the reasonable person's operation across private, public, criminal and international law. As acknowledged at the beginning of the Introduction, it is certainly the case that the precise manifestation of the concept varies across legal fields. For an in-depth study of the reasonable person's operation specifically within contract law or administrative law, it is imperative to pay attention to the particular factors that condition the concept's application in those areas. This is the approach that the overwhelming majority of commentators on the reasonable person's status in the common law has followed. My approach is different, however, since I do not seek to explain the operation of the concept in one particular field but rather across fields and to some extent across time. The assumption of this meta-perspective requires and justifies an approach that considers the reasonable person's operation in detachment from the peculiarities of specific fields of law. The adoption of this approach enables me to identify, then distinguish between, those elements of the concept that are essential and those that are attributable to circumstantial factors within specific contexts.[72]

An unusual feature of the story of the reasonable person is that its protagonist is both fictional and real. In one sense, it is a literary, poetic character, like Achilles. And, like Achilles, the reasonable person only appears in mediated form. While Virginia Woolf found it challenging enough to compose a narrative account of a life based on 'six cardboard boxes full of tailor's bills, love letters and old picture postcards',[73] there are naturally no first-hand accounts of the reasonable person. The character never speaks, never objects, never intervenes. All that we know about the reasonable person, we know from what others have said about it in cases, statutes and commentaries. It is with reference to this material that I as the biographer construct an account of the concept's life. But at the same time the concept of the reasonable person, unlike Achilles, possesses enormous legal power, which allows it to affect the lives of humans in a concrete, tangible manner. On the one hand, this means that the search for the story of the reasonable person is not just an academic adventure but also an enquiry of direct practical relevance. The way in which

[72] Mayo Moran has adopted a similar approach for similar reasons; see M. Moran, *Rethinking the Reasonable Person: An Egalitarian Reconstruction of the Objective Standard* (Oxford University Press 2003) 4, 201–2.

[73] V. Woolf, *The Letters of Virginia Woolf*, vol VI (1936–41) (N. Nicolson and J. Trautmann eds, Hogarth Press 1980) 374.

the reasonable person concept is understood matters to the practice of law. As numerous passages of the biography will show, the question of the reasonable person's identity can quite literally make the difference between a person's life or death. On the other hand, the reasonable person's mediated existence also means that, in absence of any direct knowledge of the person itself, this biography must not aim to establish the one and only truth about it. The aim is merely to establish that, with reference to the totality of the material presented, the story I tell of the reasonable person is a plausible one – while accepting that other stories could also be told.

A second unusual feature of the reasonable person's story is that this legal character has been known by many different names. Throughout history, the concept nowadays captured by the term 'reasonable person' has been referred to as a *geru maa*, a *spoudaios*, a *paterfamilias*, a reasonable man, an ordinary man, or the man on the Clapham omnibus – to give just a few examples. These different terms are not always congruent. They emphasise different aspects of the reasonable person, often in accordance with the particular features of the temporal and spatial jurisdictions in which they operated. Sometimes the terms refer to ideal types, other times to averages. Some of these characters represent egalitarian ideals, others are inherently elitist. Some are male, others are non-gendered. What all of them have in common is that the terms capture the perspective of someone else. Since this biography is told through the eyes of the concept of the reasonable person as it exists in contemporary common law jurisdictions, I have decided to refer by default to the reasonable person. However, in order to avoid concealing the often assumed maleness of the character, for instance, I will refer to the concept's relevant aliases and pseudonyms when engaging with its historical instantiations in Chapter 1, and especially when addressing 'the man on the Clapham Omnibus' in Chapter 3.

The reasonable person is an imperfect person in many ways. It is imperfect in the sense that it is human and makes mistakes. It is imperfect in the sense that it is unfinished and keeps evolving according to its time, place, and circumstances. It is imperfect in the sense that it is susceptible to abuse and cannot prevent being used for purposes that run contrary to its very rationale. But this imperfection is also part of the character's appeal. It corresponds to the imperfection of those who are judged by the standard and of those who apply it. Imperfection allows for disagreement, and is for this reason also one of the best remedies against the occasional authoritarian tendencies displayed by law and by lawyers. Most importantly, the standard's imperfection is a reminder that we must always view the imperfections of others in relation to our own. This, I hope, will make it easier for those engaged in judging others by reference to the perspective of the reasonable person to meet these others as fellow human beings – persons who must be judged, but who must nonetheless be treated with dignity and kindness.

1

The Reasonable Person in the Past

The Danish thinker Søren Kierkegaard (1813–55) observed that the history of concepts is similar to the history of individuals. Neither is able to 'resist the dominion of time'; both harbour 'a kind of homesickness for the place of their birth'.[1] If Kierkegaard is right, the nostalgic focal point of the reasonable person figure and its many variants are the arid plains of ancient Egypt. Nowadays considered a quintessentially English concept, the reasonable person was hardly the first anthropomorphised legal standard when it emerged in nineteenth-century England. Indeed, it appears that the idea of model characters, of paradigms of good, reasonable behaviour can be traced back to the oldest documents of humanity. In this first chapter I introduce three of these ancient ancestors of the reasonable person: 'the silent person' (*geru maa*) in ancient Egypt, 'the earnest person' (*ho spoudaios*) in ancient Greece, and 'the father of the family' (*paterfamilias*) in ancient Rome. There are, no doubt, many other ancestors of the reasonable person, and it is more likely than not that at least implicit anthropomorphised standards of behaviour could be found in any society at any one time. The three concepts introduced here are thus presented only by way of example; they have been selected because they form part of a large Mediterranean context in which ancient Egyptians influenced the ancient Greek world, which in turn influenced Roman culture, whose impact on modern European law and on the systems derived from it can still be felt today.[2] Each of the three figures discussed in this chapter deserves its own biography, and the analysis offered here remains fragmented. Nonetheless, the selected aspects of the lives of the *geru maa* (Section 1.1), of the *spoudaios* (Section 1.2), and of the *paterfamilias* (Section 1.3) foreshadow many of the questions, tensions and challenges with which the common law's reasonable person still struggles today.

[1] S. Kierkegaard, *Kierkegaard's Writings*, vol. 2: *The Concept of Irony, with Continual Reference to Socrates; Notes of Schelling's Berlin Lectures* (H.V. Hong and E.H. Hong eds, Princeton University Press 1989) 9.

[2] For a discussion of the interactions between ancient Greece and ancient Egypt in particular, see I. Rutherford, *Greco-Egyptian Interactions: Literature, Translation, and Culture, 500 bc–ad 300* (Oxford University Press 2016) 48–50, 52. See also J. Dillon, *The Heirs of Plato: A Study of the Old Academy (347–274 BC)* (Clarendon 2003) 219–20.

1.1 *Geru maa*: The Silent One

At the beginning of the animated discussions concerning law's reasonable person stands a silent individual. One of the oldest, if not the oldest, example of a personified standard of behaviour is ancient Egypt's *geru maa*. Literally translated, *geru* means 'silent' and *maa* means 'righteous'.[3] Accordingly, *geru maa* is often rendered as 'the silent man'[4] or, simply, 'the silent one'.[5] The *geru maa* is a paradigmatic person,[6] an ideal character,[7] a model human[8] whose example everyone should follow.[9] The *geru maa*'s key characteristics are wisdom, caution, modesty and reticence.[10] Most importantly, the silent person's character is 'infused with maat'.[11] *Maat* is 'the right order in nature and society' and reflects anything that is 'law, order, justice and truth'.[12] The preservation of *maat* is everyone's business. Not just kings, but each individual member of society is supposed to further *maat*, to be a person infused with *maat*, to be a *geru maa*.[13] Given the fragmented nature of the available sources, it is not possible to identify the function and characteristics of the *geru maa* with precision. But the few texts that do remain allow us to paint at least a rudimentary sketch of this oldest of the reasonable person's ancestors.

The first recorded reference to the virtues of the *geru maa* appears in a set of instructions addressed to the vizier Kagemni. According to the text itself, vizier Kagemni served at some point between 2637 and 2589 BC under King Huni, the last king of the Third Dynasty, and King Snefru, the first king of the Fourth Dynasty.[14] Kagemni's *Instructions* state:

The respectful man prospers,
Praised is the modest one,
The tent is open to the silent [one],
The seat of the quiet is spacious.

[3] M. Karenga, *Maat, the Moral Ideal in Ancient Egypt: A Study in Classical African Ethics* (Routledge 2004) 239.

[4] S. Morenz, *Egyptian Religion* (A.E. Keep trans., Cornell University Press 1973) 118; M. Lichtheim, *Moral Values in Ancient Egypt* (Vandenhoeck & Ruprecht 1997) 42.

[5] H.O. Lange (ed.), *Das Weisheitsbuch des Amenemope aus dem Papyrus 10, 474 des British Museum* (1925) 20.

[6] Karenga (n 3), 239.

[7] Morenz (n 4), 117. See also J. Assmann, *Ma'at: Gerechtigkeit und Unsterblichkeit im Alten Ägypten* (2nd ed., C.H. Beck 2006) 268.

[8] E. Brunner-Traut, 'Weiterleben der ägyptischen Lebenslehren in den koptischen Apophthegmata am Beispiel des Schweigens', in *Studien zu altägyptischen Lebenslehren* (E. Hornung and O. Keel eds, Vandenhoeck & Ruprecht 1979) 176.

[9] Morenz (n 4), 117. Lichtheim points out that the wise man may share characteristics with the silent man (patience, self-control), but that it would be wrong to equate the two because in ancient Egypt a '"silent man" need not be a "sage"': Lichtheim, *Moral Values in Ancient Egypt* (n 4), 6.

[10] Morenz (n 4), 118. [11] Ibid. [12] Ibid., 113. [13] Ibid., 114.

[14] M. Lichtheim, *Ancient Egyptian Literature*, vol. 1: *The Old and Middle Kingdoms* (University of California Press 1975) 6. But note that Lichtheim questions the text's own claims about its age and argues that it is more likely that it originates in the Sixth Dynasty (*c*.2345–2181 BC): ibid., 7.

Do not chatter!
Knives are sharp against the blunderer,
Without hurry except when he faults.[15]

As the Israeli American Egyptologist Miriam Lichtheim (1914–2004) explains, the tent of the silent person is described as being 'open' to indicate that it would be frequented by many, since 'quiet, modest' characters were 'well liked'.[16] The ideal of the *geru maa* features also in the *Teachings of Ptahhotep*. Ptahhotep is said to have served as a vizier about two hundred years after Kagemni (*c.*2410–2380 BC), during the Fifth Dynasty, under King Isesi.[17] In his *Teachings*, Ptahhotep observes: 'One has great respect for the silent man.'[18] A few passages later, Ptahhotep recommends:

If you are a man of worth
Who sits in his master's council,
Concentrate on excellence,
Your silence is better than chatter.[19]
Conceal your heart, control your mouth,
Then you will be known among the officials;
Be quite exact before your lord,
Act so that one will say to him: 'He's the son of that one.'[20]

The silent person's apparent deference to authority in passages like the one quoted here has prompted some to conclude that Egypt's *geru maa* was a resigned, submissive, obedient character.[21] But such an interpretation is unwarranted. The *geru maa*'s silence is not a symbol of subordination but a reflection of self-control.[22] For the Dutch Egyptologist Henri Frankfort (1897–1954), the silent person is 'patient, modest, calm, up to a point self-effacing, but above all master of himself under all circumstances'.[23] The silence of this person is 'a sign not of humility, but of superiority'[24] – a superiority attributed to the ability to master one's own temper. The *Instructions of Amenemope*, attributed to an eponymous scribe who lived under the Twentieth Dynasty of Egypt (*c.*1189–1077 BC), attempts to demonstrate the presence of these qualities in the silent person by contrasting them with the characteristics of the 'heated man':

As for the heated man in the temple,
He is like a tree growing indoors;
A moment lasts its growth of shoots,
Its end comes about in the woodshed;

15 Lichtheim, *Ancient Egyptian Literature*, vol. 1 (n 14), 59. 16 Ibid., 59, 61.

17 Lichtheim would date the *Teachings of Ptahhotep* to the Sixth Dynasty (*c.*2345–2181 BC), just as the *Instructions of Kagemni* (ibid., 62).

18 Ibid., 66. 19 Ibid., 70. 20 Ibid., 75.

21 E.A. Wallis Budge, *The Teaching of Amenem, Apt Son of Kanekht* (Martin Hopkinson 1924) 97–8.

22 Karenga (n 3), 239, 240.

23 H. Frankfort, *Ancient Egyptian Religion* (Columbia University Press 1948) 66. 24 Ibid.

It is floated far from its place,
The flame is its burial shroud.
The truly silent, who keeps apart,
He is like a tree grown in a meadow.
It greens, it doubles its yield,
It stands in front of its lord.
Its fruit is sweet, its shade delightful,
Its end comes in the garden.[25]

Thus the silent person's silence represents calmness, as opposed to the heated person's uncontrolled, 'unstable and erratic' behaviour. [26] The *geru maa*'s self-controlled and intentional conduct allows him or her to act responsibly. The heated person, by contrast, is at the mercy of their temperament and consequently acts irresponsibly. The heated person is out of place, like a tree that grows inside and dies an unceremonious death. The silent person knows their place and prospers, like a tree that grows outside and bears fruit. However, the silent person is not silent for the sake of silence, and not at any cost either.[27] This emerges clearly from a fable titled *The Eloquent Peasant* (*c*.1850 BC).[28]

The fable's protagonist is a peasant named Khunanup. He lives in Wadi an-Natrun, an oasis west of the Nile Delta, and provides for his family by exchanging the products of the oasis for corn in Egypt. One day Khunanup is preparing for a trip south. He loads his donkeys with 'all the good products'[29] of the Wadi, including rushes, grass, natron, leopard skins, wolf skins, various plants and pigeons. Shortly after departure, Khunanup is accosted by a local official who blocks his path. The official seizes his donkeys and all his goods. Khunanup protests, but the official takes 'a stick of green tamarisk', thrashes 'all his limbs with it'[30] and tells him to stop complaining. Khunanup cries out:

You beat me,
you steal my goods,
and now you take the complaint from my mouth!
O Lord of Silence,
Give me back my things,
So that I can stop crying to your dreadedness![31]

For ten days, Khunanup appeals to the official. But the official ignores the peasant's pleas. Eventually Khunanup turns to the official's superior, the region's high steward, Rensi, son of Meru, and begs him to intervene on his behalf. He petitions Rensi:

[25] M. Lichtheim, *Ancient Egyptian Literature*, vol 2: *The New Kingdom* (University of California Press 1976) 150–1. See also Lange (n 5), 42–4.
[26] S. Israeli, 'Chapter Four of the Wisdom Book of Amenemope', in S. Israelit-Groll (ed.), *Studies in Egyptology*, vol. 1 (Magnes Press 1990) 473.
[27] Brunner-Traut (n 8), 206.
[28] Lichtheim, *Ancient Egyptian Literature*, vol. 1 (n 14), 169–83.
[29] Ibid., 170.
[30] Ibid., 171.
[31] Ibid.

Do justice, O praised one,
Who is praised by the praised;
Remove my grief, I am burdened,
Examine me, I am in need![32]

Rensi remains silent. But Khunanup continues to plea. He asks: '[W]ho will punish crime if he who should rule by law commands theft?'[33] Confronted with Rensi's continued inaction and silence, Khunanup grows increasingly impatient and cries out: 'The son of Meru goes on erring. His face is blind to what he sees, deaf to what he hears; his heart strays from what is recalled to him.'[34] 'If law is laid waste and order destroyed', he says, 'no poor man can survive: when he is robbed, justice does not address him.'[35] Khunanup implores Rensi:

Speak justice [*maat*], do justice [*maat*],
For it is mighty;
It is great, it endures,
Its worth is tried,
It leads one to reveredness.[36]

Altogether, Khunanup petitions Rensi nine times. At last Rensi says: 'Don't be afraid, peasant'[37] – and gives judgment in Khunanup's favour. All the stolen goods are returned to him. The tale of *The Eloquent Peasant* makes it clear that the peasant was right to speak out when he was wronged and that Rensi, son of Meru, was right to break his silence when justice demanded it.[38] But the fable does more than confirming that a silent person was not expected to tolerate injustice; it also shows that the virtues the silent person was supposed to exhibit could be recognised and invoked by anyone. Even persons of 'humble rank',[39] like a peasant, could argue in quite explicit terms about the demands of *maat* with their superiors and could aspire to earn the characteristics of the silent person themselves.

No doubt a king was assumed to possess *maat* by virtue of being king.[40] But ultimately everyone was expected to act in accordance with *maat*. The vizier Ptahhotep remarked: 'Long-lived is the man whose rule of conduct is in accordance with maat.'[41] Kagemni also encouraged ordinary individuals to do 'maat . . . for the king', for 'maat is that which God loves! Speak maat to the king', because 'that which the king loves is maat!'[42] Anyone could have knowledge of *maat*;[43] everyone could aspire to become the silent person

32 Ibid., 172. 33 Ibid., 174. 34 Ibid., 177. 35 Ibid., 179–80.
36 Ibid., 181. See also Karenga (n 3), 70.
37 Lichtheim, *Ancient Egyptian Literature*, vol. 1 (n 14), 182.
38 A. Erman, *The Literature of the Ancient Egyptians* (A.M. Blackman trans., Benjamin Blom 1971) 85.
39 Ibid., 116. 40 Morenz (n 4), 121. 41 Ibid., 115.
42 Ibid. Morenz notes that 'God' could be a synonym for the king.
43 Lichtheim, *Moral Values in Ancient Egypt* (n 4), 12.

infused with *maat*. While the various teachings of *maat* refer to god(s), what is *maat* in a particular situation is ultimately a matter of human wisdom.[44]

The key method of acquiring the kind of wisdom that *maat* represented, of maturing into a silent person, was to listen. In the epilogue of his *Teachings*, Ptahhotep concludes:

He who hears is beloved of god,
He whom god hates does not hear,
The heart makes of its owner a hearer or a non-hearer,
. . .
The hearer is one who hears what is said,
He who loves to hear is one who does what is said,
How good for a son to listen to his father. . .[45]

Thus there are multiple aspects to listening. One aspect concerns a person's inner disposition, a person's heart.[46] One needs to be prepared to be taught the requirements of *maat*.[47] One needs to be silent in order to perceive, to take in what *maat* demands.[48] Another aspect of hearing relates to a person's taking in what is said to them by parents, by teachers, and in the various teachings referred to here, in this section.[49] The requirements of *maat* derived mostly from experiences related by elders and sages; the results or lessons from these experiences had to be applied to a given situation with the help of the teachings. Acting as a person infused with *maat* was an attainable goal, since the standard was not one of perfection[50] but simply of doing what was best in any circumstances. When determining what the circumstances might require, individuals were to take the perspective of someone firmly embedded in the community.[51] Accordingly, one of the younger texts, the *Teachings of Ani* (*c*.1250 BC), stipulates that individuals should always comply with the customs, 'which are important to society'.[52] In this way, passing on the teachings of *maat* improves not only the individual but also society as a whole: 'a good society cultivates the good person and the good person creates and sustains the good society'.[53] In this connection, the very attribute of silence has also been interpreted as an attitude that prioritises the interests of the community over private interests.[54] From this process of reflection, of internalising the experience of others and of considering one's role within and vis-à-vis society, there emerges the truly silent person who respects the laws.[55]

In this sense, the concept of *maat* was the foundation of the Egyptian legal system.[56] It 'was the truth that one ought to speak in a court of law and also

44 Frankfort (n 23), 81. 45 Lichtheim, *Ancient Egyptian Literature*, vol. 1 (n 14), 74.
46 Brunner-Traut (n 8), 202. 47 Karenga (n 3), 240. See also Morenz (n 4), 123.
48 Assmann (n 7), 269. 49 Frankfort (n 23), 81.
50 Lichtheim, *Ancient Egyptian Literature*, vol 2 (n 25), 146. 51 Morenz (n 4), 116–17.
52 Joachim Friedrich Quack, *Die Lehren des Ani: Ein neuägyptischer Weisheitstext in seinem kulturellen Umfeld* (Vandenhoeck & Ruprecht 1994) 89.
53 Karenga (n 3), 239. 54 Assmann (n 7), 268. 55 Brunner-Traut (n 8), 202.
56 Morenz (n 4), 125.

the justice which the court ought to put into practice'.[57] The viziers overseeing the administration of justice were known as priests of Maat and wore on their robes tokens that symbolised *maat*.[58] It is unclear exactly what role the silent person played in dispute settlement, but this brief introduction can outline three aspects of Egypt's *geru maa* and suggest that these are of particular interest to a prospective study of the history, role and function of the common law's reasonable person.

The first aspect is that the qualities of the *geru maa* were of a general nature in both material and personal respects. Materially, the *geru maa* was not a person with a special skill in a particular situation, but rather someone with a general quality, to be displayed in any moment of life. This is noteworthy, because most of the younger ancestors of the reasonable person are often tied to specific legal fields and specific situations. In personal terms, the standard that the *geru maa* embodied could be met by anyone. It was a universal standard, applicable to any person and to any situation. The ideal of *maat* was not a quality reserved to gods or leaders but one that anyone willing to listen could comprehend and aspire to. *The Eloquent Peasant*, a story used widely in ancient Egypt to educate not just ordinary members of society but also administrative decision makers, shows that even the leaders of Egyptian society were expected to answer for their actions and were accountable to their subjects. Just how radically egalitarian the concept of *maat* was understood to be emerges clearly from a passage in Ptahhotep's *Instructions*:

> Be not arrogant because of thy knowledge, and have no confidence in that thou art a learned man. Take counsel with the ignorant as with the wise, for the limits of art cannot be reached, and no artist fully possesseth his skill. And good discourse is more hidden than the precious green stone, and yet is it found with slave-girls over the mill-stones.[59]

Adolf Erman (1854–1937), a German Egyptologist, explains that 'slave-girls over the mill-stones' are meant to represent the poorest of the poor.[60] In other words knowledge, wisdom and virtue are not reserved to particular persons but can be found across all genders and all levels of society. In light of the subsequent manifestations of the reasonable person in law, it is phenomenal that the ancient Egyptians were of the view that anyone, regardless of class or gender, could access the virtues that infuse a society's model human.

The second aspect of the *geru maa* that is relevant to my purpose concerns the socially minded nature and orientation of the standard it represents. Being a person infused with *maat* was not simply a matter of maintaining an optimal bilateral relation between oneself as an individual and *maat*, understood as

[57] Ibid., 119.

[58] G. Möller, 'Das Amtsabzeichen des Oberrichters in der Spätzeit' (1920) 56 Zeitschrift für Ägyptische Sprache und Altertumskunde 67, 67–8; Morenz (n 4), 125.

[59] Erman (n 38), 56. [60] Ibid.; see also 116.

god-inspired but ultimately human wisdom. It was very much a triangular relationship between an individual who strove to be his or her best self, that individual's society, whose interests were paramount, and the ethical ideal of *maat*, to which both society and the individual were oriented. As we shall soon see, when accurately construed, the reasonable person shares this social mindedness with the *geru maa*.

The third relevant aspect that emerges from the brief history of ancient Egypt's *geru maa* is that the practice of using archetypal human characters as tools to relate abstract norms to concrete situations can be traced back to the oldest texts of humanity. By comparison with the monotheist religions that began emerging in the first millennium BC, the Egyptians did not strive to provide individuals with norms for every eventuality in life.[61] Instead, Egypt's *geru maa* represents a pragmatic, casuistic approach, which pinned the responsibility to find the best answer in a given situation on the individuals who confronted it: 'The silent person', writes Amenemope, 'sails with the wind.'[62] Follow the silent person 'and you will find life'.[63]

1.2 *Ho spoudaios*: The Earnest One

One of the oldest Greek ancestors of what was long known as law's reasonable man is a queen fighting for a Persian king. The year was 480 BC. The Persian king Xerxes the Great (*c*.518–465 BC) was attempting to achieve what his father had failed to bring about twelve years earlier: the conquest of Greece. During the first half of 480, Xerxes had emerged victorious from a number of battles. The cities of Thespiae and Plataea had been destroyed; Athens was torched, the Acropolis razed. It was looking good for Persia. In the autumn of 480, the remaining forces of the alliance of city-states formed to preserve their autonomy were retreating. The Greek fleet had relocated to the island of Salamis. Greek land forces were preparing to defend the Isthmus of Corinth – the passage that connected the Peloponnese with the mainland. Aware of these movements, Xerxes convened his council of war to determine the next move: should Persian forces attack the Greeks by sea, by land, or both ways, simultaneously? Reportedly every commander was in favour of engaging the fleet at Salamis. The Persian fleet was significantly larger than the Greek fleet, hence a battle at sea appeared to be a sensible proposal. One person, however, disagreed. Artemisia of Caria (*c*.520–460 BC), queen of Halicarnassus, accomplished military commander (Figure 1.1), and an ally

[61] Morenz (n 4), 117.

[62] Lange (n 5), 56. While Lange replaces 'the silent one' with 'the humble one', Irene Shirun-Grumach preserves the original term in her translation: I. Shirun-Grumach, 'Bemerkungen zu Rhythmus, Form und Inhalt in der Weisheit', in E. Hornung and O. Keel (eds), *Studien zu altägyptischen Lebenslehren* (Vandenhoeck & Ruprecht 1979) 336.

[63] Lange (n 5), 45–6. See also Lichtheim, *Ancient Egyptian Literature*, vol. 2 (n 25), 151.

Figure 1.1 Queen Artemisia of Halicarnassus fights in the Battle of Salamis in 480 BC. [Credits: Grafissimo/Getty Images]

of the Persians against the Greeks, counselled against a naval battle. According to Herodotus (*c*.484–425 BC), Artemisia said:

> Spare your ships, and offer no battle at sea ... why must you at all costs imperil yourself by fighting battles on the sea? Have you not possession of Athens, for the sake of which you set out on this march, and of the rest of Hellas? No man stands in your path; they that resisted you have come off in such plight as beseemed them ... If you make no haste to fight at sea, but keep your ships here and abide near the land, or even go forward into the Peloponnese, then, my master, you will easily gain that end wherefor you have come.[64]

Herodotus reports that Xerxes was very pleased to receive Artemisia's advice. Xerxes 'had ever deemed her a woman of worth and now held her in much higher esteem'.[65] Nonetheless, Xerxes decided that the advice given by the majority of his counsellors should be followed.[66] Accordingly, he gave the order to prepare for a sea battle. In the fight that ensued, it became clear very quickly that the narrow strait of Salamis, where the Persians met their Greek opponents, neutralised the advantage of the larger Persian fleet. Moreover, the

[64] Herodotus, book 8, chapter 68; Herodotus is quoted here passim from Herodotus, vol. 4 (A.D. Godley trans., William Heinemann 1930) 65–7.

[65] Herodotus 8.69, p. 67 Godley. [66] Herodotus 8.69–70, pp. 67–9 Godley.

Greek ships, smaller than the Persian ones, found it easier to navigate the crowded, narrow waters. By the end of the day the Greek forces emerged victorious. Xerxes was defeated.

The battle of Salamis marked the beginning of the end of Xerxes' attempt to conquer Greece. But, for the purposes of our legal biography of the reasonable person, the importance of this battle is related to the way in which Herodotus describes Queen Artemisia. In referring to her, Herodotus employs the adjective *spoudaios* in the feminine, *spoudaia*.[67] This adjective derives from the noun *spoudē*, which originally meant 'haste', 'zeal', 'eagerness', also 'earnestness', 'diligence'[68] and later came to designate what is morally good.[69] The qualifier *spoudaia* thus identifies the queen as an earnest, diligent and intrepid advisor.[70] This is of interest because the *spoudaios* is said to be the Greek precursor of Roman law's *bonus paterfamilias*, [71] whom we shall encounter in the final section of this chapter.

Originally an adjective, *spoudaios* soon becomes a noun – *ho spoudaios*, 'the *spoudaios* person' (in the masculine) – that designates the individual who possesses the characteristics of earnestness, diligence, eagerness and seriousness.[72] To Aristotle, the term describes the '"mature" rational and ethical person, the fully developed human being capable of intelligent thought and responsible decision and action'.[73] The *spoudaios* becomes 'an ethical exemplar',[74] a 'mannequin'[75] used to flesh out ethical ideals.

The *spoudaios*, says Aristotle, 'judges each case correctly, and in each case what is true appears to him'.[76] In doing so, the *spoudaios* does not need to possess a maximum of wisdom but rather, much like the Egyptian *geru maa*,[77] an understanding of what is required under the circumstances of a specific situation.[78] The *spoudaios* must not remain aloof but prove himself in practice. Aristotle explains:

[67] Herodotus 8.69, p. 66 Godley. Rudolf Schottlaender cites Herodotus' account of the battle of Salamis as an example of the pre-Aristotelian use of the term; see R. Schottlaender, 'Der aristotelische "spoudaios"' (1980) 34 Zeitschrift für philosophische Forschung 385, 392.

[68] Schottlaender (n 67), 385. See also G. Duke, *Aristotle's Legal Theory: The Politics of Nomos* (Cambridge University Press 2019) 160.

[69] Schottlaender (n 67), 385. [70] Ibid., 392.

[71] W. Kunkel, 'Diligentia' (1925) 45 Zeitschrift der Savigny-Stiftung für Rechtsgeschichte: Romanistische Abteilung 266, 344.

[72] Schottlaender (n 67), 385.

[73] E. Webb, *Eric Voegelin: Philosopher of History* (University of Washington Press 1981) 288.

[74] Duke (n 68), 162.

[75] E. Schwartz, *Ethik der Griechen* (K.F. Koehler 1951) 169. See also Aristotle, *Nikomachische Ethik* (F. Dirlmeier ed., 8th ed., Akademie Verlag 1983) 285.

[76] Aristotle, *Nicomachean Ethics* (*NE*), book 3, ch. 4, 1113a30, p. 51 in the Bartlet and Collins translation quoted here. See also Schottlaender (n 67), 385; Duke (n 68), 159.

[77] As Lichtheim has pointed out, however, in substantive terms – that is, in terms of the qualities he possessed, the *geru maa* is much closer to the Greek *sophron* – the temperate person – than to the Greek *spoudaios*. See Lichtheim, *Moral Values in Ancient Egypt* (n 4), 7.

[78] Schottlaender (n 67), 385–6. See also Duke (n 68), 160.

> For just as it is not the noblest and strongest who are crowned with the victory wreath in the Olympic Games but rather the competitors (for it is certain of these who win), so also it is those who act correctly who attain the noble and good things in life.[79]

The figure of the *spoudaios* who knows what is good and right and acts accordingly was meant to serve both as an example of virtuous character, a model that one could follow, and as a tool that allowed ordinary citizens to determine how best to act; for citizens would do so by pondering what the *spoudaios* would do in their place. Foreshadowing the function of the concept of the reasonable person in nineteenth-century Britain, discussed in the next chapter, the act of contemplating the *spoudaios* wrests individual decision makers from their 'egocentric selfishness',[80] thus allowing for a more accurate assessment of a given situation. As with the Egyptian *geru maa*, we must take care not to exaggerate the likeness between the Greek *spoudaios* and the common law's reasonable person. While George Duke argues that the legal function of Aristotle's *spoudaios* was similar to that of the reasonable person in modern tort law,[81] it is unlikely that the *spoudaios* played a decisive part in Greek legal proceedings. Indeed, very little is known about the exact role and characteristics of the *spoudaios*. This figure shares the fate of many other legal archetypes discussed in the present book: 'their history has yet to be written'.[82]

Nonetheless, a look at the *spoudaios* as an ancient relative of the reasonable person is instructive, since it highlights at least three of the challenges that still haunt the reasonable person eighteen centuries later. These challenges concern the character's subjectivity, objectivity and inclusivity.

With respect to the first feature, the *spoudaios* illustrates a certain kind of risk: appeal to an exemplary character who makes casuistic judgements – in lieu of, say, codified rules, or virtues that prescribe how to behave – leads to judgements' becoming personalised or subjective, in the sense that a judge's perspective unduly conditions the outcome of his or her deliberations.[83] Different people who try to imitate Artemisia's example and start by asking 'What would *spoudaia* Artemisia do?' can reasonably reach different conclusions. If the disparity between the conclusions reached grows too large, the underlying standard risks becoming arbitrary. Aristotle was aware of this challenge and tried to introduce a degree of objectivity into the standard by appealing to a version of human common sense. He observes:

79 Aristotle, *NE* 1.8, 1099a3–7, p. 16 Bartlett–Collins.

80 V.J. Bourke, 'The Ethical Role of the Impartial Observer' (1978) 6 The Journal of Religious Ethics 279, 284. Duke draws an explicit parallel between the common law's reasonable person and the *spoudaios*; see Duke (n 68), 162.

81 Ibid. Duke discusses Aristotle's distinction between voluntary and involuntary conduct.

82 Editorial comment by Dirlmeier in his edition of the *Nicomachean Ethics*: Aristotle (n 75), 284 (my translation).

83 Schottlaender (n 67), 387.

> To the serious person, then, the object of wish exists in a true sense, whereas to the base person, it is whatever chances to appear good, just as is the case also with bodies: to those who are in good condition, things that are truly healthful appear to be such, whereas to those who are sick, the healthful things appear to be different from these, as is similarly the case with what is bitter, sweet, hot, cold, and each of the rest.[84]

Thus, just as the healthy person can distinguish bitterness from sweetness and heavy things from light, the virtuous person 'judges each case correctly, and in each case what is true appears to him'.[85] In other words, whether something is sweet or virtuous is not up to the individual to determine but is regulated by a general sense of what is sweet or virtuous.[86] The risk of linking what is right to the views or sensations of the majority is illustrated by the events that surround the battle of Salamis. Most members of Xerxes' war council would have agreed on the difference between sweetness and bitterness, and yet they disagree as to the best way of engaging the Greek forces. Queen Artemisia's was a lone voice of wisdom among Xerxes' counsellors – that of a *spoudaia* woman. Accordingly, the comparison between a healthy person's taste and a healthy person's understanding of the difference between right and wrong is misleading – lest one construe virtue as that which the majority believes to be right. As we shall see,[87] the question whether reasonableness is determined by reference to an average or to the majority view in society or is anchored in objective criteria detached from people's beliefs is still relevant to contemporary debates about the reasonable person.

With respect to the *spoudaios*, however, Aristotle makes it clear that this is not a character whose virtue is based on the views of the many.[88] Aristotle makes another analogy to communicate this point: 'Hence it is in fact a task to be serious, for in each case it is a task to grasp what resides in the middle. For example, to grasp the middle of a circle belongs not to everyone but to a knower.'[89]

It takes a knower to do it: this view gives an alternative strategy for avoiding an unduly subjective notion of virtue. The centre of a circle is an objectively verifiable point. It is not up to an individual, or even a majority, to determine where that point is. Only Queen Artemisia possessed the wisdom to warn Xerxes against attacking the Greeks by sea; only the *spoudaios* knows where the centre of the circle is. While this conceptualisation avoids allowing virtue to degenerate into what the majority thinks is right, this answer to the challenge of subjectivity has its own problems. If the centre of the circle can

[84] Aristotle, *NE* 3.4, 1113a25–29, p. 50 Bartlett–Collins. [85] Ibid., 1113a29–33.
[86] See also Schottlaender (n 67), 387. [87] See Chapters 3(2), 4(2) and 6.
[88] L. Zwiffelhoffer, *Die Figur des Durchschnittssmenschen im Verwaltungsrecht* (Mohr Siebeck 2020) 44.
[89] Aristotle, *NE* 2.9, 1109a24–25, p. 40 Bartlett–Collins.

be found only by those who know, then, by extension, only those can be *spoudaioi* who either are *spoudaioi* or are aware of what it means to be a *spoudaios*.[90] Thus, acting virtuously would presuppose that one knows what virtuous conduct demands. There are different ways in which this apparent circularity can be resolved.[91] Aristotle explains, for example, that the ability to 'see' what is right can be acquired over time.[92] However, for our purposes, it suffices to observe that variants of this conundrum continue to plague the life of the reasonable person until today.

The third characteristic that the *spoudaios* shares with the common law's reasonable person relates to the standard's inclusivity. Although one of the earliest references to the Greek ancestor of the reasonable person is to a female character, the qualities of the *spoudaios* became associated with the social class of male property owners.[93] They are egalitarian only in the sense that the standard does not explicitly distinguish between the status of different male property owners.[94] In principle, the standard was informed by the conviction that, 'until otherwise proven, wealth and nobility are bound together with ethical virtues'.[95] At least for this reason, it is fitting that one of the standard's first representatives was not a commoner but a noble queen. Just like Egypt's *geru maa*, the Greek *spoudaios* was an exemplary character, whose perspective helped individuals act and judge virtuously in an explicitly casuistic manner.[96] However, unlike Egypt's *geru maa*, whose virtues could be exhibited by slave girls and humble peasants, the *spoudaios* was construed in significantly more aristocratic, if not discriminatory, terms. The discriminatory potential of personified reference points becomes particularly apparent in classical Roman law, which is the home of one of the most sophisticated ancestors of the reasonable person – and the first distinctly legal one.

1.3 *Paterfamilias*: The Head of the Family

The Egyptian *geru maa* and the Greek *spoudaios* appeal to more or less abstract ideal figures, who could serve as social and ethical role models in society. Thus we encountered Rensi, son of Meru, the eloquent peasant, and Queen Artemisia. In many respects *paterfamilias* – the Roman ancestor of the reasonable person[97] – served a similar function. In the context of agriculture, for example, the Roman writer Columella (*c.*AD 4–70) observes that an 'attentive' *paterfamilias*, one

[90] See Duke (n 68), 163. [91] See, e.g., ibid., 165. [92] Schottlaender (n 67), 388–90.

[93] Zwiffelhoffer (n 88), 43. [94] Duke (n 68), 160; Schottlaender (n 67), 385.

[95] R. Fiori, 'The *vir bonus* in Cicero's *De officiis*: Greek Philosophy and Roman Legal Science', in A.M. Shirvindt (ed.), *Aequum ius* (Statut 2014) 189.

[96] Schottlaender (n 67), 391.

[97] For a contemporary introduction to the function and significance of *paterfamilias*, see Katharina Stypulkowski, *Der bonus paterfamilias im klassischen Römischen Recht: Soziales Abbild und Rechtsbegriff* (Dr Kovac Verlag 2017).

> whose heart is set on pursuing a sure method of increasing his fortune from the tillage of his land, will take especial pains to consult on every point the most experienced farmers of his own time; he should study zealously the manuals of the ancients, gauging the opinions and teachings of each of them, to see whether the records handed down by his forefathers are suited in their entirety to the husbandry of his day or are out of keeping in some respects.[98]

However, apart from this more general function as a social role model, *paterfamilias* was also understood in more concrete, legal terms. In the digest of Roman law compiled by Emperor Justinian I (AD 530–3), *paterfamilias* is defined as 'the father of a family who has authority over the household'.[99] This authority of the father over the members of his household (wife, children, grandchildren, slaves)[100] was extensive,[101] since the law's jurisdiction did not normally penetrate the outer walls of a private household.[102] *Paterfamilias* was tasked not only with protecting the interests of his family but also with settling disputes among the members of his household at his own discretion.[103] Like his two predecessors, the Roman *paterfamilias* also represents an ethical and social ideal figure.[104] But unlike them, he has a clearly defined legal personality, as the paradigmatic subject of Roman law from the classical period onwards (*c.* AD 1–250).

In that capacity, *paterfamilias* not only enjoyed particular rights and privileges but also matured into 'the first anthropomorphised legal standard'.[105] To the question which abode could qualify as a home, Justinian's Digest replied: 'every residence in which the paterfamilias lives'.[106] In cases of legal uncertainty – concerning wills, for example – the customs of the *paterfamilias* were to be consulted.[107] Most importantly, however, the figure of *paterfamilias* was invoked to determine whether someone behaved in a manner in which they should have behaved.

For example, according to Justinian's Digest, when a person who is trimming a tree throws down a branch, if that branch kills a slave who happens to

[98] Lucius Iunius Moderatus Columella, *De re rustica*, 1.1.3.

[99] D.50.16.195.2, quoted passim from Alan Watson's edition: here A. Watson (ed), *The Digest of Justinian*, vol. 4 (University of Pennsylvania Press 1998) 464. See also M. Kaser, *Das römische Privatrecht: Erster Abschnitt* (CH Beck 1955) 56. The historical origin of the concept remains disputed; see Zwiffelhoffer (n 88), 41.

[100] Kaser (n 99), 56, 51.

[101] Zwiffelhoffer (n 88), 47. See also Kaser (n 99), 46.

[102] Only the protection of common interests – including 'military matters, honouring the Gods or crimes against the society' – could justify interfering with the autonomy of a *paterfamilias*: Kaser (n 99), 46.

[103] Ibid., 19.

[104] Kunkel (n 71), 344, 285–6.

[105] Zwiffelhoffer (n 88), 41 (my translsation). See also R.P. Saller, 'Paterfamilias, Mater Familias, and the Gendered Semantics of the Roman Household' (1999) 94 Classical Philology 182, 186.

[106] D.47.10.5.5, vol. 4, pp. 286–7 Watson.

[107] D.34.2.32.2, in A. Watson (ed), *The Digest of Justinian*, vol. 3 (University of Pennsylvania Press 1998) 154. Note how this requirement compares to that of the Egyptian *geru maa*, who was encouraged to follow not the example of a particular group of persons but of society as a whole: Quack (n 52), 89.

pass under the tree at just that moment, the person who threw the branch is liable for the slave's death only when what *paterfamilias*[108] could have foreseen was not foreseen, or 'when a warning was shouted too late for the danger to be avoided'.[109] One should not, the Digest continues, 'throw anything at someone . . . passing by', but one 'is not to be deemed blameworthy' when they 'could not have guessed that someone was about to pass through that place'.[110]

Likewise, when a question concerning a reasonable timeframe for making a payment at a particular location arises, the person who promised to make the payment needs to meet the standard of the diligent *paterfamilias*. In case of a dispute, an arbiter 'will estimate how much time the diligent head of a household would require to be able to accomplish what he had promised to do'. Specifically, a diligent *paterfamilias*

> would not be compelled to travel at great speed day and night, and continue his journey regardless of every kind of weather; nor should he travel so leisurely as to appear worthy of blame; but the season, as well as the age, sex, and condition of health of the promisor, should be taken into account, in order that he may act so as to arrive promptly, that is to say, within the time that most men of his rank would ordinarily consume in making the journey.[111]

Finally, if a slave whom a person has sold breaks a leg before he has been transferred to his new owner, the seller is responsible for the slave's injury if that seller had compelled the slave to perform some 'dangerous work' – such as walking down a tightrope or going into a sewer, 'which a cautious and careful head of a household would not order that slave to do'.[112] In all these fictional situations listed in Justinian's Digest, *paterfamilias* serves as an example of model citizen behaviour and as a point of reference that citizens can use to determine how to conduct themselves in particular situations.[113]

[108] The original passage uses the term 'diligent man' instead of *paterfamilias*. But the terms can be taken to refer to the same standard. See P.J. du Plessis, *Borkowski's Textbook on Roman Law* (Oxford University Press 2020) 328; H. Hausmaninger, 'Diligentia quam in suis: A Standard of Contractual Liability from Ancient Roman to Modern Soviet Law' (1985) 18 Cornell International Law Journal 179, 180; P. Birks, *The Roman Law of Obligations* (E. Descheemaeker ed., Oxford University Press 2014) 205.

[109] D.9.2.31, in A. Watson (ed.), *The Digest of Justinian*, vol. 1 (University of Pennsylvania Press 1998) 288.

[110] D.9.2.31, ibid. For a discussion of the precise relationship between wrongfulness, *culpa*, and *paterfamilias*, see also Birks (n 108), ch 9 (esp. 204–6).

[111] D.45.137.2.2, vol. 4, p. 189 Watson.

[112] D.19.1.54, in A. Watson (ed.), *The Digest of Justinian*, vol. 2 (University of Pennsylvania Press 1998) 100. In the context of a discussion of Roman contracts *consensu*, Peter Birks observes that 'the modern reasonable man is taken to behave much in the same way as the notional *paterfamilias*': Birks (n 108), 79, 117. With reference to contracts *re*, Birks notes that defendants were 'judged by the standard of the reasonable man, the *bonus paterfamilias*', even though it is uncertain whether 'the *bonus paterfamilias* and our man on the Clapham omnibus are anthropomorphic conceptions of the same standard' (ibid., 138).

[113] It is in this latter function that Kunkel sees a difference between the related concepts of a Roman *bonus vir* and a Roman *paterfamilias*: while *paterfamilias* is meant to serve as an

Specifically, *paterfamilias* was used to identify whether a particular person's conduct was blameworthy.[114]

It is not entirely clear when the transformation of *paterfamilias* and of the related concept of *bonus vir* ('the good man')[115] from a socio-ethical standard into a legal standard occurred.[116] What is clear is that Roman law gradually began to shift from a system in which persons were individually responsible for the damage they caused (and this included liability for accidents) to a system in which persons were responsible for the damage they caused if the conduct they had engaged in was blameworthy (and this excluded liability for accidents).[117] By Justinian's time, one way to establish blameworthiness was to ask whether a particular type of action with detrimental consequences could have been avoided if reasonable care had been taken.[118] Consequently, it became important to specify what reasonable care in a given situation required.[119] One way of defining standards of care is to codify explicit standards of behaviour that persons in different situations have to follow. Roman law, however, was inherently casuistic in nature. Situations were assessed not with reference to predetermined, explicit provisions of law, but on a case-by-case basis. Instead of asking whether a defendant had foreseen a particular kind of damage,[120] Roman lawyers asked

> whether, more generally, the defendant had been at fault; whether, in other words, he had behaved as he should not have behaved; and that, in turn,

imaginary actor whose example one should follow, *bonus vir* is meant to be a third person, invoked to determine contractual liabilities; see Kunkel (n 71), 307. On *bonus vir* as a precursor to *paterfamilias*, see also Zwiffelhoffer (n 88), 45–6.

114 Zwiffelhoffer (n 88), 42. For the purposes of determining *culpa* in the context of *damnum iniuria datum*, Peter Birks observes that the relevant question was whether a person accused of causing damage to another '[c]ould … have foreseen it as a *paterfamilias* of sound judgment and intelligence possessing the skills necessary for the proper conduct of the operation in question': Birks (n 108), 206.

115 Charlotte Stopes notes that, unlike terms such as *homo*, *vir* – 'man' – was traditionally used when referring only to men, as opposed to humans (*homines*, men and women) generally; see C. Stopes, *The Sphere of 'Man' in Relation to That of 'Woman' in the Constitution* (Fisher Unwin 1907) 5. See also the discussion concerning the meaning of 'man' at the beginning of the third section of Chapter 3.

116 Compare e.g. Kunkel (n 71), 275, 311 and J.W. Jones, *The Law and Legal Theory of the Greeks* (Clarendon 1956) 274 with H. Honsell, T. Mayer-Maly and W. Selb, *Römisches Recht* (4th edn. Springer 1987) 229, D. Daube, *Roman Law: Linguistic, Social and Philosophical Aspects* (Edinburgh University Press 1969) 171, and M. Kaser, *Das römische Privatrecht: Zweiter Abschnitt* (C.H. Beck 1975) 351.

117 Zwiffelhoffer (n 88), 48–9. See also Daube (n 116), 171–2 and R. Zimmermann, *The Law of Obligations: Roman Foundations of the Civilian Tradition* (Oxford University Press 1996) 1005–7.

118 Zimmermann (n 117), 1008. Zimmermann observes that the 'crucial issue was whether … the defendant had behaved as he should not have behaved'.

119 Zwiffelhoffer (n 88), 42.

120 Helen Scott has argued that reasonable foreseeability was nonetheless important to Roman lawyers and might have influenced the development of modern tort law. See H. Scott, 'The History of Foreseeability' (2019) 72 Current Legal Problems 287, 293–7.

depended on an evaluation of all the circumstances of the case and tended to be determined from an objective point of view.[121]

One source of this objective point of view was the figure of *paterfamilias*.[122] Adjectives used to describe his behaviour include *prudens*, *studiosus* and *idoneus*[123] – that is, 'wise', 'eager' and 'proper'. A *paterfamilias* was not expected to be an expert but had to listen to expert advice.[124] He should not 'roam the world' but reside in Rome or in a province.[125] He should not be frequently mistaken[126] and should be able to act in a prescient manner, owing to his acute understanding of situations.[127] As head of a family, he acted by definition on behalf of others and with reference to their interests. As Zwiffelhoffer observes, beyond these attributes and apart from the various examples offered in Justinian's Digest, the actual standard of care to be expected of a *paterfamilias* remained relatively imprecise.[128]

It is this imprecision – or, put more positively, the standard's dynamic nature – that explains the impressive versatility of the *paterfamilias* concept. The lack of precise, codified criteria allowed for the standard to be applied across a nearly unlimited number of situations. Its rootedness in social norms and social ethics made it relatable to a wide variety of legal actors. The fact that the standard appealed to an established figure without claiming to have a verifiable empirical basis permitted the law to impose normative demands without appearing to be detached from reality. Similarly, the concession that the law's model human is not a superhero but possesses qualities to which everyone can realistically aspire meant that the standard could claim to be of a significant action-guiding nature.

Against this background, it is maybe not surprising that the standard of the *paterfamilias* has been in use more or less uninterruptedly throughout the past two thousand years.[129] A comparatively recent South African case, for example, explains:

> One does not expect of a *diligens paterfamilias* any extremes such as Solomonic wisdom, prophetic foresight, chameleonic caution, headlong haste, nervous timidity, or the trained reflexes of a racing driver. In short, a *diligens paterfamilias* treads life's pathway with moderation and prudent common sense.[130]

[121] Zimmermann (n 117), 1008.
[122] Zwiffelhoffer (n 88), 48; Zimmermann (n 117), 1008–9.
[123] Zwiffelhoffer (n 88), 50.
[124] Ibid. See also Columella 1.1.3.
[125] D.38.1.20.1, vol. 3, p. 323 Watson.
[126] D.22.3.25, vol. 2, p. 189 Watson.
[127] Zwiffelhoffer (n 88), 50.
[128] Ibid. See also Kaser (n 116), 351. Simon Stern, by contrast, describes the *bonus paterfamilias* as a comparatively rigid, static figure; see S. Stern, 'R v Jones (1703)', in P. Handler, H. Mares and I. Williams (eds), *Landmark Cases in Criminal Law* (Hart 2017) 59.
[129] For an overview of the development of the *paterfamilias* figure in Late Antiquity and the Middle Ages, see Zwiffelhoffer (n 88), 52–3.
[130] J.A. Holmes in *S v Burger 1975 (4) SA 877 (A)* [879D–E], as quoted by Zimmermann (n 117), 1008–9.

French (*en bon père de famille*),[131] Spanish (*un buen padre de familia*),[132] Portuguese (*um bom pai de familia*)[133] and also Maltese law[134] continue to refer each to its own version of *paterfamilias*.[135] But, as already mentioned, the *paterfamilias* standard has always also had a significant discriminatory potential. The standard was, at least in Roman times, linked to the conduct of property-owning classes.[136] The customs of the lower classes were not worthy of consideration when it came to setting social and legal norms.[137] It is telling in this regard that Justinian's Digest illustrates the duties of a *paterfamilias* by reference (*inter alia*) to a slave who injured himself before being transferred to a new owner. Moreover, the standard was essentially patriarchal in nature.[138] It is by no means certain that it always excluded women.[139] Indeed, one of the passages of Justinian's Digest did allow for the sex of a person to be considered when assessing their conduct. Nonetheless, the concept of *paterfamilias* is and was nearly universally interpreted to refer predominantly to male members of society.[140]

For this reason, it is noteworthy that the nineteenth-century architects of the 1900 German Civil Code (Bürgerliches Gesetzbuch) decided to replace the expression *paterfamilias* with a general standard of care.[141] Earlier drafts of the Civil Code that contained references to the German variant of *paterfamilias* (*der ordentliche Hausvater*) had been deemed anachronistic. In particular, it was argued that it would be a 'strange imposition' to expect everyone – 'male and female', 'housewives', 'sons and daughters', 'students', 'domestic servants', 'actresses', 'female dancers', 'female chefs' – to act as if they were men presiding over a household.[142] The relevant provision now reads: 'Negligent is one who fails to exercise reasonable care.'[143]

Subsequently, the German legal tradition developed specialised standards of care that were tailored to the needs and practices of specific individuals or

[131] See e.g. the French Civil Code 1804, section 1728. In 2014 the reference to *bon père de famille* was replaced by a reference to *raisonnablement*: see section 26 of Loi n° 2014-873 du 4 août 2014 pour l'égalité réelle entre les femmes et les hommes.

[132] See e.g. Spanish Civil Code 1889, section 1094.

[133] See e.g. Portuguese Civil Code 1867, section 1446.

[134] See e.g. Maltese Civil Code 1870, section 1124A (4)(a).

[135] See also Hausmaninger (n 108), 180. For a relatively late reference to *paterfamilias* in England, see W. Jones, *An Essay on the Law of Bailments* (Charles Dilly 1781) 5–6.

[136] Zwiffelhoffer (n 88), 51–2. [137] Ibid. [138] Kaser (n 99), 46.

[139] Saller (n 105), 187. See also Stypulkowski (n 97), 194–8.

[140] See Kaser (n 99), 46; also Larry Siedentop, *Inventing the Individual: The Origins of Western Liberalism* (Harvard University Press 2014) 18.

[141] Zwiffelhoffer (n 88), 38.

[142] Otto von Gierke, *Der Entwurf eines bürgerlichen Gesetzbuches und das deutsche Recht* (Duncker & Humblot 1889) 39. Curiously, even a contemporary German scholar of Roman law observes that to assess a defendant's blameworthiness by asking whether they 'exercised the care of a *bonus paterfamilias*' is 'hardly a meaningful test question to determine issues of wrongfulness': Zimmermann (n 117), 1007.

[143] German Civil Code 1900, section 276(2).

professions[144] and that 'were not based on a minority of fathers presiding over a household but rather on the notion of an average of all citizens'.[145]

As mentioned earlier, this introduction to the precursors of the reasonable person is far from comprehensive. Each of the three figures or 'characters' discussed here deserves its own legal biography. Egypt's *geru maa*, in particular, has received almost no attention from legal researchers so far, despite the fact that there are numerous indications that this figure played a crucial role in ancient Egypt's system of law.

Even so, the brief review presented here allows me to draw a number of conclusions that help me to contextualise the discussions in the following chapters. First, anthropomorphised standards and models of behaviour can be found in Greek philosophy, in ancient Roman law, and even in the earliest records of human history in ancient Egypt. Second, the concrete manifestation of these standards differs from society to society and from epoch to epoch. Egypt's *geru maa* was conceived of in a comparatively egalitarian spirit. Men and women, rich and poor could relate to and embody the standard it represented. The Greek *spoudaios* and the Roman *paterfamilias*, by contrast, were predominantly male and anchored to the property-owning classes. This indicates that the standard tends to reflect the conditions and characteristics of the society in which it develops. This makes sense, since a standard's ability to guide the action of ordinary humans presupposes that the standard in question relates to conditions that people of a certain time and place can predict, at least to some extent.[146] And this brings me to my third conclusion: each of the figures we encountered was indeed linked to its society, in at least two ways. On the one hand, every figure tapped into established societal notions of what is the good, proper and right conduct. The *geru maa*, for example, was 'infused' with *maat* – the body of social norms that governed society as a whole. Likewise, the *spoudaios* and *paterfamilias* were so deeply anchored in their respective societies that there was no need to specify their characteristics or make them explicit.[147] This embeddedness of the figures allowed them to function in practice despite their relatively imprecise character. On the other hand, all three were also linked to their respective societies in the sense that the substantive virtues they represented were tied to the welfare of society.[148] In other words, the interests of society influenced what was deemed good,

[144] Von Gierke (n 142), 39. These standards can appear in anthropomorphised forms. Among the figures that Zwiffelhoffer discusses are *der besonnene Polizist* ('the conscientious policeman'), *der pflichtgetreue Durchschnittsbeamte* ('the prudent average state official') and *der Durchschnittsbürger* ('the average citizen'). For an overview of comparable figures in Dutch law, see A.G. Castermans et al. (eds), *De maatman in het burgerlijk recht* (Kluwer 2008).

[145] Zwiffelhoffer (n 88), 39.

[146] Accordingly, Gustav Radbruch has observed that a legal system 'collapses' if it relies on an 'inaccurate conception' of the individual. See G. Radbruch, 'Law's Image of the Human' (2020) 40 Oxford Journal of Legal Studies 667, 674.

[147] Zwiffelhoffer (n 88), 50. [148] Ibid., 43.

right and proper; someone aspiring to follow the example of a *geru maa*, a *spoudaios*, or a *paterfamilias* had to actively consider how the collective interests could be reconciled with their own. Finally, it also became apparent that the explicit use of a universal human paradigm to determine levels of legal fault is not a necessary component of every legal system. The German example showed that it is possible to replace an anthropomorphised standard with an abstract, non-personified formula. The next chapter explains why there is an important difference between the use of an abstract formula and the use of an anthropomorphised standard and what this difference has to do with the emergence of the common law's reasonable person in nineteenth-century England.

2

The Reasonable Person in Birmingham

On 21 February 1855, the River Severn near Birmingham was covered by an ice-sheet so thick that 'an enormous concourse of spectators' was able to gather upon it to witness the roasting of two sheep.[1] It was only the third time in recorded history that the Severn had completely frozen over. The British winter of 1855 was particularly harsh, the frost of February 1855 being the severest on record since 1659.[2] On Saturday 24 February 1855, three days after the sheep had been roasted on the Severn, a leaking water pipe set in motion events that would lead to one of the first explicit references to the reasonable person in common law. The pipe in question had been laid in 1830 by the Birmingham Waterworks Company 18 inches (*c.*45 cm) below Woodcock Street in central Birmingham. For twenty-five years, the pipe functioned as it should and provided the street's residents with fresh water. Owing to the exceptionally low temperatures of February 1855, however, a portion of the pipe froze. The expanding ice pushed out a plug that had been inserted into the pipe for the purpose of allowing quick access to water in the event of a fire.[3] The plug having been pushed out, water was now able to escape from the pipe into the soil around it and, eventually, into the cellar of the nearby house of Mr Blyth.[4] There it brought about 'considerable mischief'.[5] It damaged property stored in the basement and, as the *Birmingham Gazette* (but none of the law reports) relates, caused Mr Blyth's four children to contract 'severe colds'.[6] Subsequently Mr Blyth sued the Birmingham Waterworks Company for the damages he sustained. Almost one year after

[1] 'County News', *Birmingham Gazette* (Birmingham, 26 February 1855), 1.

[2] G. Manley, 'Central England Temperatures: Monthly Means 1659 to 1973' (1974) 100 Quarterly Journal of the Royal Meteorological Society 389, 396.

[3] For an illustration of how such a fire plug was meant to function, see G.G. Flexer, 'From Fire Plug to Fire Hydrant' (1966) 58 Journal (American Water Works Association) 1417, 1417.

[4] In 2022, I travelled to Birmingham in search of Mr Blyth's house. However, the oldest surviving building of Woodcock Street is a bath house (now part of Aston University), which first opened in 1860, four years after Mr Blyth's basement was flooded.

[5] 'Blyth vs. The Birmingham Waterworks Company' (1856) 4 The American Law Register 570, 571.

[6] 'Blyth v. The Birmingham Water Works Company', *Birmingham Gazette* (Birmingham, 6 February 1856), 4.

the pipe leakage, on 6 February 1856, the Court of Exchequer handed down its judgment. Finding in favour of the Birmingham Waterworks, Sir Edward Hall Alderson, Baron of the Exchequer, held that the key question for determining the responsibility of the waterworks company had been

> whether the facts proved shew that the defendants [the Birmingham Waterworks Company] were guilty of negligence. Negligence is the omission to do something which a reasonable man, guided upon those considerations which ordinarily regulate the conduct of human affairs, would do, or doing something which a prudent and reasonable man would not do. The defendants might have been liable for negligence, if, unintentionally, they omitted to do that which a reasonable person would have done, or did that which a person taking reasonable precautions would not have done.[7]

And thus, on page 784 of the 1856 Exchequer Reports, that variant of the reasonable person known as 'the reasonable man' entered the stage of the common law. As the previous chapter established, at the time of its birth, the reasonable man was only the latest in a long line of paradigmatic figures that reaches back to ancient Egypt. And yet the reasonable man, and later the reasonable person, were to become particularly successful, if not the most successful, representatives of this family of legal characters. This chapter asks why this particular legal figure was born at that particular time and in that particular place. The attempt to answer this question begins at the site of the leaked water pipe, in Woodcock Street, Birmingham (Section 2.1). I then consider the prevailing intellectual currents of the time (Section 2.2), before I turn to Baron Alderson, the very judge who brought the reasonable man to life (Section 2.3).

2.1 Mr Blyth

The events that triggered *Blyth v Birmingham Waterworks* unfolded in Woodcock Street, Birmingham. For almost a century, this city in the British West Midlands had been at the heart of the industrial revolution (see Figure 2.1). The roller-spinning machine, which mechanised the process of turning cotton into yarn, was patented here in 1732. The Soho Manufactory in Birmingham pioneered the assembly line principle, and in 1776 James Watt and Matthew Boulton launched the first industrial steam engine at the Soho Foundry. As a result of Birmingham's rapid economic development, the city's population increased significantly, tripling from about 70,000 to more than 230,000 in the first half of the nineteenth century.[8] When the French

[7] *Blyth v The Company of Proprietors of the Birmingham Waterworks* (1856) 11 Exch 781 (Court of Exchequer) 784 (Alderson B).

[8] Encyclopaedia Britannica (ed.), 'Birmingham', *The Encyclopaedia Britannica* (11th ed., Cambridge University Press 1910) 983, 985; A. de Tocqueville, *Journeys to England and Ireland* (J.P. Mayer ed., G. Lawrence and K.P. Mayer trans., Yale University Press 1958) 99.

Figure 2.1 Birmingham in 1898. The city was at the centre of the British industrial revolution of the eighteenth and nineteenth century.
[Credits: Hulton Archive/Getty Images]

publicist Alexis de Tocqueville visited Birmingham in June 1835, he described the city as

> an immense workshop, a huge forge, a vast shop. One only sees busy people and faces brown with smoke. One hears nothing but the sound of hammers and the whistle of steam escaping from boilers. One might be down a mine in the New World. Everything is black, dirty and obscure, although every instant it is winning silver and gold.[9]

While the industrial revolution affected cities and societies as a whole in different ways,[10] de Tocqueville's impression is largely representative of the fundamental changes triggered by the new conditions brought about by technological innovations in the eighteenth and nineteenth centuries. On the one hand, cities turned into workshops with massive workforces. On the other hand, as de Tocqueville neatly observes, the industrial revolution generated a lot of wealth. Both these aspects matter if we wish to understand the advent of the reasonable man at this particular time.

[9] Tocqueville (n 8), 94.

[10] Tocqueville notes, for example, that the conditions in Manchester were considerably worse than those in Birmingham, ibid., 104.

The period of urbanisation, which began in the eighteenth century and continued at least until the late nineteenth century, resulted in a larger number of people inhabiting and moving about in much smaller spaces than they had done previously. Before the onset of the industrial revolution, people largely lived where they worked.[11] Highly skilled artisans lived above their workshops, in medieval towns; peasants lived in the countryside, on the land they farmed. As industrialisation unfolded, this changed. Farmers either commuted to cities or relocated to them, to work in the factories. While efforts were made to house workers as close as possible to factories,[12] both skilled and unskilled labourers tended to have longer journeys to work than they had previously had. The clearer division between places of work and places of private life also meant that people had to travel further in search of entertainment or recreational pursuits.[13] Classes and professions previously clearly separated were suddenly in 'constant contact'.[14] In short, people lived in more crowded conditions and were much more on the move than in pre-industrial times. Life had become more complex and cities had become 'unpredictable' sites of 'coincidences, crimes, collisions and catastrophes'.[15]

As a result of the high density of peoples' living quarters, the number of people in motion, and the increasing use of novel technologies such as the steam engine, the number of accidents also rose.[16] Not only were there more accidents but they also differed in kind and scale from those of the pre-industrial period.[17] A glance at the pages of the *Birmingham Gazette* published in the weeks just before and just after 24 February 1855, the day the pipe burst in Woodcock Street, reveals the sheer variety and frequency of accidents that shaped an ordinary person's life at the time. On 26 February, the explosion of a boiler in the house of a certain Edward Atkison 'severely injured four persons, two of whom' were left 'in a very precarious state'.[18] Omnipresent construction works put not only ordinary people at risk but also the Lord Chancellor, who narrowly escaped certain death when 'a stone of considerable size . . . fell through the ceiling of one of the corridors' of the House of Lords in late March 1855. New chemicals, too, caused frequent injuries – for example, a

[11] P. Bairoch, *Cities and Economic Development: From the Dawn of History to the Present* (University of Chicago Press 1988) 279–80.

[12] Ibid., 271. [13] Ibid., 279–80.

[14] M.L. Frazer, *The Enlightenment of Sympathy: Justice and the Moral Sentiments in the Eighteenth Century and Today* (Oxford University Press 2010) 54.

[15] P. Fyfe, *By Accident or Design: Writing the Victorian Metropolis* (Oxford University Press 2015) 31.

[16] J.G. Williamson, *Coping with City Growth during the British Industrial Revolution* (Cambridge University Press 2002) 231; J. Hinshaw and P.N. Stearns, *Industrialization in the Modern World: From the Industrial Revolution to the Internet*, vol. 1 (ABC-CLIO 2013) 3.

[17] Hinshaw and Stearns (n 16), 3; N. Jansen, 'Deliktsrecht: Allgemeines und lex Aquilia', *Handwörterbuch des Europäischen Privatrechts* (Max Planck Institute for Comparative Public Law and International Law 2009). https://hwb-eup2009.mpipriv.de.

[18] 'General Intelligence', *Birmingham Gazette* (Birmingham, 26 February 1855), 4.

dinner of oatmeal was determined to have contained traces of arsenic, causing 'violent illness' and at least one death.[19] Chemicals are also a good example of the fact that accidents could have large-scale consequences.[20] Just a few months before the events in Woodcock Street, Birmingham Waterworks reported that the Birmingham water network had been 'temporarily contaminated by ammoniacal liquour', which had been 'poured into it from the Willenhall Gas Works'.[21] All readers of the *Birmingham Gazette* were thus requested to abstain from drinking the contaminated water and not to use it for the purposes of preparing food.

The main cause of accidents was not, however, chemical pollution, exploding boilers, or stones dropped from construction sites. The single most important source of accidents was the transportation sector.[22] In 1855 hardly a day went by without the *Birmingham Gazette* reporting the details of transport-related accidents. One particularly striking example is the newspaper train due to depart from Rugby at 06:15 on 22 February 1855. Before the train had even had a chance to leave the station, it was hit by an empty locomotive, 'severely shaking one gentleman', who had to stay behind at Rugby. When the train eventually left Rugby half an hour late, its first car jumped off the tracks, 'taking with it the next two carriages'. These carriages then crashed into an embankment and destroyed a telegraph post. 'Many of the passengers sustained concussions' but, miraculously, the train eventually arrived at Derby, merely 'upwards of an hour late'.[23] Then, when the train departed Derby, the 'tires of the leading wheels of the engine flew off',[24] bringing traffic once more to a halt. Two weeks earlier, a train on the Oxford and Birmingham line derailed, collided with a bridge and caused a truck that was crossing the bridge to crash through the roof of a nearby home.[25] To borrow the words of one legal historian, '[e]arly railway trains ... were notable neither for speed nor for safety. They killed any object from a Minister of State to a wandering cow.'[26] On the waterways, too, steam-powered vehicles caused accidents. The *Gazette* of 26 March 1855, for example, describes in considerable detail how a horse, a waggoner, a woman, a child and a shopkeeper were killed as a result of a 180-ton steamship (the *John*) 'coming into contact with' and subsequently 'totally destroying' a bridge

[19] 'General Intelligence', *Birmingham Gazette* (Birmingham, 16 April 1855), 4. But a reasonable person may wonder whether the arsenic had truly found its way into the meal in question by accident (as the *Gazette* reports) or whether the chef, a 'lady named Evans' who herself did not consume the meal, could have mixed it in intentionally.

[20] Jansen (n 17).

[21] 'Birmingham, Sept. 1854', *Birmingham Gazette* (Birmingham, 18 September 1854), 3.

[22] Michael Lobban, 'Common Law Reasoning and the Foundations of Modern Private Law' (2007) 32 Australian Journal of Legal Philosophy 39, 53–4.

[23] 'General Intelligence' (n 18). [24] Ibid.

[25] 'General Intelligence', *Birmingham Gazette* (Birmingham, 12 February 1855), 2.

[26] P.H. Winfield, 'The History of Negligence in the Law of Torts' (1926) 42 Law Quarterly Review 184, 195.

near Bath.[27] And, naturally, a fair share of accidents also occurred on ordinary roads. On 4 June 1855, for instance, a certain Mr Amphlett and his servant were driving in a horse-drawn carriage when their horse 'took fright from some unexplained cause, dashed down a hill and violently collided with a waggon, throwing Mr Amphlett and his servant out of their vehicle'.[28] The passengers sustained concussions and were rendered 'insensible'.[29]

The increased frequency of accidents and their novel scale triggered the emergence of the modern tort of negligence.[30] A person was found to have acted negligently if they failed to comply with a duty of care towards another and, importantly, if they did so in a blameworthy manner.[31] One way or another, the law had always taken a defendant's level of care into account when determining how to address harm caused by one person to another.[32] As we saw in the previous chapter, the ancient societies of Egypt, Greece and Rome already grappled with the question of distinguishing blameworthy from blameless negligence. But the industrial revolution fundamentally changed the parameters that used to apply to questions of negligence. In pre-industrial societies, it might have been tolerable that rulers made law in the same way as 'wild beasts eat – hurriedly, when and how they can, careless of what the food is so long as it fills them for the moment'.[33] It might also have been possible for disputes between neighbours concerning, for instance, wandering animals[34] to be settled locally, in an ad hoc fashion.[35] In pre-industrial times, harm was ordinarily caused by 'one person's private sphere being invaded by the act of another'.[36] The law of tort – the law dealing with the civil (as opposed to criminal) consequences of illegal acts – resembled 'a system of corrective justice simple, in which any disturbance of the existing set of rights had to be corrected by the person who invaded the right'.[37]

Industrialisation upset this established approach in at least four ways. First, as we have seen, it brought with it accidents of a frequency and scale not witnessed before. Harm was caused not by actions resembling trespass but by

[27] 'General Intelligence', *Birmingham Gazette* (Birmingham, 26 March 1855), 1.

[28] 'General Intelligence', *Birmingham Gazette* (Birmingham, 4 June 1855), 3. [29] Ibid.

[30] Winfield (n 26), 184, 195; Lobban (n 22), 54; R.L. Rabin, 'The Historical Development of the Fault Principle: A Reinterpretation Symposium: Modern Tort Theory' (1980) 15 Georgia Law Review 925, 947.

[31] Winfield (n 26), 184.

[32] P.H. Winfield, 'The Myth of Absolute Liability' (1926) 42 Law Quarterly Review 37, 37–8; Winfield (n 26), 191; David Daube, *Roman Law: Linguistic, Social and Philosophical Aspects* (Edinburgh University Press 1969) 171–2; M.J. Prichard, 'Trespass, Case and the Rule in Williams v. Holland' (1964) 22 Cambridge Law Journal 234, 235; Lara Zwiffelhoffer, *Die Figur des Durchschnittssmenschen im Verwaltungsrecht* (Mohr Siebeck 2020) 42.

[33] Winfield (n 32), 38. [34] Prichard (n 32), 235. [35] Winfield (n 26), 184–5.

[36] Lobban (n 22), 53–4.

[37] Ibid. Ogorek makes a similar observation about the German context at the time; see Regina Ogorek, *Untersuchungen zur Entwicklung der Gefährdungshaftung im 19. Jahrhundert* (Böhlau 1975) 23.

malfunctioning technical appliances in the public sphere. Second, the parties affected in a dispute were not usually acquainted. The most serious disputes did not arise between neighbours familiar with each other but between producers of machinery located in one part of the country and consumers or innocent bystanders who lived in cities and villages far removed from a company's place of incorporation. This also meant that, third, disputes could not be settled locally, by arbiters familiar with the parties, but by judges who had to apply general and objective rules. Fourth, as observed by de Tocqueville in the passage quoted earlier, the adjudication of accidents in industrialised Britain came with extremely high financial stakes. In pre-industrial Britain it might have been practical to apply rules resembling strict liability[38] – that is, not to pay much attention to questions of fault and blameworthiness and to impose duties of compensation on those who caused harm, regardless of whether they could indeed be blamed for what had caused the harm.[39] But such an approach was no longer tenable in an age where the machines of companies regularly harmed ordinary people.[40] If every railway corporation were strictly liable for any harm caused to one of its employees or passengers, the ensuing financial burdens would have made the enterprise of running a railway so costly that few would have been willing or able to undertake it.[41]

The events of 24 February 1855 in Woodcock Street, Birmingham are a good illustration of the four aspects of the change that industrialisation brought about. The harm was caused by a leaking waterpipe buried on public ground, to the urban home of Mr Blyth (and his children), who had probably never met the proprietors of the Birmingham Waterworks. The case was heard by a bench of judges who had travelled to Birmingham from London; and they had to balance the needs of Mr Blyth against the (public) interests represented by the waterworks company.[42]

The satisfactory resolution of such disputes required a standard of negligence that compensated the persons harmed by new technologies for their injuries, while also distinguishing harm caused by ordinary risks from harm caused by unusual risks in order to ensure that the industrial enterprises of the time remained lucrative. Moreover, the standard of care had to be of a general character, so as to be applicable by judges not familiar with the parties

[38] W.S. Holdsworth, *A History of English Law*, vol. 3 (Methuen 1909) 299, 303–4; M. Bateson (ed.), *Borough Customs*, vol. 2 (Seldon Society 1906) xl. It is nearly universally accepted that criminal law, unlike civil law, had always (or in any event much earlier) distinguished between harm caused intentionally and harm caused by accident. See e.g. Holdsworth 295, 298.

[39] Lobban (n 22), 53–4. Rabin proposes an alternative theory. He argues that the emergence of modern negligence law was not a shift from strict liability to fault-based liability but rather a transition from no liability to fault-based liability: see Rabin (n 30), 960. For our purposes, it is not necessary to pass judgement on the comparative merits of these theories, since both agree on the importance of the industrialisation for the emergence of negligence law.

[40] D. Ibbetson, *A Historical Introduction to the Law of Obligations* (Oxford University Press 2001) 164.

[41] Lobban (n 22), 57. [42] Ibid.

before them; it had to be sufficiently dynamic to accommodate a multiplicity of legal and factual situations,[43] and it had to be as predictable as possible, so as to provide legal certainty both to enterprises that engaged in hazardous activities and to ordinary people whose interests such hazardous activities would affect.

The legal system's response to this demand was to introduce a personified standard of care in the late eighteenth century.[44] Writing in 1781 and making a thinly veiled reference to the notion of *paterfamilias* in Roman law, the judge and philologist Sir William Jones (1746–94) argued that the standard of care should be that which '*every person of common prudence and capable of governing a family*' would exhibit.[45] In 1837, in the case of *Vaughan v Menlove*, the court deliberated whether a defendant had acted negligently when stacking hay so that it ignited and burned down his neighbour's dwelling; and it ruled that the defendant had acted negligently if he had failed to act in the way in which a 'man of ordinary prudence' would have acted.[46] Eventually Baron Alderson made the first explicit reference to 'reasonable man' in 1856. Subsequently negligence was defined as

> the omission to do something which a reasonable man, guided upon those considerations which ordinarily regulate the conduct of human affairs, would do, or doing something which a prudent and reasonable man would not do.[47]

Ultimately the industrial revolution required a novel and sophisticated yet relatable standard of care, and this need resulted in the emergence of the modern law of negligence. The modern law of negligence in turn required a method to identify whether a given defendant had in fact acted negligently. In its most perfected form, such a method was provided by Alderson's 'reasonable man'. This is where the attempts to explain the emergence of the standard of the reasonable person ordinarily end. But the events triggered by the industrial revolution are only one half of the answer to the question why the reasonable person standard developed in early nineteenth-century Britain. After all, as we have seen in the previous chapter, modern negligence law can do without an explicitly personified standard of care. Merely a few years after the advent of Britain's 'reasonable man', the drafters of the 1900 German Civil Code explicitly decided against the use of an anthropomorphised standard of

[43] O.M. Reynolds Jr, 'The Reasonable Man of Negligence Law: A Health Report on the Odious Creature' (1970) 23 Oklahoma Law Review 410, 414.

[44] S. Stern, 'R v Jones (1703)', in P. Handler, H. Mares and I. Williams (eds), *Landmark Cases in Criminal Law* (Hart 2017) 59.

[45] W. Jones, *An Essay on the Law of Bailments* (Charles Dilly 1781) 5–6. See also Ibbetson (n 40), 164.

[46] *Vaughan v Menlove* 132 ER 490 (Court of Common Pleas). Notably, Baron Alderson was involved in this case, too.

[47] *Blyth v The Company of Proprietors of the Birmingham Waterworks* (1856) 11 Exch 781 (n 7), 784.

care, opting instead for a definition of negligence that merely required persons to 'exercise reasonable care'.[48]

In order to understand the difference between the common law's personified standard of care and standards of care phrased in abstract terms, we must consider the thoughts of numerous Scottish thinkers whose scholarship shaped the metaphysical world of industrial Britain.

2.2 The Scottish Sentimentalists

When Britain's industrial revolution began in the eighteenth century, another revolution – the Enlightenment, a revolution of the intellect – was already in full swing. As this section will show, the thinkers of the Enlightenment period played an important role in the emergence of the modern standard of the reasonable person in England. Spanning roughly the period between 1650 and 1800, it is not easy to offer an uncontroversial and comprehensive account of the ideas that the European Enlightenment represented.[49] Even the use of a definite article, the singular form of the noun, and its capitalisation are disputed.[50] But in the most general sense it might be said that the thinkers of the Enlightenment period questioned the established norms and dogmas of their time and by so doing placed the 'onus of intellectual and moral responsibility on every human being'.[51] According to the German philosopher and theologian Moses Mendelssohn (1729–86), for instance, the term 'Enlightenment' refers to the process of honing an individual's ability to reason.[52] For the German philosopher Immanuel Kant (1724–1804), the period of the Enlightenment marked 'mankind's exit from its self-incurred immaturity' caused by its 'inability to make use of one's own understanding.'[53] 'Sapere aude!', wrote Kant: 'have the courage to make use of your ability to reason!'[54] While it is generally accepted that the Enlightenment challenged convention and encouraged individuals to reflect critically upon the state of the world and the societies they inhabited, thinkers were divided over what exactly it meant to employ one's ability to reason and how exactly moral principles were identified.[55] As we shall see, this debate concerning how moral

[48] German Civil Code 1900, section 276(2).

[49] For an overview of different interpretations and perspectives, see F. Oz-Salzberger, 'Enlightenment, National Enlightenments, and Translation', *The Routledge Companion to Eighteenth Century Philosophy* (Routledge 2017); Dorinda Outram, *The Enlightenment* (Cambridge University Press 2013) ch. 1.

[50] Oz-Salzberger (n 49), 37.

[51] Ibid., 36. See also M. Foucault, 'What Is Enlightenment?' in P. Rabinow (ed.), *The Foucault Reader* (Pantheon Books 1984) 38.

[52] M. Mendelssohn, 'Ueber die Frage: was heißt aufklären?' (1784) Berlinische Monatsschrift 193, 194.

[53] I. Kant, 'Beantwortung der Frage: Was ist Aufklärung?' (1784) Berlinische Monatsschrift 481, 481.

[54] Ibid. [55] Frazer (n 14), 4, 8.

principles are identified is connected to the emergence of the reasonable person in modern common law.

One cluster of authors, later labelled 'rationalists', argued that moral principles could be identified by reason alone.[56] Rationalists such as the German philosopher Christian Wolff (1679–1754)[57] considered that moral truths were 'built into the universe independent[ly] of human psychology';[58] they merely had to be discovered through rational deduction. To a pure rationalist, 'the criterion of truth is not sensory but intellectual and deductive'.[59] The image that emerges from this approach is that of a singular individual directly confronting the universe from which she attempts to deduce principles of rightful conduct. In very general terms,[60] this 'rationalist' view reflects the approach of measuring someone's conduct by asking whether what that person did was itself 'reasonable', 'prudent' or 'negligent' – as opposed to asking whether what that person did is something that a reasonable person, a prudent person or a negligent person would have done.

This approach can be contrasted with the view advanced by thinkers associated with the sentimental variant of Enlightenment. For them, the Enlightenment was not just the age of reason but also the age of feeling.[61] They agree that the cognitive, analytical faculty of the mind is important. Yet, crucially, they maintain that moral principles are not deduced through reason alone but also through emotional responses to experiences and observations. More specifically, moral sentimentalists argue that individuals possess a 'moral sense'[62] that allows them to determine whether a given characteristic or a given action is morally desirable. This moral sense not only responds to the feelings of the person who is assessing a given situation but, importantly, connects to 'community sentiment'[63] and to 'feelings shared among individuals'.[64] Stated in general terms again, this view reflects the approach of measuring the conduct of persons by asking whether what someone did is

[56] Ibid., 8.

[57] Immanuel Kant is frequently associated with the rational Enlightenment. Notably, however, Kant rejected the ideas of the sentimental Enlightenment only in the last quarter of his life (ibid., 112).

[58] Ibid., 34.

[59] V.J. Bourke, 'Rationalism', in D.D. Runes (ed.), *The Dictionary of Philosophy* (Philosophical Library 1951) 263.

[60] As acknowledged throughout this chapter, one must not overstate the differences between rationalist and sentimental Enlightenment thinking. I describe here two ends of the spectrum, but they overlap in many respects.

[61] S. Moyn, 'Empathy in History, Empathizing with Humanity' (2006) 45 History and Theory 397, 399.

[62] Or 'moral taste ', as David Hume calls it. See D. Hume, *A Treatise of Human Nature* (L.A. Selby-Bigge ed, Clarendon 1896) 581. On the links between the Scottish common sense philosophy and the development of the common law more generally, see Chloë Kennedy, '"Ungovernable Feelings and Passions": Common Sense Philosophy and Mental State Defences in Nineteenth Century Scotland' (2016) 20 Edinburgh Law Review 285.

[63] Chloë Kennedy, 'Declaring Crimes' (2017) 37 Oxford Journal of Legal Studies 741, 768.

[64] Frazer (n 14), 4.

something that a reasonable person, a prudent person or a negligent person would have done – as opposed to asking whether what someone did was itself 'reasonable', 'prudent' or 'negligent'.

A particularly high concentration of sentimentalist thinkers was to be found in eighteenth-century Scotland. One of the first[65] Scottish sentimentalists was David Hume (1711–76). According to him, 'the minds of men are mirrors to one another', they reflect 'each other[']s emotions . . . passions, sentiments and opinions'.[66] Hume explains:

> When I see the *effects* of passion in the voice and gesture of any person, my mind immediately passes from these effects to their causes, and forms such a lively idea of the passion, as is presently converted into the passion itself.[67]

For Hume, the assessment of whether or not a given act or characteristic is morally desirable 'proceeds entirely from moral taste, and from certain sentiments of pleasure or disgust, which arise upon the contemplation and view of particular qualities or characters.'[68] To ensure that an individual's 'moral taste' is not unduly influenced by the individual's subjective preferences, Hume writes that an individual must

> depart from his private and particular situation, and must choose a point of view, common to him with others: [h]e must move some universal principle of the human frame, and touch a string, to which all mankind have an accord and symphony.[69]

We must, says Hume, 'fix on some *steady* and *general* points of view; and always, in our thoughts, place ourselves in them, whatever may be our present situation'.[70] In the eighteenth century, the general point of view adopted here – that of touching a string connected to all mankind, of placing oneself in the shoes of another – would have been described as recommending an act of sympathy. But if sympathy is defined as 'the active will to identify with others',[71] what we are dealing with here is most accurately described today as an act of empathy.[72]

Some have argued that the idea that human sentiments should influence the identification of moral principles was entirely novel. The US literary critic Ronald S. Crane (1886–1967), for instance, claimed that sentimentalism 'was something new in the world' – something that 'representatives of every school

65 Though certainly not the earliest; see Frazer (n 14), ch. 1.

66 Hume, *A Treatise of Human Nature* (n 62), 365. 67 Ibid., 576. 68 Ibid., 581.

69 D. Hume, *An Enquiry Concerning the Principles of Morals: A Critical Edition* (Tom L. Beauchamp ed., Clarendon 2006) 75.

70 Hume, *A Treatise of Human Nature* (n 62), 581–2.

71 L. Hunt, *Inventing Human Rights: A History* (W.W. Norton 2007) 65.

72 On the etymology and the relationship between the terms 'sympathy' and 'empathy', see Moyn (n 61), 399–400. See also Karsten Stueber, 'Empathy', in Edward N. Zalta (ed.), *The Stanford Encyclopedia of Philosophy* (Metaphysics Research Lab, Stanford University 2019). https://plato.stanford.edu/archives/fall2019/entries/empathy.

of ethical or religious thought' would have rejected a century earlier.[73] When commenting on the importance of pity in philosophical reasoning, the German philosopher Friedrich Nietzsche (1844–1900) argued along similar lines. He opined that before the modern era 'philosophers have been at one as to the *worthlessness* of pity'.[74] One has to treat such views with caution – especially in light of the three ancient precursors of the reasonable person introduced in the previous chapter.[75] The capacity for sympathy – or empathy, as I will from now on call it – is a universal human characteristic,[76] and it is unlikely that the Scottish sentimentalists were the first to acknowledge the importance of human emotions, of empathy, in connection with moral judgments. But they certainly put forward a particularly sophisticated theory of empathy's significance that, I argue, also informs the function of the reasonable person in the common law.

The connection between the Scottish sentimentalists and the common law's reasonable person becomes clearer when one considers that Hume and his successors did not merely advocate the adoption of a general perspective but anthropomorphised this point of reference. In doing so, they encouraged individuals to engage in acts of perspective taking as they assessed a given situation. In other words they encouraged people to consider a given situation not from their own but from some other person's point of view.

In this regard, one of the earliest sentimentalists, Anthony Ashley-Cooper (1671–1713), the third Earl of Shaftesbury, employed the concept of 'the common honest Man'.[77] The Anglican bishop and theologian Joseph Butler (1692–1752) counselled that we should 'place ourselves at a due distance', assuming the perspective of 'good men'.[78] Hume himself proposed that one should strive to conform one's conduct to 'the model of a character' that one 'approves' of.[79] But it is Hume's Scottish compatriot, the philosopher Adam Smith (1723–90), who presented the most refined account of a personified standard for judging one's own and others' behaviour.

[73] R.S. Crane, 'Suggestions toward a Genealogy of the "Man of Feeling"' (1934) 1 ELH 205, 206–7.

[74] F. Nietzsche, *On the Genealogy of Morals* (Walter Kaufmann and RJ Hollingdale trans., Vintage Books 1989) 19. Less absolute but also sceptical is H. Arendt, *On Revolution* (17th edn, Penguin Books 1990) 70–1; H. Arendt, 'Lectures on Kant's Political Philosophy', in R. Beiner (ed.), *Lectures on Kant's Political Philosophy* (University of Chicago Press 1982) 43.

[75] Concerning the significance of the emotions of compassion and fear to the *spoudaios*, see e.g. Rudolf Schottlaender, 'Der aristotelische "spoudaios"' (1980) 34 Zeitschrift für philosophische Forschung 385, 394. Aristotle explicitly stated that the question whether 'a person is censurable' is determined 'in the sensitive part of the soul' (*Nicomachean Ethics* 2.9, 1109b23).

[76] Hunt (n 71), 39. See also R. Niebuhr, *Moral Man and Immoral Society: A Study in Ethics and Politics* (Charles Scribner's Sons 1932) xi–xii; R. Crouter, *Reinhold Niebuhr: On Politics, Religion, and Christian Faith* (Oxford University Press 2010) 48–9.

[77] A.A. Cooper, *Characteristicks of Men, Manners, Opinions, Times*, vol. 1 (Philip Ayres ed., Clarendon 1999) 72.

[78] J. Butler, *The Works of Bishop Butler* (D.E. White ed., University of Rochester Press 2006) 100.

[79] D. Hume, *Essays: Moral, Political, and Literary* (Lewis 1889) 158.

In *Theory of Moral Sentiments*,[80] first published in 1759, Smith develops a comprehensive theory of how our moral sense influences our judgements. Smith begins by explaining that humans must judge the propriety of their own behaviour and of the behaviour of others[81] by reference to an imaginary 'impartial spectator'. Adopting the perspective of an impartial spectator when we assess our own or others' actions means that we remove or distance ourselves

> from our own natural station, and endeavour to view them [*sc.* those actions] as at a certain distance from us. But we can do this in no other way than by endeavouring to view them with the eyes of other people, or as other people are likely to view them. Whatever judgment we can form concerning them, accordingly, must always bear some secret reference, either to what are, or to what, upon a certain condition, would be, or to what, we imagine, ought to be the judgment of others. We endeavour to examine our own conduct as we imagine any other fair and impartial spectator would examine it.[82]

The impartial spectator is meant to facilitate the forming of judgments by providing a point of reference that allows us to look at a given situation from an imaginary external point of view. Accordingly, Smith writes that we must 'divide' ourselves 'into two persons':[83] a spectator and an agent. The spectator is the judge, the agent is the person being judged. The imaginary judge, the impartial spectator, is familiar with the particular circumstances of the situation under review and with the feelings and characteristics of the person to be judged.[84] The spectator's views are informed by the views of society at a particular point in time, but they need not be an identical reflection of them.[85] The impartial spectator is not an idealised superhuman but an 'imperfect',[86] an 'ordinary'[87] – or, as Smith writes on at least one occasion, a 'reasonable' – 'man'.[88] Crucially, the spectator is different from the agent. They are an other to each other. Their thoughts, their feelings are those of an other.[89]

In order to adopt the impartial observer's perspective, individuals must do two things: use their imagination; and empathise. Imagination is important, because the impartial spectator is not an actual third party whose views one

[80] A. Smith, *The Theory of Moral Sentiments* (D.D. Raphael and A.L. Macfie eds, Clarendon 1976).

[81] Smith focuses at times on self-assessment, at times on passing judgement on others. But he maintains that both types of assessment are governed by the same principle (ibid., 109).

[82] Ibid., 110.

[83] Ibid., 113. See also D.D. Raphael, *The Impartial Spectator: Adam Smith's Moral Philosophy* (Clarendon 2007) 36.

[84] Raphael (n 83), 36.

[85] Ibid., 129; Kennedy (n 63), 768.

[86] Frazer (n 14), 96. See also Tom Campbell, *Adam Smith's Science of Morals* (Routledge 2012) 136.

[87] Campbell (n 86), 134.

[88] Smith, *The Theory of Moral Sentiments* (n 80), 70.

[89] In this regard see also Edith Stein's observation that the subject as addressee of an act of empathy differs from the subject who engages in an act of empathy: E. Stein, *Zum Problem der Einfühlung* (Buchdruckerei des Waisenhauses 1917) 10.

could try to gauge.[90] The impartial spectator is a creation of the mind of an individual who attempts to gain an accurate understanding of a given situation.[91] In assuming the perspective of the impartial spectator, 'we put ourselves in his situation and imagine how he would respond to the situation, how he would think and feel about it'.[92] 'When we imagine with figures' in this manner, Maksymilian Del Mar explains,

> we explore what values, vulnerabilities and interests might be at stake in a certain case and in cases like it in the future. This is a highly casuistic way to make normative insight. As a process of imagining, it is also one involving high degrees of affective, sensory and kinesic involvement.[93]

Thus, when invoking the image of a figure such as the impartial spectator, we imagine not only what this impartial spectator might think about a given state of affairs but also what he would sense and feel about it. Accordingly, empathy is important here because what is morally required in a given situation is judged not by reference to some independent abstract standard, but by reference to the concrete sentiments that an impartial spectator would deem it appropriate for me and for society to entertain in a given situation. If imagination and empathy are used in this way, the spectator's perspective can be invoked *ex post*, to judge a given act or circumstance that has already occurred – for example, when assessing a defendant's conduct in court. It can also be used to generate standards of behaviour *ex ante* with respect to acts or circumstances that have yet to occur – for example, when an individual is deliberating how to behave in a given situation.[94]

One may wonder what Smith's impartial observer has to do with the common law's reasonable person. After all, Smith aimed to develop a theory of how to make moral judgements,[95] a theory that would be an alternative to the rationalist accounts of morality mentioned at the beginning of this section.[96] In his *Lectures on Jurisprudence*, however, Smith explicitly links the concept of impartial observer to at least three fields of law: property law, contract law, criminal law.[97] With respect to property law, he observes, referring to his *Theory of Moral Sentiments*:

> an injury was done one when an impartial spectator would be of opinion he was injured, would join with him in his concern and go along with him when he defend(ed) the subject in his possession against any violent attack, or used force to recover what had been thus wrongfully wrested out of his hands.[98]

[90] See generally M. Del Mar, 'Common Virtue and the Perspectival Imagination: Adam Smith and Common Law Reasoning' (2018) 9 Jurisprudence 58.

[91] Raphael (n 83), 35. [92] Stueber (n 72).

[93] M. Del Mar, *Artefacts of Legal Inquiry: The Value of Imagination in Adjudication* (Hart 2020) 339.

[94] Del Mar (n 90), 64. [95] See Raphael (n 83), 10. [96] Ibid., 49. [97] Ibid., 12.

[98] A. Smith, *Lectures on Jurisprudence* (R.L. Meek, D.D. Raphael and P.G. Stein eds, Clarendon 1978) 17.

This would be the case, Smith explains, if one person 'wrested' an apple from another person, who had just picked the apple from a tree.[99] And thus, in light of an impartial spectator's disapproval of such an act, it would be proper to conclude that it is not permissible to wrest apples from other people. Note that the impartial spectator's empathy with the owner of the apple is not itself the foundation of the apple picker's right to the apple. The impartial spectator's empathy merely 'confirms the apple picker's judgement'.[100] The ground for the apple picker's right to the apple is the apple picker's reasonable expectation to acquire title to property by occupying it.[101] However, it is through empathy with the apple picker that this foundation becomes apparent. To Smith, property is, then, 'a reflective outgrowth of our sympathy with the reasonable expectations of our fellows'.[102]

Similarly, in the context of contract law, Smith argues that only such promises are enforceable that an impartial spectator considers to have arisen in connection with the promisor's intention to enter into legal relations with the person to whom a given thing was promised.[103] Only when a person makes an 'open and plain declaration that he desires the person to whom he makes the declaration to have a dependance on what he promises'[104] would an impartial spectator accept the emergence of a contractual relationship between the promisor and the promisee.

Smith refers to the impartial spectator in the context of criminal law, too. Here the spectator's 'concurrence ... with the resentment of the injured' determines the 'measure of punishment to be inflicted on the delinquent'.[105] For example, if the 'injury is so great as that the spectator can go along with the injured person in revenging himself by the death of the offender, this is the proper punishment'.[106] On the other hand,

> If the spectator could not concur with the injured if his revenge led him to the death of the offender, but could go along with him if he revenged the injury by a small corporal punishment or a pecuniary fine, this is the punishment that ought here to be inflicted. In all cases a punishment appears equitable in the eyes of the rest of mankind when it is such that the spectator would concur with the offended person in exacting it.[107]

Thus Adam Smith explicitly acknowledged the transferability of the concept of impartial spectator from the field of morality to the field of law. The Scottish impartial spectator is not identical with the English reasonable man. They have their own history and context. Importantly, the spectator's perspective is necessarily impartial, whereas the reasonable person's perspective is not

99 Ibid., 16–17. 100 Raphael (n 83), 110. 101 Smith, *Lectures on Jurisprudence* (n 98), 17.
102 Frazer (n 14), 107. 103 Smith, *Lectures on Jurisprudence* (n 98), 87. 104 Ibid.
105 Ibid., 104. 106 Ibid. 107 Ibid.

necessarily so.[108] Nevertheless, a look at the scholarship of Scottish sentimentalists such as Smith helps us to answer the question raised at the end of the previous section, namely whether there is a difference between asking whether a given action is reasonable and asking whether a given action is what a reasonable person would have done. In light of the brief introduction to the Scottish sentimentalists, I argue that there is a significant difference and that it corresponds to the difference between the rationalist and the sentimentalist thinkers of the Enlightenment. Answering whether a given action conforms to the behaviour of a reasonable person invites us to engage in perspective taking. It compels us to consider our own situation from an external point of view and from a distinctly social one. Since the idea of an imaginary figure invokes the image of others (real or imaginary), it reminds the person who assesses a given situation of her connectedness to a specific kind of social–environmental context. The reasonable person can function as a 'companion in thought' even to someone who lives alone on an island.[109] When the latter is asked to imagine what a reasonable person might do in a given situation, the figure of the reasonable person invites him to reflect on his role not just as a single individual but as a member of that species called 'human'. These implications are absent from the question whether a given act is reasonable. Del Mar has rightly pointed out that this process of imagining an other is not automatic but is contingent upon recognising the reasonable person as an artefact.[110] Failure to recognise the artifactuality of the reasonable person means that the figure becomes a mere shorthand for reasonableness.[111] For that reason, it is important to avoid conflating references to reasonableness and references to the reasonable person.[112] One could of course answer the question what it means to be reasonable via perspective taking, but the abstract notion of reasonableness appeals more obviously to objective truths built into the universe that are accessed not through empathy but through rational deduction.

The geographic distribution of the different varieties of the Enlightenment appears to lend support to this argument. In Germany – home to many thinkers of the rationalist Enlightenment – references to a personified general standard of reasonableness were dropped in the nineteenth century and replaced by an abstract notion of reasonableness.[113] To a system informed by rational thinking and claiming to be founded on objective maxims discovered by reason alone, references to empathy-inspiring abstract persons are an irritation. But on the British Isles, home to many thinkers of the

[108] Whether the reasonable person's calibrated perspective is impartial depends on the circumstances. See the discussion of the three steps of empathetic perspective taking in the Conclusion.

[109] Del Mar (n 93), 344. [110] Ibid., 331–2. [111] Ibid., 331.

[112] For a different approach, see Michael Saltman, *The Demise of the Reasonable Man: A Cross-Cultural Study of a Legal Concept* (Transaction Publishers 1991) 1.

[113] As mentioned in Chapter 1, however, personified standards survive in specialised areas of German law.

sentimentalist Enlightenment, the eighteenth and the nineteenth centuries saw the emergence of the most robust and most refined personified standard of behaviour to date.[114]

Apart from the temporal and spatial proximity between the Scottish sentimentalists and the reasonable man as a new arrival in nineteenth-century Britain, there are at least three reasons why the former can be seen as a precursor to the common law's anthropomorphised standard of reasonableness. First, the concept of an imaginary, personified standard responded to the need for a functional standard in negligence cases triggered by the industrial revolution. As a concept, the personified standard was instantly relatable, yet appropriately objective. It was transferable across many different situations, yet functionally stable and predictable.

Second, an empathy-based standard of behaviour must have appeared to be particularly plausible in nineteenth-century Britain, where the new media of the novel and, as we saw above, of the newspaper familiarised their readers with the suffering of fellow humans.[115] It was a time 'when such authors as Charles Dickens and Harriet Beecher Stowe gave "eloquent recital" to the sufferings of the poor and enslaved'.[116] Novels that narrated the experiences and feelings of ordinary characters invited readers 'to empathize across class, sex, and national lines.'[117] Well-known examples are Samuel Richardson's (1689–1761) *Pamela, or Virtue Rewarded* (1740), which relates the story of the fifteen-year old maid Pamela Andrews, who struggles with abusive employers and seeks to find her place in society, and *Clarissa, or The History of a Young Lady* (1748), in which Richardson details how the book's heroine, Clarissa Harlowe, tries to remain virtuous in an increasingly corrupt society. Going beyond class and gender relations in a domestic setting, Amelia Opie's (1769–1853) *The Quaker, and the Young Man of the World*[118] (1818) and her poem *The Black Man's Lament* (1826) addressed the question of slavery and of the ultimate unity of human beings.

Books like these aimed to communicate that 'all people are fundamentally similar because of their inner feelings'; they created a 'sense of equality and empathy through passionate involvement in the narrative'.[119] But people were not just reading about one another. As we have seen, the ongoing

[114] As Frazer points out, one must be careful with such a generalization, since there were notable exceptions to this geographic division – for example Johann Gottfried Herder (1744–1803) in Germany and William Wollaston (1659–1724) in Britain: see Frazer (n 14), 4. Note also that numerous elements of Kant's political theory are compatible with the claim that one's own perspective can be calibrated and rendered less partial through the adoption of the perspective of imaginary others; see Arendt (n 74), 42–4.

[115] Moyn (n 61), 401. In this regard, Maksymilian Del Mar has suggested that there might also be a connection between the emergence of figural tests and the 'rich tradition of character writing in England'; see Del Mar (n 93), 336.

[116] Frazer (n 14), 54. [117] Hunt (n 71), 38.

[118] A. Opie, *The Quaker, and the Young Man of the World: A Tale of Trials* (Longman 1818).

[119] Hunt (n 71), 39.

industrialisation and subsequent urbanisation also 'brought the classes into constant contact'.[120] Fittingly, the first sentence of Opie's book *The Quaker* reads: 'There is nothing, perhaps, which occasions so curious a mixture of heterogenous characters, as travelling in stage coaches, and persons meet there, whom the chances of life could not well bring together in any other place.'[121] Social fluidity 'meant that the person who is one day one's inferior may the next be one's equal'.[122] The US author, sociologist and civil rights activist William Edward Burghardt du Bois (1868–1963) has called the nineteenth century 'the first century of human sympathy'.[123] He describes it as an age

> when half wonderingly we began to descry in others the transfigured spark of divinity which we call Myself; when clodhoppers and peasants, and tramps and thieves, and millionaires and – sometimes – Negroes, became throbbing souls whose warm pulsing life touched us so nearly that we half gasped with surprise, crying, 'Thou too! Hast Thou seen Sorrow and the dull waters of Hopelessness? Has Thou known Life?' And then all helplessly we peered into those Other-worlds, and wailed, 'O World of Worlds, how shall man make you one?'[124]

The figure of the reasonable person could be seen as an attempt to negotiate these other worlds, to facilitate the ability of individuals to touch that string of David Hume's, through which all mankind have an accord and a symphony. It is one of the main objectives of the following chapters to determine to which extent the concept of the reasonable person was able to achieve that aim. But, for now, it suffices to note a third connection between the Scottish sentimentalists and the common law's reasonable man. That connection is the figure's proverbial father: Baron Alderson.

2.3 Baron Alderson

In the previous two sections we encountered two metatrends that shaped the period in which the sympathetic character of the reasonable man was born: industrialisation and the sentimental Enlightenment. To speak of metatrends, however, risks forgetting that they do not have lives of their own. In fact they have no lives at all, being mere reflections of the combined experiences of countless individuals to whom a certain label is retrospectively assigned. Thus, in order to understand how industrialisation and the Scottish Enlightenment may have influenced the emergence of the reasonable man, one must consider how these trends manifested themselves in the life of individual human beings. In our case, that individual human being is Edward Hall Alderson, subsequently Baron Alderson – the judge to whose judicial opinion one can trace

[120] Frazer (n 14), 54. [121] Opie, *The Quaker, and the Young Man of the World* (n 118), 1.
[122] Frazer (n 14), 54. [123] Ibid.
[124] W.E.B. du Bois, *The Souls of Black Folk* (2nd ed., McClurg 1903) 218. Note, however, that du Bois also points out that sympathy is no necessary consequence of proximity (ibid., 183–5).

the first reference to the reasonable man. It should be noted from the outset that the choice of focusing on Alderson in this section is not meant to suggest that Alderson was a singular, unique character, a *sine qua non* factor, an entity without which the reasonable man would never have seen the light of day. Alderson's involvement in one of the first cases that refer explicitly to the reasonable man certainly distinguishes him from many of his contemporaries. However, he was selected not because of his unique biography but, on the contrary, because his life and thinking can be considered representative of the life and experiences of an early nineteenth-century judge.

Alderson was born on 11 September 1787 in Great Yarmouth, Norfolk, in the East of England. Throughout his life he remained 'fondly proud' of this 'fishy town'.[125] He returned to it frequently and it delighted him to 'point out to his children the house where he first drew breath'.[126] After completing school in 1805, he went to study classics and mathematics at Gonville and Caius College, Cambridge. There he made himself known not only as a student of extraordinary competence, winning numerous prizes, but apparently also for his ability to prepare a 'brimming bowl of punch, in the admixture of which he was pronounced to excel'.[127] Alderson graduated from Cambridge in 1809, moved to London to study law and was called to the bar in 1811. He joined the Northern Circuit, served as an editor of the law reports from the King's Bench Division and was appointed common law commissioner. In 1830 he was appointed judge of the Court of Common Pleas, then knighted, and in 1834 his legal career reached its climax through elevation to the position of Baron of the Exchequer. In 1823 he married Georgina Catherine Drewe (1791–1871), with whom he had six children. Relatives and colleagues describe Alderson as well organised, humorous – even 'witty'[128] – and unusually curious, 'picking up information at all times and on all points, the most varied and dissimilar'.[129] Alderson died on 27 January 1857, at the age of 69, less than a year after handing down the decision in *Blyth v Birmingham Waterworks*.

Both sentimentalism and industrialisation left their mark on Alderson's life. With respect to sentimentalism, all (available) sources suggest that in his private and professional life Alderson embraced both its core elements: sympathetic perspective taking and an appreciation of the importance of empirical facts and experiences.

In his private relations, Alderson was known as a 'large-hearted' man[130] who empathised with the pain of his dying brother,[131] with a cousin's feelings occasioned by the passing of her aunt,[132] or with the 'suffering and distress'

[125] C. Alderson, 'Life and Literary Remains of Baron Alderson' (1859) 9 The Monthly Christian Spectator 206.
[126] C. Alderson, *Selections from the Charges and Other Detached Papers of Baron Alderson* (John W. Parker and Son 1858) 85.
[127] Ibid., 11. [128] Ibid., 161, 165, 24–5. [129] Ibid., 6. [130] Ibid., 111–12.
[131] Ibid., 30. [132] Ibid., 104. 'I enter completely', Alderson writes to Opie, 'into your feeling'.

sustained by his seafaring friends in 'humbler walks of life'.[133] Having lost his own mother when he was four years old,[134] Alderson wrote to a close relative whose children had lost their mother to an illness: 'I feel for your children more than they can, poor babes, feel for themselves as yet. They are, as I was, without a mother's care at an early period of life, and I know how much of advantage they lose, and of the purest pleasure.'[135] Alderson's son later reported that Alderson had a 'heart which emphatically could sympathize with the joys and sorrows of others'.[136]

Alderson also had a habit of 'poetizing his feelings';[137] he read widely, drafted a drama on the siege of Calais and produced numerous translations of Horace from Latin and Sophocles from Greek.[138] When his sister Isabella – 'his earliest companion and friend'[139] – died of an illness in 1807, Alderson expressed his sentiment in the following lines:

So have I seen the canker's deadly power
E'en in its pride destroy the lovely rose,
While, sweet in death, the slowly withering flower
Around its stem a parting fragrance throws.[140]

When Alderson left the family summer retreat in Norwich for London, to commence his legal studies there in 1809, he wrote:

As one condemned on unknown seas to sail,
When from the port his little bark he steers,
Grazes awhile – his eyes suffused with tears
Ere yet he spreads his canvas to the gale,
So do I now forsake with anxious fears,
Home of my forefathers, thy peaceful dale;
For other prospect to my view appears,
Half hid beneath futurity's deep veil.
Me now the busy world's unceasing strife,
The throng of cities and the hum of men,
And all the crowded walks of active life,
Call from thy rustic Muse, and silent glen;
Oh! when shall I from cares like these be free,
To dream of pleasure, and revisit thee![141]

Other surviving poems mark the birth and confirmation of his children,[142] family vacations,[143] or a temporary lack of work.[144] A frequent recipient of

[133] Ibid., 86.

[134] Ibid., 2. Alderson's son reports that the 'premature loss of that maternal superintendence which exercises so salutary an influence upon childhood' caused Alderson a 'lifelong regret.'

[135] Ibid. [136] Ibid., 160, 110. [137] *The Monthly Christian Spectator* (n 125), 208.

[138] Alderson (n 126), 7. A collection of Alderson's translations is reprinted at the end of the biography prepared by his son (ibid., 246–66).

[139] Alderson (n 126), 12–13. [140] Ibid., 12. [141] Ibid., 15–16. [142] Ibid., 93–94.

[143] Ibid., 83–84. [144] Ibid., 23–24.

Alderson's texts was his already mentioned cousin, the writer and novelist Amelia Opie, *née* Alderson. Opie not only was very active in the anti-slavery movement but also authored numerous works that addressed the social conditions prevalent in early nineteenth-century Britain more generally. Her novel *Valentine's Eve*,[145] for example, focuses on a young lady's struggle to live virtuously in a thoroughly corrupted society and has been described as a 'bleaker'[146] version of Samuel Richardson's *Clarissa*. Opie's first book published under her name,[147] *The Father and Daughter*[148] (1801), addressed the same subject matter. The reader follows the story of the heroine, Agnes Fitzhenry, who is seduced by an aristocratic womanizer, gives birth to his illegitimate son, is abandoned, and, returning to her paternal home, seeks her father's forgiveness. The Scottish writer and historian Walter Scott (1771–1832), himself greatly influenced by the works of the Scottish sentimentalist Adam Smith, with whom he was acquainted,[149] later told Opie that he 'had cried over [the book] more than he ever cried over such things'.[150] In the spirit of the sentimental Enlightenment, Opie's works emphasised 'common humanity and sentimentalized criticism of social differences that produce inequality and suffering'.[151]

Amelia Opie moved in the most progressive circles of her time, calling the German explorer and scientist Alexander von Humboldt (1769–1859) an 'old and valued acquaintance'[152] and entertaining friendly relations with the English writer and feminist Mary Wollstonecraft (1759–97) and her husband, the philosopher William Godwin (1756–1836).

Opie and Alderson met regularly and on numerous occasions she, the progressive author, exposed him, the more conservative judge, to her circle of friends and to the texts she read. In the letters they exchanged, they discussed the transformation of prisons from sites of punishment to places of reform,[153] the unequal distribution of wealth in England,[154] the despotic nature of lynch law in America,[155] and the latest feminist literature.[156] They also discussed Alderson's cases and his work as a judge, which brings us to the point of considering the importance of empathy in Alderson's professional life.

[145] A. Opie, *Valentine's Eve* (Longman 1816).

[146] I.M. Cosgrave, '"White Lies": Amelia Opie, Fiction, and the Quakers' (University of Exeter 2014) 159–60.

[147] The first book authored by Amelia Opie, *Dangers of Coquetry*, was published anonymously in 1790.

[148] A. Opie, *The Father and Daughter with Dangers of Coquetry* (K. Shelley and J.B. Pierce eds, Broadview Press 2003).

[149] A. Smith, *The Correspondence of Adam Smith* (Ernest Campbell Mossner and Ian Simpson Ross eds, Oxford University Press 1987) 258; Kathryn Sutherland, 'Fictional Economies: Adam Smith, Walter Scott and the Nineteenth-Century Novel' (1987) 54 ELH 97, 100.

[150] A. Opie and C.L. Brightwell, *Memorials of the Life of Amelia Opie: Selected and Arranged from Her Letters, Diaries, and Other Manuscripts* (Fletcher and Alexander 1854) 175.

[151] G. Kelly, 'Opie [Née Alderson], Amelia', *Oxford Dictionary of National Biography* (Oxford University Press 2004).

[152] Opie and Brightwell (n 150), 253. [153] Alderson (n 126), 66. [154] Ibid., 73–4.

[155] Ibid., 73. [156] Ibid., 87–8.

In Alderson's professional life, his empathetic character appears to have clashed occasionally with the comparative harshness of the day-to-day administration of justice. Alderson's son observes: 'it cost [Alderson] a painful effort, from the outset to the close of his judicial career, to check the tendency of an unusually indulgent and sympathizing temper'.[157] In a letter written shortly after he became a judge in 1830, Alderson reports:

> The truth is, I am thoroughly sick of this business, and hate it. We have such a terrible responsibility, and I feel to be ashamed and angry with myself for suggesting, as I must do, that the life of this or that man should be sacrificed.[158]

Accordingly, the *Oxford Dictionary of National Biography* remembers Alderson as being 'particularly astute in finding technical reasons to avoid the application of the death penalty'.[159] His biographer relates that 'few things delighted him more than to be instrumental in obtaining a merciful consideration for circumstances which allowed, with propriety, of such intervention'.[160] Even in the later stages of his life, when Alderson had been an experienced judge for some time, his cousin Opie, on hearing that Alderson escaped a trial that could have led to the imposition of the death penalty, wrote that she was 'glad to find thou wast not likely to try the case; because I . . . was perfectly aware what suffering was inflicted on thee whenever thou wast forced in duty to convict capitally'.[161] Alderson even struggled with sentences falling short of capital punishment. In a letter addressed presumably to his wife and dated January 1831, he writes:

> What most moves my pity in the case of these poor felons is their being sent far away from their wives and children; for I think of the agony I should feel in parting from you and my dear children, to meet no more probably in this world. Alas! People think little of any punishment but death, and yet transportation for life seems to be nearly as bad.[162]

There is, however, no indication that Alderson's sentiment caused him to forget his duty as a judge. And when severe penalties could not be avoided, he did impose them, albeit not without expressing his regret. Addressing a group of men convicted of conspiracy and rioting in 1848, Alderson said:

> probably many of you have wives and children; they will suffer in your suffering. I feel for them; I feel for you. I am sorry it is my duty to inflict severe punishment upon you, but I must do it. The law must be vindicated, and people must be convinced that these are dangerous offences for them to commit. Therefore, you must all of you, I am sorry to say, suffer severe punishment.[163]

The importance Alderson attached to empathy in a professional context is also reflected in the following passage taken from his instruction to the jury

[157] Ibid., 50. [158] Ibid.

[159] Steve Hedley, 'Alderson, Sir Edward Hall', *Oxford Dictionary of National Biography* (Oxford University Press 2014). www.oxforddnb.com.

[160] Alderson (n 126), 108. [161] Ibid., 107. [162] Ibid., 53. [163] Ibid., 194.

charged with deciding the fate of those same rioters. Alderson proposed that the rioters be met with a 'uniform course of kind and affectionate conduct towards them':

> The gentleman of estate, with his labourers – the opulent manufacturer, with his workmen – the tradesman, with his apprentices – the clergy, in their more extended sphere, with their flocks – in short, all of us, with our respective dependents, must make men feel that we sympathize with their sufferings and wish their real good; that we seek not theirs, but them; and that with us the name of brother is not a mere empty sound, but denotes in our vocabulary a member of Christ our Head, and a fellow-heir of immortality.[164]

This last passage also indicates the central role of Alderson's Christian faith – a religion that some consider to be the source of the sentimentalist approach.[165] The Christian faith was no doubt important to Alderson (as it was to Opie, a Quaker, and to many other sentimentalists, too).[166] But his own faith was such that it did not prevent him from subscribing to one of the other credos of the sentimentalists: the unity and equality of all humans. Asking himself the question whether there is something that unites 'the Negro, the Carib, the Esquimaux, the Calmuck, the Hindoo, the European', he replies to himself: 'Whatever may be their religion, government, manners, progress in arts or sciences ... still they are one, if they have the same breath of life, origin, redemption, partaking of one common humanity which belongs to the whole race.'[167] This did not mean, however, that law should not take into account those differences that do exist between human beings. In connection with a case concerning whether a Jewish member elect of the House of Commons could omit the words 'on the true faith of a Christian' from an oath, Alderson 'most seriously regret[ted]' to conclude that an oath omitting those words is 'not taken at all'.[168] However, in the same judgment, he also proclaimed that the law must consider the actual human being to which it aims to relate. In the case at hand, Alderson opined that the stipulation that every oath had to include the Christian phrase had entered the law without any heed to people who might not share the Christian faith and strongly recommended that the legislature remedy the legal status of non-Christians in that regard.[169]

While Alderson cherished the certainty and justice of 'general rules' as opposed to the 'imaginary particular justice of each case',[170] he was suspicious of the 'destructive power' of 'systematizing and dogmatizing'.[171] Thus he aimed to combine general norms with empirical facts. In his personal affairs, this meant judging 'not by reference to any ideal standard of his own, but the aggregate results at which the experience of a lifetime conversant with every

164 Ibid., 186. 165 Moyn (n 61), 399.

166 One of Alderson's obituaries remembers him as 'a gentleman, a judge, and, above all, an eminent Christian', *The Monthly Christian Spectator* (n 125), 207.

167 Alderson (n 126), 146. 168 *Miller v Salomons* 155 ER 1036 (Court of Exchequer) 1064.

169 Alderson (n 126), 272–3. 170 Ibid., 123. 171 Ibid., 137.

side of human nature enabled him to arrive'.[172] In his legal affairs, this meant trying to persuade the rioters of the comparative benefit of protesting peacefully, and doing so with the help of a booklet[173] of statistics produced by the first Earl of Lovelace[174] (1805–93) that showed how the average population tends to be affected by unrest and disturbances much more than the wealthy members of society.[175] With respect to sentimentalism, Alderson's biography reflects both its core elements – sympathetic perspective taking and an appreciation of the importance of empirical facts and experience.

Turning now to the period's second metatrend, Alderson dealt with industrialisation-related cases of such importance that it has been said that a list of 'the leading civil cases in which Alderson gave judgment . . . reads like a broad survey of the legal problems of emerging capitalism'.[176] He heard cases concerning the patenting of innovations,[177] the legal character of company shares[178] and the legal consequences of breach of contract.[179] Alderson's most important encounter with industrialisation occurred in 1825, in connection with what his biographer has called the 'first railway case'.[180] The matter concerned a hearing, by a parliamentary committee at Westminster, concerning the proposed construction of a railway line between Liverpool and Manchester across Chat Moss, a stretch of marshland widely assumed not be able to support heavy railroads tracks. The proponents of the railway were relying on a survey prepared by the 'father of the railway', the engineer George Stephenson (1781–1848). The opponents, owners of the land across which the railway was to be built and representatives of canal companies, were determined to protect their commercial interests against competition from the railways. They instructed Alderson to represent these interests during the committee stage of the proposed bill that authorised the construction of the railway. Alderson's task was to call into question the survey prepared by Stephenson. As the hearing started, the proponents presented evidence that, despite the construction of railways in other places and contrary to popular belief, 'horses have not started, nor the cows ceased to give their milk, nor have ladies miscarried at the sight of these things going forward at the rate of four miles and a half an hour'.[181]

The question of speed was of central importance to the opponents of the railway and, accordingly, also formed the subject matter of one of Alderson's cross-examinations of Stephenson. The brief excerpt below gives the reader a

[172] Ibid., 111–12. [173] W.K.-N. Lovelace, *The Agricultural Statistics of France* (Batten 1848).
[174] William King-Noel, the first earl of Lovelace, was the husband of Ada Lovelace (née Byron), who authored one of the first algorithms to be executed by a computation machine.
[175] Alderson (n 126), 112. [176] Hedley (n 159).
[177] *Russell v Cowley* 149 ER 1331 (Court of Exchequer).
[178] *Bligh v Brent* (1836) 2 Y & C Ex 268; 160 ER 397 (Court of King's Bench).
[179] *Hadley and Another v Baxendale and Others* [1854] EWHC J70 (Court of Exchequer).
[180] Alderson (n 126), 32.
[181] S. Smiles, *The Life of George Stephenson, Railway Engineer* (John Murray 1859) 161–2.

good idea of society's struggle to come to terms with the constantly accelerating speed of industrialisation:

ALDERSON:	Of course, when a body is moving upon a road, the greater the velocity, the greater the momentum that is generated?
STEPHENSON:	Certainly.
ALDERSON:	What would be the momentum of forty tons moving at the rate of twelve miles an hour?
STEPHENSON:	It would be very great.
ALDERSON:	Have you seen a railroad that would stand that?
STEPHENSON:	Yes.
ALDERSON:	Where?
STEPHENSON:	Any railroad that would bear going four miles an hour: I mean to say, that if it would bear the weight at four miles an hour, it would bear it at twelve.
ALDERSON:	Taking it at four miles an hour, do you mean to say that it would not require a stronger railway to carry the same weight twelve miles an hour?
STEPHENSON:	I will give an answer to that. I dare say every person has been over ice, when skating, or seen persons go over; and they know that it would bear them at a greater velocity than it would if they went slower; when it goes quick the weight in a manner ceases.
ALDERSON:	Is not that upon the hypothesis that the railroad is perfect?
STEPHENSON:	It is; and I mean to make it perfect.[182]

Alderson's interventions on behalf of the railway's opponents and his claim that Stephenson's railway would inevitably sink 'into the shades of eternal night'[183] delayed the project for a while. Ultimately, however, Stephenson was permitted to construct his railway across the moss, where it still runs today. Nonetheless, despite Stephenson's insistence to the contrary, the railway was of course not perfect, and neither were the pipes of the Birmingham Waterworks. It is in no small part because these inventions were not perfect that the concept of the reasonable person emerged.

As I tried to show in this chapter, the emergence of the concept of the reasonable man in *Blyth v Birmingham Waterworks* can be understood as a result of the interplay between the social changes triggered by industrialisation and the prevailing theories of the sentimental Enlightenment, both of which manifested themselves in the person of judge Edward Hall Alderson. Against that background, it might be surprising to learn that Alderson's role in *Blyth v Birmingham Waterworks* is not mentioned in the available obituaries or in his biography. In fact, one of the first references to Alderson in connection with the reasonable man occurs only at the beginning of the twentieth century, when the legal historian Percy H. Winfield (1878–1953) speaks of 'Baron

[182] Ibid., 165–6. [183] Ibid., 178.

Alderson's "reasonable man"'.[184] That Alderson's contemporaries attached little importance to his statement in *Blyth v Birmingham Waterworks* merely confirms, however, what I argued at the beginning of this chapter, namely that Alderson's biography and views were not unique but representative of a general legal trend. There are other cases, such as *Tindall v Bell*,[185] for example – another case in which Alderson had been involved – that referred to the reasonable man. And there were other judges and legal thinkers who had similar ideas. For instance the legal historian Sir William Jones, mentioned earlier in this chapter, played an instrumental role in connection with the emergence of the reasonable man standard and modern negligence law.[186] As a contemporary of Adam Smith and co-member of the famous Literary Club founded in London in 1764, it is likely that Jones, too, was influenced by the scholarship of the Scottish sentimentalists.

The story of the emergence of the reasonable man can thus be told with reference to different characters. But ultimately it remains the same story: that of a hypothetical figure designed to assist those who exercised a degree of discretion in judging others by inviting them to adopt the perspective of another via their own imagination and empathy. Thus construed, the reasonable person is a hybrid figure. It is used as a model or prototype of a human, yet that human possesses no extraordinary virtues or skills. The figure is meant to be grounded in actual sentiments of people who belong to a given society at a given time, yet the standard it represents is not one that can be verified empirically. The reasonable person is a legal standard; but by making space for human sentiments, for a social common sense, the standard also allows for a variety of other considerations to enter the process of judging. Finally, the reasonable person's perspective is invoked by a person who aims to pass judgment in a court of law, but it is also a perspective informed by the views of those who are being judged and by the society in whose midst the judgment is being passed. Understood in this manner, the concept promised to be a standard that could allow for a benevolent, empathetic evaluation of the behaviour of people across social, economic and cultural divides. Alas, as we move from the birth of the reasonable man to look at the life of this figure in the next chapters, it will become apparent that the standard's application all too often led not to an enhanced understanding of and to empathy with the other but rather to discrimination against that other.

[184] Winfield (n 26), 185. Similarly, Lord Bowen's association with the 'man on the Clapham omnibus', to be discussed in Chapter 3, is not addressed in Lord Bowen's biography but imputed to him only later by another judge. See S. Stern, 'From Clapham to Salina: Locating the Reasonable Man' (2023) Law & Literature 1, 9.

[185] *Tindall v Bell* 152 ER 786 (Court of Exchequer).

[186] R. Young, 'Sir William Jones and the Translation of Law in India', in M. Wan (ed.), *Reading the Legal Case* (Routledge 2012).

3

The Reasonable Person in Clapham

'Great men lived here; great deeds were done here in the cause of suffering humanity. True religion throve and flourished here; this was the home of great enthusiasts.'[1] The object of these words of praise is Clapham, a district in south London. In the early nineteenth century, Clapham resembled a rural 'residential resort for solid City people'[2] at the edge of the English capital. One of Clapham's 'great enthusiasts' referred to by John William Grover (1836–92) in the quotation above was the scientist Henry Cavendish (1731–1810). Having retired to Clapham, it was apparently there that Cavendish determined the density of the earth.[3] Other great Claphamites include the journalist John Walter (1739–1812), founder of the *Times* newspaper, and the members of the Clapham Saints, a circle of social reformers and anti-slavery campaigners that counted among them the minister Henry Venn (1725–97) and the politician William Wilberforce (1759–1833) together with his son Samuel (1805–73), Bishop of Oxford. But, writing in 1892, Grover was speaking about the Clapham of the 'great men' already in past tense. The establishment of a more regular omnibus connection between Clapham and London by the mid-1800s enabled the district to 'become a residence for men having occupation in the City'.[4] Much to Grover's dismay, this led to the replacement of the 'great old houses'[5] with 'comfortable middle-class dwellings'[6] (or 'formal, ugly terraces', as Grover described them)[7] inhabited by people who commuted daily into town.

It must have been these daily commuters that Lord Bowen (1835–94)[8] had in mind when he directed those in search of the characteristics of the reasonable man to imagine the passengers on the Clapham omnibus. In what terms exactly he referred to the man on the Clapham omnibus and why he did so is difficult to ascertain. Lord Bowen's alleged reference occurred in unrecorded proceedings related to the 1872 Tichborne[9] case and, as Simon Stern has

[1] J.W. Grover, *Old Clapham* (2nd ed., Bachhoffner 1892) 5–6.

[2] C.L. Graves, *The Life and Letters of Sir George Grove* (Macmillan 1903) 5. See also H.E. Malden, 'Parishes: Clapham', in H.E. Malden (ed.), *A History of the County of Surrey*, vol. 4 (Victoria County History 1912).

[3] Malden (n 2). [4] Grover (n 1), 95. [5] Ibid., 11. [6] Ibid., 95. [7] Ibid., 11.

[8] *McQuire v Western Morning News Co Ltd* [1903] 2 KB 100 (Court of Appeal) 109 (Collins MR).

[9] *Tichborne v Lushington* (Court of Common Pleas, 1872).

recently shown, none of the surviving records linked to the case contains any reference to Lord Bowen's use of a phrase such as 'the man on the Clapham omnibus'.[10] Lord Bowen's uncertain relationship with this hypothetical referent is a good illustration of the fact that the line between truth and fiction or between fable and fact is frequently difficult to locate when writing the biography of the reasonable person (or indeed when writing any biography).

The first recorded association of the reasonable man with the man on the Clapham omnibus appears in *McQuire v Western Morning News Co Ltd*,[11] a 1903 case where Lord Collins MR (1842–1911) likens the opinion of 'the ordinary reasonable man' to that of 'the man on the Clapham omnibus'.[12] In *Healthcare at Home Ltd v The Common Services Agency*, a UK Supreme Court decision of 2014, Lord Reed recently confirmed the reasonable man's association with the man on the Clapham omnibus.[13]

The inspiration for Lord Bowen's original location of the reasonable man on an omnibus may have been a book by the English journalist and writer Walter Bagehot (1826–77), who was one of Bowen's contemporaries in London's liberal Century Club.[14] In his 1867 work *The English Constitution*,[15] Bagehot equated 'the bald-headed man at the back of the omnibus' with 'the ordinary mass of educated, but still commonplace mankind'.[16] Having outlined in the previous chapter the context in which the concept of the reasonable person emerged in nineteenth-century Britain, I aim to explore here who the reasonable person was or had become by the end of the century that witnessed the arrival of this figure in law reports. I begin my search by considering the relationship between the reasonable person and the passengers on the Clapham omnibus (Section 3.1). I then ask whether the reference was meant to pick up an average or an extraordinary passenger (Section 3.2), and to what extent it was supposed to include non-male passengers (Section 3.3).

3.1 Omnès Omnibus

The original omnibus was introduced in 1826 on the route between Nantes in France and a nearby bath house. It was a horse-drawn bus operated by the

[10] S. Stern, 'From Clapham to Salina: Locating the Reasonable Man' (2023) Law & Literature 1, 9.

[11] *McQuire v Western Morning News* (n 8).

[12] Ibid., 109 (Collins MR).

[13] *Healthcare at Home Limited v The Common Services Agency* [2014] UKSC 49 (Supreme Court) [1–2]. Other cases equating the reasonable man with the man on the Clapham omnibus are *Wilson v Coll (Listing Officer)* [2011] EWHC 2824 (Admin.); [2012] PTSR 1313 (Queen's Bench Division (Administrative Court)) 1316 (Singh J); *Bland v Archdeacon of Cheltenham* [1972] Fam 157 (Arches Court of Canterbury) 162–3 (Sir Cecil Havers).

[14] C.A. Kent, 'Century Club', in *Oxford Dictionary of National Biography* (Oxford University Press 2006).

[15] W. Bagehot, *The English Constitution* (Chapman & Hall 1867).

[16] Ibid., 50. In an 1856 text, Bagehot uses the same phrase but attributes it to 'an able Whig': W. Bagehot, 'Average Government' (*The Saturday Review, 29 March 1856*), 428, 429.

owner of the bath house – a retired officer under Napoleon by the name of Stanislas Baudry (1777–1830) – with the aim of increasing the number of people who frequented his establishment. The omnibus was large by comparison with other vehicles of the time, offering space for up to 16–18 passengers who sat along the sides of the vehicle, facing each other.[17] As it turned out, the omnibus quickly attracted many customers, although the bath house remained empty. People were using the omnibus not as a shuttle for the bath house but as a general means of getting around. Accordingly, Baudry closed the bath house and focused exclusively on setting up additional omnibus routes, first in Nantes and subsequently in Paris.[18] Just why Baudry named his vehicles 'omnibuses' has become the subject of various speculations and fictitious accounts.[19] One such legend involves a French businessman by the name of Omnès, who allegedly owned a hat business[20] or a grocery store[21] called Omnès omnibus – with a play on the Latin echo of the owner's name (*omnes* 'all', *omnibus* 'for all'). This shop was located near the first omnibus station, or maybe somewhere else in Nantes, not near a bus stop at all; and it was well known to the city's inhabitants. Another legend attributes the name to a law student called Omnès who in 1789 convinced his fellow students in Nantes to join the Revolution and received the nickname Omnibus after he rescued two people from drowning.[22] Whatever the true origins of the word 'omnibus' might be, the son of Baudry's accountant, writing in 1892, reports that the decision to use this name communicated the intention that the omnibuses be directed at a broader and more diverse group of people[23] than the rather exclusive *carosses*, for instance.[24]

The first omnibuses arrived in London in 1829 and were built by George Shillibeer (1797–1866), an Englishman who had earlier worked for Baudry in

17 For the etymology of 'omnibus' and for additional references, see W. von Wartburg (ed.), 'Omnis', in *Französisches etymologisches Wörterbuch (Online)* (Mohr 1948) 352–4; Oxford English Dictionary Online, s.v. 'Omnibus', https://www.oed.com/view/Entry/131228; F.A. Brockhaus (ed.), 'Omnibus', in *Allgemeine deutsche Real-Encyklopädie für die gebildeten Stände: Conversations-Lexikon* (8th ed., Brockhaus 1835).

18 Musée des Transports, 'Stanislas Baudry et Les Omnibus de Nantes En 1825', https://amtuir.org/03_htu_generale/htu_1_avant_1870/htu_1.htm#top; E. Amann, *The Omnibus: A Cultural History of Urban Transportation* (Springer Nature 2023) 20–1.

19 For an overview, see S. Winick, 'The Legend of Monsieur Omnès' (*Folklife Today (Library of Congress)*, 12 February 2020), https://blogs.loc.gov/folklife/2020/02/the-legend-of-monsieur-omnes.

20 Musée des Transports (n 18).

21 WTM, 'Omnibus' (1879) 11 Notes and Queries 455, 455; H.C. Moore, *Omnibuses and Cabs: Their Origin and History* (Chapman & Hall 1902) 8.

22 N. Déplanche, 'From Young People to Young Citizens: The Emergence of a Revolutionary Youth in France, 1788–1790' (2011) 45 Journal of Social History 225, 228 (the episode about Omnès's heroic rescue is recounted in note 22).

23 M. Dagault, 'Bureau des voitures Dames blanches dites omnibus' (1892) 31 Bulletin de la Société Archéologique de Nantes 116, 119.

24 Oxford English Dictionary Online (n 17).

Paris. On 7 July 1829, the *Morning Post* of London described the arrival of the omnibus in the following manner:

> Saturday the new vehicle, called the *Omnibus*, commenced running from Paddington to the City, and excited considerable notice, both from the novel form of the carriage and the elegance with which it is fitted out. It is capable of accommodating 16 or 18 persons, all inside; and we apprehend it would be almost impossible to make it overturn, owing to the great width of the carriage. It was drawn by three beautiful bays a-breast, after the French fashion. The *Omnibus* is a handsome machine, in the shape of a van, with windows on each side, and one at the end.[25]

A few days later another newspaper, *The Standard*, reported that London's Lord Mayer had remarked that the 'civility, in particular' of the conductors of omnibuses 'was a charm with which those who travelled the Paddington road were not accustomed to meet from the coachmen'.[26] He thought that 'the Omnibus might tend to reform the manners of these well-known gentlemen of the whip'.[27]

It was on one of these 'handsome machines' that Lord Bowen sought to place the reasonable man. As we have seen, the omnibus was not just any vehicle. It was a relatively new invention by comparison with more established means of transport such as the stagecoach or the steam-powered boat. And it was a vehicle that aimed to offer comfortable transportation to a large section of the public. However, upon closer inspection, the omnibus was not as egalitarian as its name suggests. As the historian Donald Read notes, omnibuses 'were always middle-class vehicles', since 'the fares were high . . . and most services started too late (normally about 8 a.m.) to suit working people'.[28] Similarly, Elizabeth Amann, author of a cultural history of the omnibus, observes that its passengers represented 'the common-sense consensus of the commercial middle-class'.[29] Thus, to say that the reasonable man travels on an omnibus singled him out as a member of the urban middle classes. These were people who could afford to pay the omnibus fare instead of having to rely on the seemingly unruly stagecoach operators at Paddington station; people who had the means to move around in relative comfort, but did not own or have access to a private carriage; people who embraced modernity and the ongoing transport revolution.[30]

The following excerpt clearly expresses the association of the omnibus with the middle class – situated between the high society that gathered in a club in Pall Mall and the 'man on the street' who frequented local pubs:

[25] 'Police Intelligence', *Morning Post* (London, 7 July 1829), 3.

[26] 'Multiple News Items', *The Standard* (London, 13 July 1829), 4.

[27] Ibid.

[28] D. Read, *England, 1868–1914: The Age of Urban Democracy* (Longman 1979) 62.

[29] Amann (n 18), 157.

[30] J. Thompson, *British Political Culture and the Idea of 'Public Opinion', 1867–1914* (Cambridge University Press 2013) 36.

> If you want to know what one newspaper will say, ask the first hundred men who come out of a club in Pall Mall, and put the opinion of the majority into rather smarter language, deck it out with a few antitheses and illustrations, and provide it with a short irrelevant preface; – that will be the leading article for one newspaper. For another we must go a degree further down, and gather our samples in an omnibus; or drop yet another degree, and find out what people are saying at the bars of public-houses.[31]

In other words, the man travelling on the omnibus between Clapham and London was not one of Grover's great men, and he most likely did not live in one of Clapham's great houses.[32] He was sufficiently well off to travel and to have occasion to travel, but not sufficiently wealthy to do so in his own vehicle. The most concrete description of who these commuters would have been comes from the 1866 novel *Land at Last*[33] by Edmund Yates (1831–94), who describes the passengers on the Clapham omnibus as people

> who married and settled, and paid taxes and tradesmen's bills, and had children, and went to bed before morning, and didn't smoke clay pipes and sit in their shirt-sleeves.[34]

An important aspect of placing the reasonable man on the Clapham omnibus is that this figure moves about in public. By comparison with persons who had access to carriages or, even better, possessed carriages of their own – judges such as Baron Alderson, for example[35] – or with a figure such as the male head of a household, who reads his newspaper 'over breakfast',[36] in the privacy of his home, the reasonable man enjoyed a high degree of visibility. One had a chance of encountering him on one's way to work in the morning, or of seeing him descend on the pavement of Grace Church Street in London. Accordingly, an anonymous letter published by the satire magazine *Punch* in 1855 encouraged Prime Minister Lord Palmerston to listen to 'the Voice of the Omnibus':[37] 'give up your carriage and condescend to the bus', the author tells the prime minister, since it is on the bus that one can ascertain 'the feeling of the middle class' inhabiting the 'wide world outside of Belgravia, Piccadilly, May Fair, Whitehall, and the Houses of Parliament'.[38]

31 L. Stephen, 'Anonymous Journalism', in A. King and J. Plunkett (eds), *Popular Print Media, 1820–1900*, vol. 2 (Routledge 2004) 580. The text first appeared in the monthly magazine *Saint Paul's*, in May 1868.

32 See also K.P. Tobia, 'How People Judge What Is Reasonable' (2018) 70 Alabama Law Review 293, 334–5. Kevin Tobia suggests that the reasonable man might have been 'both a statistically average person and a prescriptively praiseworthy person'.

33 E. Yates, *Land at Last* (2nd ed., Chapman & Hall 1867).

34 Ibid., 102.

35 For example, Amelia Opie recounts an evening when, to her great excitement, Baron Alderson, her cousin, invited her to ride along in his carriage, together with a chaplain and the High Sheriff; see A. Opie and C.L. Brightwell, *Memorials of the Life of Amelia Opie: Selected and Arranged from Her Letters, Diaries, and Other Manuscripts* (Fletcher and Alexander 1854) 355.

36 Thompson (n 30), 37.

37 Punch, 'The Voice of the Omnibus' (1855) 28 *Punch* 179.

38 Ibid.

While the passengers on the omnibus itself might have belonged to the middle class, the reasonable man's perspective is also informed by what he sees while travelling on it. The following lines, from a poem dedicated to the London omnibuses, relate the heterogenous scenery that an omnibus passenger would have observed. The author begins by noting: 'the true observatory, / Whence you may view this London's shame and glory / . . . / Its goodness, meanness, tumult, fogs and fuss / Come near – I whisper – is – an – OMNIBUS!'.[39] Having boarded the bus, the author describes what one observes while travelling through London:

Here walk, or stagger, lie, or crouch, or stand,
Men of all colours and of every land:
Here every costume, custom, class, or sect,
Finds some to wear it, follow, or protect:
And all the ages, by some elfin power,
Are here compressed into a single hour.
Savage or cultured, fierce or mild or mad;
Lazarus all sores, and he in purple clad;
Greeks, Russians, Yankees, Jews, Australians, Tartars,
Thugs, Magis, Sophists, Cannibals, and Martyrs;
Wretches who dyed their blades in Pompey's blood,
And laughed at Noah just before the flood;
And white-robed saints, angels in human guise,
Who staid, when Adam fled from Paradise;
All, all, are here – each shadow, type, and mystery,
Terrific Drama of man's tragic history,
As, day by day, the mighty town repeats
The world's vast record on its echoing streets.[40]

Thus, crucially, the reasonable man could not only be seen in public but also see others in public. The fact that he travelled by bus meant that he was in motion, passing through different parts of town, and that, while doing so, he would encounter many others – not just fellow middle-class passengers. In light of the ever-fluctuating group of passengers who travel on public transport, the reasonable person, construed as a passenger on an omnibus, is familiar with many different people (see Figure 3.1). This makes him relatable and, importantly, also enables someone in that position to relate to others.

The fluctuating character of passengers on an omnibus also meant that the ultimate identity of the reasonable man remained to some extent indeterminate. Depending on season, time of day or city, the passenger one could encounter would look different – not radically different, since the earlier observations and hints concerning class and gender limit the range of persons that could fit the description, but nonetheless sufficiently different to avoid the impression that the man on the Clapham omnibus could ever be just one

[39] Anonymous, *The Omnibus: A Satire* (Trubner 1865) 4–5. [40] Ibid., 9.

Figure 3.1 *The Bayswater Omnibus* (1895), by George William Joy (1844–1925). On omnibuses, persons met 'whom the chances of life could not well bring together in any other place' (Amelia Opie).
Credits: Heritage Images / Getty Images

particular person. In this connection it might be worth recalling the opening passage from Amelia Opie's *The Quaker, and the Young Man of the World* – where, reflecting a sentiment akin to the one expressed in the lines of the poem quoted earlier, she observes that there are few places that can compare to means of public transport where 'so curious a mixture of heterogenous characters . . . meet . . . whom the chances of life could not well bring together in any other place'.[41] Consequently the precise characteristics of the reasonable man must be diffuse to some extent. As one judge put it in a case from the 1940s, 'there is room for diversity of view'[42] when it comes to the characteristics of the reasonable man. Regrettably, the legal potential of such a heterogenous, visible, inclusive, relatable and indeterminate legal standard has not always been recognised in this manner. As we will see in the following

[41] A. Opie, *The Quaker, and the Young Man of the World: A Tale of Trials* (Longman 1818) 1. Opie's observation refers to a stagecoach, but it is just as applicable to the omnibus, the stagecoach's successor. Similarly, Elizabeth Amman observes that the introduction of the omnibus caused 'the population . . . to mix in unprecedented ways': Amann (n 18), 3.

[42] *Glasgow Corporation v Muir and Others* [1943] AC 448 (House of Lords) 457 (Lord Macmillan). Thus one must approach with caution any claims that the reasonable person standard is an expression of the view that there 'can be one ideal, one truth, one and only one appropriate behaviour in any given situation': R. Martin, 'A Feminist View of the Reasonable Man: An Alternative Approach to Liability in Negligence for Personal Injury' (1994) 23 Anglo-American Law Review 334, 342.

subsections and in the forthcoming chapters, the relative heterogeneity of the standard either has attracted fierce criticism for being at once too broad and too narrow or has simply been ignored, in the absence of a more fixed notion of reasonableness. But before we turn to consider these aspects in more detail we must consider what standard of behaviour one could actually expect from passengers on the omnibus. We now know, albeit only roughly, who the passengers could be, but we do not yet know whether they are ideal or ordinary representatives of their group.

3.2 Adolphe Quetelet

The case of *Blyth v Birmingham Waterworks* indicates that the applicable standard is not that of an ideal person but that of an ordinary person with ordinary capabilities and aspirations. In *Blyth* the court was asked to determine whether a reasonable man would have acted the way the defendant – Birmingham Waterworks Company – did. Specifically, the question was whether a reasonable man could have prevented the leakage of the waterpipes. Baron Alderson concluded that the reasonable man 'would act with reference to the average circumstances of the temperature in ordinary years'[43] and, consequently, that the severe frost that caused the leakage was 'a contingency against which no reasonable man can provide'.[44] Thus, he reasoned, the injuries sustained by Mr Blyth and his children were not a result of Birmingham Waterworks' negligence. This is a plausible finding; and it is one that indicates that the standard of the reasonable man was not an ideal person but rather an ordinary, average person. This is so because *de facto* it would have been possible to avoid the accident. For example, if the severe temperatures had caused the company to survey its pipes and fire plugs more regularly, daily maybe, or at least if the company had acted immediately when it had cause to suspect a leakage (i.e. when the ice appeared around the fire plug, some time before the leakage), the injury to Mr Blyth's children and the damage to his property could have been prevented. Such a course of conduct might have been time-intensive and costly. But one could argue that a perfect or 'ideal' man would have readily incurred the additional cost and would have invested the extra time, in the interest of preventing harm to others.

Despite occasional suggestions to the contrary,[45] subsequent decisions confirmed that the reasonable man standard is best understood as referring

[43] *Blyth v The Company of Proprietors of the Birmingham Waterworks* (1856) 11 Exch 781 (Court of Exchequer) 784.

[44] Ibid., 784–5.

[45] William Prosser argues, for instance, that the reasonable person is 'always up to standard' (W.L. Prosser, *The Law of Torts* (4th ed., West Publishing 1971) 150–1). Alan Patrick Herbert famously described the reasonable man as being '[d]evoid . . . of any human weakness, with not one single saving vice': A.P. Herbert, *Uncommon Law* (Methuen 1948) 4. This characterisation can make for good entertainment, but is misleading at best.

not to an ideal individual but to a man of 'ordinary care and skill',[46] that the reasonable man 'is presumed to be free both from over-apprehension and from over-confidence',[47] and that he is an 'ordinary man',[48] a 'man of ordinary prudence',[49] 'the common man',[50] 'the average person'.[51] Similarly, the author of the *Oxford Companion to Law* observes that the reasonable man 'has not the courage of Achilles, the wisdom of Hercules, nor has he the prophetic vision of a clairvoyant'.[52] He is 'reassuringly ordinary'[53] or, in the words of Maksymilian Del Mar, 'chock-full of average humanity'.[54] In this way the reasonable man once more resembles Adam Smith's impartial observer, who similarly appealed to 'so weak and imperfect a creature as man'[55] as opposed to a perfect being[56] such as 'the great Superintendant of the universe'.[57] Just like the abilities of Smith's impartial spectator, those of the reasonable man are 'fully human, and he possesses these only to the degree which is common in the average person'.[58]

The reasonable man's association with the 'average person' has prompted some to argue that the characteristics of this construct can be established by collecting empirical information about the actual behaviour of human beings. Support for the contention that these characteristics were meant to be empirically verifiable comes from a theory that relates the emergence of the reasonable man to the publication of a book by the Belgian astronomer, statistician and sociologist Adolphe Quetelet (1796–1874). At about the same time as the concept of the reasonable man began to appear in English law reports, Quetelet published in Paris a book entitled *A Treatise on Man and the Development of His Faculties*.[59] In the book, Quetelet set out to identify the

46 *Heaven v Pender, Trading as West India Graving Dock Company* (1883) 11 QBD 503 (Court of Appeal) 507–10 (Brett MR).
47 *Glasgow Corporation v Muir and Others* [1943] AC 448 (n 42), 457 (Lord Macmillan).
48 *Bolam v Friern Hospital Management Committee* [1957] 1 WLR 582 (Queen's Bench Division) 586 (McNair J).
49 *Vaughan v Menlove* 132 ER 490 (Court of Common Pleas) 493 (Tindall CJ).
50 *Indyka v Indyka* [1967] P 233 (Court of Appeal) 264–5 (Russel LJ).
51 *Bland v Archdeacon of Cheltenham* [1972] Fam 157 (n 13) 162–3 (Sir Cecil Havers).
52 D.M. Walker, *The Oxford Companion to Law* (Clarendon 1980) 1038, 288. The limited ability of the reasonable man to predict the future was also pointed out by Romer LJ in *Hawkins v Coulsdon and Purley Urban DC* [1954] 1 QB 319 (Court of Appeal) 341 (Romer LJ).
53 M. Moran, *Rethinking the Reasonable Person: An Egalitarian Reconstruction of the Objective Standard* (Oxford University Press 2003) 18.
54 M. Del Mar, 'Common Virtue and the Perspectival Imagination: Adam Smith and Common Law Reasoning' (2018) 9 Jurisprudence 58, 61.
55 A. Smith, *The Theory of Moral Sentiments* (D.D. Raphael and A.L. Macfie eds, Clarendon 1976) 77.
56 Ibid. 57 Ibid., 292.
58 T. Campbell, *Adam Smith's Science of Morals* (Routledge 2012) 137.
59 The original book (*Sur l'homme et le développement de ses facultés, ou essai de physique sociale*) was published in 1835. The first English translation appeared in 1842: A. Quetelet, *A Treatise on Man and the Development of His Faculties* (R. Knox trans., William and Robert Chambers 1842).

characteristics of *l'homme moyen* – the average person. Himself not only a sociologist but also an astronomer, Quetelet aimed to study the characteristics of the average person in the same manner as he would have studied stars: through careful observation.[60] Thus he compiled statistics, across various European states, of the rate of human reproduction, the physical strength of individuals and their height, weight, death rates, productivity, gender ratio, age of marriage, and crime rates. According to Quetelet, the potential of the statistical method was not limited to the identification of the average person's physical characteristics but could also be applied to the average person's moral characteristics:

> To attain a knowledge of the general laws regulating these latter (moral) faculties, a sufficient number of observations must be collected, in order to bring out what is constant, and to set aside what is purely accidental.[61]

The temporal proximity between the advent of Quetelet's 'average person' and the emergence of the reasonable man has invited some to argue that the 'early idea of the reasonable person borrowed heavily from the concept of *l'homme moyen*',[62] that 'the reasonable man is average man's descendant',[63] and that 'the average man and the reasonable man are historically intertwined'.[64] As plausible as this theory might seem, there are important differences between the common law's reasonable person and Quetelet's *homme moyen*. Maybe confusingly, Quetelet's average human was not 'average' in the ordinary sense (an arbitrary mean of human behaviour) but was an ideal to be aspired to. Quetelet's average person was society's 'centre of gravity'[65] and, much like the Egyptian *geru maa*, represented 'all which is beautiful – all which is good'.[66] Coming close to conflating the distinction between how things are and how things ought to be, Quetelet argued that individual humans should, and that they *de facto* do, approach the human average type in their behaviour.[67] The common law's reasonable man, by contrast, is above the average but more ordinary than Quetelet's archetypal person, who represents all that is good and beautiful. In any event, an analysis of the case law quickly reveals that the reasonable man was not meant to be a normative standard that could be empirically verified, but rather a standard controlled by the courts.

60 Ibid., 8. 61 Ibid., 6.

62 A.D. Miller and R. Perry, 'The Reasonable Person' (2012) 87 New York University Law Review 323, 370. See also G. Shajobi-Ibikunle, 'The Concept of a Reasonable Man in Tort Law: A Need for a Paradigm Shift?' (2018) 2 Kampala International University Law Journal 267, 268.

63 B. Cooper, *Family Fictions and Family Facts: Harriet Martineau, Adolphe Quetelet and the Population Question in England, 1798–1859* (Routledge 2007) 5.

64 T. Hyde, *Ugliness and Judgment: On Architecture in the Public Eye* (Princeton University Press 2019) 81.

65 Quetelet (n 59), 8. 66 Ibid., 100, 108.

67 Ibid., 108. For a discussion of the phenomenon whereby 'the typical becomes the admirable simply by virtue of its typicality', see Stern (n 10), 2–4.

Once again, *Blyth v Birmingham Waterworks* provides a suitable illustration. When Baron Alderson was presented with the question whether a reasonable person would have acted as the Birmingham Waterworks did, he did not survey how waterworks companies normally protect people against severe temperatures. He simply assessed the Waterworks' conduct with reference to the reasonable person standard. In other words, it was Baron Alderson and his brother judges – Baron Martin (1801–33) and Baron Bramwell (1808–92) – who controlled how the question concerning the reasonableness of the behaviour of this particular waterworks company should be answered. At the time, one of the main reasons for the judges' determination to retain control over the characteristics of the reasonable person as opposed to leaving these characteristics to be determined by empirically verifiable facts was the concern that juries were too ready to convict and too prepared to impose substantial fines upon companies responsible for causing injuries to members of the public.[68] And indeed, in *Blyth*, Baron Alderson and his brother judges overturned the lower-instance judgment, including the findings of the lower court's jury, which had concluded that the Birmingham Waterworks had in fact acted negligently and that they should compensate Mr Blyth and his four children for the injuries and damage they sustained.[69] A recent UK Supreme Court decision confirmed that the approach of the judges in *Blyth* is still being followed today. In the decision *Healthcare at Home Ltd v The Common Services Agency*[70] (mentioned earlier in this chapter), Lord Reed explains:

> the behaviour of the reasonable man is not established by the evidence of witnesses, but by the application of a legal standard by the court. The court may require to be informed by evidence of circumstances which bear on its application of the standard of the reasonable man in any particular case; but it is then for the court to determine the outcome, in those circumstances, of applying that impersonal standard.[71]

As Lord Reed's comment indicates, the exact characteristics of the reasonable man are determined by the courts. The reasonable man is, then, not an average person in any statistical sense, or in any sense that could be otherwise empirically verified.[72] Accepting Lord Bowen's invitation to associate the

[68] M. Lobban, 'Common Law Reasoning and the Foundations of Modern Private Law' (2007) 32 Australian Journal of Legal Philosophy 39, 57. See also C. Dent, 'The Reasonable Man, His Nineteenth-Century Siblings, and Their Legacy' (2017) 44 Journal of Law and Society 406, 415–16; C.K. Allen, 'The Judge as Man of the World' (1930) 46 Law Quarterly Review 151, 154.

[69] Some even suggest that the standard of the reasonable man was specifically introduced to limit the discretion of juries when determining whether companies had acted negligently; see Dent (n 68), 416.

[70] *Healthcare at Home Limited v The Common Services Agency* [2014] UKSC 49 (n 13).

[71] Ibid., [3].

[72] Accordingly, it is misleading when Goddard LJ (as he then was) equates the views of the reasonable man with the views of 'most people'; see *English and Scottish Co-Operative Properties Mortgage and Investment Society Ltd v Odhams Press Ltd* [1940] 1 KB 440 (Court of Appeal) 459–60 (Goddard LJ). See also Thompson (n 30), 40; S. Stern, 'R v Jones (1703)', in

reasonable man with the man on the Clapham omnibus thus does not mean searching for actual passengers on that bus, but rather imagining the perspective of ordinary people of average capacity who might travel on public means of transport. However, when imagining who these people might be and what characteristics they might possess, judges (or we, when assessing others) do not enjoy unlimited discretion. The creations of imagination must still be anchored to reality. As we saw in the previous chapter, the Enlightenment sentimentalists – whose school of thought, I argued, informed the emergence of the reasonable man standard – were 'united in their insistence that the modern, a posteriori or "experimental" approach be applied'[73] not just to 'natural subjects' such as Quetelet's stars but also to moral questions. Hutcheson held that 'a true scheme of morals could not be the product of genius and invention, or of the greatest precision of thought in metaphysical reasonings, but must be drawn from proper observations upon the several powers and principles which we are conscious of in our bosoms'.[74]

In contrast to Quetelet, the Scottish sentimentalists did not believe that experiments, statistics or empirical studies could conclusively identify what is morally right and what is morally wrong. Observations and insights gained through empathy needed to be filtered. They 'must always bear', as Smith put it, 'some secret reference, either to what are, or to what, upon a certain condition, would be, or to what, we imagine, ought to be the judgment of others'.[75] This 'secret reference' is meant to ensure that judges do not simply project their own characteristics onto the reasonable man. What exactly this secret reference could be is difficult to determine in general terms. In *Barry*, a 1997 House of Lords decision, Lord Lloyd of Berwick suggested that the perspective of the reasonable person must be rooted in 'the standards of civilised society'.[76] Others have proposed that the standard should relate to some 'pre-existing societal consensus',[77] to 'community expectations',[78] or to an 'organic sense of custom'.[79] In any event, the ultimate function of Smith's 'secret reference' is to ensure that the multiplication of perspectives involved

P. Handler, H. Mares and I. Williams (eds), *Landmark Cases in Criminal Law* (Hart 2017) 66; Tobia (n 32), 335; O.M. Jr Reynolds, 'The Reasonable Man of Negligence Law: A Health Report on the Odious Creature' (1970) 23 Oklahoma Law Review 410, 421.

73 M.L. Frazer, *The Enlightenment of Sympathy: Justice and the Moral Sentiments in the Eighteenth Century and Today* (Oxford University Press 2010) 17.

74 W. Leechman, 'Preface', in F. Hutcheson, *A System of Moral Philosophy, in Three Books*, vol 1 (A. Millar 1755) xiv.

75 Smith (n 55), 110.

76 *R v Gloucestershire CC Ex p Barry* [1997] AC 584 (House of Lords) 598 (Lord Lloyd of Berwick). See also *Owens v Owens* [2017] EWCA Civ 182 (Court of Appeal) [41] (Sir James Munby P).

77 N. Ehrenreich, 'Pluralist Myths and Powerless Men: The Ideology of Reasonableness in Sexual Harassment Law' (1990) 99 Yale Law Journal 1177, 1181.

78 R.L. Rabin, 'The Historical Development of the Fault Principle: A Reinterpretation Symposium: Modern Tort Theory' (1980) 15 Georgia Law Review 925, 931.

79 Ibid., 930.

in perspective taking truly is a multiplication of perspectives rather than an egocentric replication of the judge's own stand. And yet, for the longest part of the concept's existence, the reasonable person has been thought of as a male figure, a figure that possesses the same gender as the judges who resort to it. It is to this core characteristic that we now turn.

3.3 Eileen Sayers

Baron Alderson spoke of the reasonable man, Bagehot of the bald-headed man, Lord Bowen of the man on the Clapham omnibus. The archetypal legal person that these commentators had in mind was clearly male. On the basis of the term's etymology, one could construe 'man' also in a way that captures human beings in general, as opposed to men only.[80] A study by the Scottish writer and feminist Charlotte Stopes (1840–1929) noted:

> For centuries . . . the word 'man' was practically treated as a common noun, like freeholder, resident, taxpayer, merchant, trader, shopkeeper, pauper, prisoner, traitor, criminal benefactor. In short 'man' was held as equivalent to person or individual, the unit in the collective noun 'people'.[81]

In 1850, the English parliament even passed a law that stipulated that all words 'importing the Masculine Gender shall be deemed and taken to include Females . . . unless the contrary as to Gender . . . is expressly provided'.[82] Nonetheless, in *Chorlton v Lings*,[83] a case from 1868, the Court of Common Pleas determined that the formulation '[e]very Man shall . . . be entitled to be registered as a Voter' in section 3 of the 1867 Representation of the People Act[84] was not meant to extend the right to vote to women, despite the absence of any express provision to the contrary. The court held that only in scientific works on 'zoology or fossil organic remains', or in 'abstract . . . philosophical or religious disquisitions', would the term 'man' cover women as well.[85] '[I]n almost every other connection, the word "man" is used in contradistinction to "woman".'[86] Stopes herself observed that, in practice, nineteenth-century lawyers 'decided . . . that the word "man" always includes "woman" when

[80] Oxford English Dictionary Online, s.v. 'Man'. On the supposed gender neutrality of the term 'man', see also L. Bender, 'A Lawyer's Primer on Feminist Theory and Tort' (1988) 38 Journal of Legal Education 3, 22; R.K.L. Collins, 'Language, History and the Legal Process: A Profile of the Reasonable Man' (1976) 8 Rutgers Camden Law Journal 311, 32.

[81] C. Stopes, *The Sphere of 'Man' in Relation to That of 'Woman' in the Constitution* (Fisher Unwin 1907) 6. For a comprehensive overview of the various meanings attributed to 'man' and how this word has been used to exclude woman, see in M. Beard, 'Attitudes of Man', in her *Woman as a Force in History* (Macmillan 1946).

[82] Interpretation Act 1850, section 4. The full title of the act was An Act for Shortening the Language Used in Acts of Parliament.

[83] *Chorlton v Lings* (1868) LR 4 CP 374 (Court of Common Pleas).

[84] Representation of the People Act 1867, section 3.

[85] *Chorlton v Lings* (1868) LR 4 CP 374 (n 83), 392 (Byles J).

[86] Ibid.

there is a penalty to be incurred, and never includes "woman" when there is a privilege to be conferred'.[87]

A close look at the metaphors used to describe the reasonable man also reveals that the judges really had their male contemporaries in mind when they described the reasonable person as the man on the Clapham omnibus.[88] A nineteenth-century member of society who did not work at home but in the city and who 'returns home to dinner, tired, care-worn; his mind in his ledger and his banker's book ... very bad company for his wife; perhaps cross; perhaps sleepy'[89] was clearly a male individual.[90] Describing the reasonable person in this way means thinking of the reasonable person as a man. Thinking of the reasonable person as a man risks othering all those who are not men. Accordingly, many have asked whether there can also be reasonable women.[91] We have seen in Chapter 2 that the nineteenth century has been described as the century of sympathy. However, Lynn Hunt has pointed out that, while '[s]ympathy and sensibility worked in favor of many disenfranchised groups',[92] it did not do so for women. Up until the end of the nineteenth century it remained true that, as the English jurist William Blackstone (1723–80) remarked in 1765, a woman's marriage 'suspended' her 'very being or legal existence'[93] and that, legally, women could be considered 'inferior' beings at best.

Writing extrajudicially about two hundred years later, Lord Denning declared that gender equality had been 'completed' thanks to a series of legal reforms that commenced in 1870. In 1980 he stated that even married women were able to 'own property and earnings ... stocks ... wedding presents' and to 'go out to work and earn' their own living.[94] To many, Lord Denning's proclamation would have seemed premature. In any event, his account neatly summarises the position of (married) women before 1870: they were not able to own property or dispose of it, or to go to work and earn a living. Women could not vote and played a negligible role in economic affairs.[95] The judges, lawyers, clerks in court were, of course, all men. Women played only a minor role in judicial proceedings, if any. Once again, *Blyth* can make a suitable illustration. The case was heard by a male bench. The claimant was Mr Blyth,

[87] Stopes (n 81), 5. [88] Collins (n 80), 312.

[89] Calcutta Review, 'Review of: The Letters of Civis on Indian Affairs from 1842–1849 by Henry Russell', *Calcutta Review (XXV/XIII)* (Sanders, Cones and Co 1850) 416.

[90] L.M. Finley, 'A Break in the Silence: Including Women's Issues in a Torts Course' (1989) 1 Yale Journal of Law and Feminism 41, 58. See also Joanne Conaghan, 'Tort Law and the Feminist Critique of Reason', in Anne Bottomley (ed.), *Feminist Perspectives on the Foundational Subjects of Law* (Cavendish Publishing 1996) 52.

[91] Herbert (n 45), 5. [92] L. Hunt, *Inventing Human Rights: A History* (W.W. Norton 2007) 66.

[93] W. Blackstone, *Commentaries on the Laws of England*, vol. 1 (Clarendon 1765) 430.

[94] A. Denning, *The Due Process of Law* (Oxford University Press 1980) 200. See also C. Smart, *Feminism and the Power of Law* (Routledge 1989) 12.

[95] W. Parker, 'The Reasonable Person: A Gendered Concept?' (1993) 23 Victoria University of Wellington Law Review 105, 108. See also Collins (n 80), 316.

who sought compensation for damage to his property. The property was stored in the house he owned and inhabited with his four children and – presumably – with the children's mother, his wife. Yet there is no mention of Mr Blyth's wife (or of any other woman, for that matter) in any of the law reports or newspaper articles related to the incident in question.

In the few cases on record where the conduct of a woman was at issue, courts tended to employ the reasonable man standard so that it 'othered' women in at least two ways. One tendency was to other women explicitly, by claiming that the standard of the reasonable man clearly could not be applied to them.[96] In these cases, courts were 'equating the degree of diligence required of women with that which the law expected of children or incompetents'.[97] In the American case of *Daniels v Clegg*, for instance, Mr Clegg sought to recover damages from Mr Daniels after 'a horse and buggy' driven by Mr Clegg's twenty-year-old daughter 'in great haste to find her father on account of the dangerous illness of a sister' had collided with a carriage driven by Mr Daniels.[98] Apart from the fact that it is the father who brings the action on behalf of his daughter (whose name the court reports do not care to mention), it is noteworthy that Chief Justice Christiancy holds that no one could expect

> from a young woman ... the same amount of knowledge, skill, dexterity, steadiness of nerve, or coolness of judgment, in short the same degree of competency, which he would expect of ordinary men under like circumstances.[99]

And he continues: 'The incompetency indicated by her age or sex ... was less in degree ... than in the case of a mere child; but the difference is in degree only, and not in principle.'[100]

Alongside these explicit forms of exclusion, the standard of the reasonable man was also used to discriminate more indirectly against women. For example in *Tucker v Henniker*,[101] another case from the United States, the court was asked to determine whether the conduct of women was meant to be judged with reference to a standard of care usually exercised by women. The facts of the case were similar to those of *Daniels v Clegg* and involved a woman losing control of her horse, which subsequently injured another. The court concluded that there was only one standard of care – 'that degree of diligence which men in general exert in respect to their own concerns'.[102] Ultimately the court phrased its judgment in seemingly neutral terms, by stipulating that the standard of care must correspond to 'that degree of care, skill and prudence which persons of common prudence, or mankind in general, usually

[96] Parker (n 95), 108; Collins (n 80), 316. [97] Collins (n 80), 316.
[98] *Daniels v Clegg* 28 Mich 32 (1873) (Michigan Supreme Court) [34]. [99] Ibid., 42.
[100] Ibid. See also Collins (n 80), 316.
[101] *Tucker v Henniker*, 41 NH 317 (1860) (Superior Court of Judicature of New Hampshire).
[102] Ibid., 321.

exercise'.[103] But, as others have pointed out,[104] in view of the prevailing practices at the time, this meant that women were generally judged 'according to the level of skill and strength of grown men'[105] and, specifically in *Tucker v Henniker*, against 'the standard of experienced carriage drivers, most of whom were male'.[106]

On the basis of a review of cases dealing with allurement,[107] Mayo Moran argues that a similar tendency can be identified in the judicial assessment of the conduct of boys by comparison with that of girls. Contrasting how courts assess cases in which children were injured when engaging in risky conduct (e.g. playing around trains), Moran concludes that courts appear to deem it 'reasonable . . . and thus non-culpable, for boys to be seduced into danger. But there does not appear to be a similar apparatus to forgive the girl who is careless of her own safety.'[108] In *Gough v National Coal Board*,[109] for example, a boy trespassed onto the property of the National Coal Board, played on and jumped off a tram operated by the Board, and was seriously injured as a result. The court found for the boy and against the National Coal Board, taking the view that, despite the fact that the boy had been told numerous times not to play around the tram and conceded that he knew it was wrong to do so,[110] the tram was a 'very real allurement', 'very tempting and attractive'.[111] Therefore the court concluded that the National Coal Board should have done more to preclude the possibility of young boys getting injured on its premises. Moran contrasts the conclusion reached in *Gough* with the conclusion reached in *O'Connell v Town of Chatham*.[112] In the latter, a girl – Dolores O'Connell – had been seriously injured when sliding down an icy street of her home town of Chatham.[113] Being aware that children frequently slid down town streets, the town had started to erect barricades that partially blocked the steepest roads whenever the weather was particularly suitable for coasting. Counsel for the girl argued that these barricades created an allurement and caused the girl to think that it would be safe to coast down the hill.[114] The court rejected this argument and found for the town. According to the judgment, the barricades made it clear 'for anybody to see'[115] that it would be dangerous to slide down the streets. 'The result', Moran summarises, 'in contrast with *Gough* and many other cases . . . involving the playing boy, is that any indication that the girl knew of the danger seems to operate to preclude her

[103] Ibid., 321–2. [104] Conaghan (n 90), 53; Finley (n 90), 59. [105] Finley (n 90), 59.
[106] Conaghan (n 90), 53. [107] Moran (n 53), 92–130. [108] Ibid., 94, 99.
[109] *Gough v National Coal Board* [1954] 1 QB 191; [1953] 3 WLR 900 (Court of Appeal).
[110] Moran (n 53), 103.
[111] *Gough v National Coal Board* [1954] 1 Q.B. 191; [1953] 3 WLR 900 (n 109), 205 (Birket LJ quoting Finnemore J's judgment of the lower instance).
[112] *O'Connell v Town of Chatham* 1949 CanLII 550; 24 MPR 36 (Supreme Court of New Brunswick).
[113] Ibid., 40–1. [114] Ibid., 41. [115] Ibid., 68.

recovery . . . Unlike her male counterpart, it seems the reasonable girl would never be tempted.'[116]

In different ways, the cases cited here illustrate the historical maleness of the reasonable person. In *Daniels*, the court removed women categorically from the class of reasonable persons; in *Tucker* it subjected them to a standard of care that derives from the customs of male members of society. In this way, the cases support the widely acknowledged claim that the passengers on the Clapham omnibus who are relevant to identifying the reasonable person were men. At the time of its emergence, the standard of the reasonable man was not meant to be all-encompassing. Rather it was tailored, more or less exclusively, to male members of society.[117]

For some, these cases – together with the fact that women were, 'by and large', absent from the reasonable man's 'birth and subsequent upbringing'[118] –mean that the reasonable person is inherently male, that such a figure can never be anything but a reflection of masculine norms.[119] If one traces the birth of the reasonable person to nineteenth-century England and considers, if anything, only its Roman legal history, this conclusion is not implausible. But, as I argued earlier, one should look at the reasonable man not in isolation, but rather as a particular instantiation of an old dynasty of personified legal standards. In a moderately egalitarian society like that of ancient Egypt, the *geru maa* was characterised in relatively egalitarian terms. When the US ethnographer George A. Dorsey (1868–1931) compared and contrasted the status of women in ancient Egypt and in Blackstone's England, he remarked that, while 'English law . . . practically denied woman's existence as a personality after marriage', the 'Code of Hammurabi showed not only a high order of society but a high status of woman, and such recognition of her rights as a human being as are hardly equalled on earth today'.[120] In a comparatively inegalitarian society like that of nineteenth-century Britain, which considered only men to be legal subjects in the fullest sense of the term, the characteristics of the reasonable person reflected the characteristics of a man.[121] Whether and to what extent the reasonable person's deference to prevailing social norms is inevitable will be explored in later chapters. There are good reasons to believe that, at heart,

[116] Moran (n 53), 112–13. [117] Finley (n 90), 59. [118] Conaghan (n 90), 52.

[119] R. West, 'Jurisprudence and Gender' (1988) 55 The University of Chicago Law Review 1, 2; Bender (n 80), 22; Stern (n 10), 4.

[120] G.A. Dorsey, *Man's Own Show: Civilization* (Harper & Brothers 1931) 565.

[121] Collins (n 80), 319. In this connection, John Gardner has remarked: 'If the reasonable person often ends up giving effect to a male standard of justification that is not because he sets a male standard of justification. It is because he sets no particular standard of justification': J. Gardner, 'The Many Faces of the Reasonable Person' (2015) 131 Law Quarterly Review 563, 568). Instead, the standard gives effect to the justifications considered acceptable at the particular time and place of the standard's application.

the reasonable person standard is a champion of equality and inclusivity. But for now it suffices to note that the reasonable person certainly tends to incorporate the values of the society whose legal system it relates to.

Importantly, this means that the characteristics of the reasonable person are dynamic and change over time.[122] More than a century after the reasonable man's first appearance in the law reports, the judges were still exclusively male, but the cases suggest that women formed part of the class of reasonable persons. The decision in *Sayers v Harlow UDC*[123] is a good example. Mrs Eileen Sayers and her husband were intending to travel by omnibus from Stow Harlow in Essex to London, at 8.32 in the morning. Having arrived at the station a little early, Mrs Sayers left her husband behind 'in order to visit the public lavatory', 'went to the furthest cubicle', 'opened the door, went in, and found that the door had shut and left her with no means from inside of re-opening it'. She then spent some ten or fifteen minutes 'trying to attract attention orally and visually from the window in the lavatory; and, having failed, she tried to see if she could escape over the door, or make her presence known from over the door'.[124]

Having pulled herself up on one side of the cubicle, Mrs Sayers noticed that an escape over the door was an impossibility. Subsequently she 'allowed some of her weight to be on the toilet roll, and her balance to depend upon it. The toilet roll rotated, which disturbed her equilibrium, and she fell and sustained injury.'[125] The question that arose during a subsequent trial was whether Mrs Sayers's chosen course of action – the attempt to escape by climbing over the cubicle door – was reasonable. The court's ensuing analysis has been described as an example of 'phallocentrism'[126] – since three 'elderly male Judges were called upon to put themselves in the position of a woman, dressed in tight skirt and high heeled shoes, locked in a lavatory while her impatient husband waited for her at the bus stop'.[127] But there is evidence that, by comparison with early case law, here the court construed the reasonable person standard in more inclusive terms. Finding for Mrs Sayers, the court held that it would be 'asking too much of the so-called reasonable man or woman to suppose that he or she would just remain inactive until her husband . . . chose to come and look for her'.[128]

No doubt law's image of the reasonable person changes slowly, and many would agree that, despite Lord Denning's enthusiastic declaration to the contrary, gender inequality within and outside of the law continues to persist. However, a survey of the current case law reveals that the woman on the underground is occasionally hailed as the modern successor of the man on the

[122] Reynolds (n 72), 420.
[123] *Sayers v Harlow Urban DC* [1958] 1 WLR 623 (Court of Appeal). [124] Ibid., 624.
[125] Ibid. [126] Martin (n 42), 348–9. See also Moran (n 53), 200. [127] Martin (n 42), 348–9.
[128] *Sayers v Harlow Urban DC* [1958] 1 WLR 623 (n 123), 626–7.

Clapham omnibus.[129] Along with women generally, mothers,[130] patients,[131] and adherents of various kinds of religions – Jehovah's Witnesses, humanists, Roman Catholics, Protestants of Anglo-Saxon descent[132] – have now also boarded the bus. And, as mentioned in the Introduction, since Lord Bowen's first description of the reasonable man as the man on the Clapham omnibus, the bus itself has been transformed into various means of public transport.[133]

These changing depictions and, by extension, the changing characteristics of the reasonable person account for the concept's remarkable versatility, but they are also a potential weakness. With respect to versatility, it is imperative and unavoidable that the reasonable person standard, as a perspective-taking device, relates to and reflects the norms of the society in which it is applied. The reasonable person is substantively an ever-changing standard. As John Gardner noted, '[i]f the reasonable person often ends up giving effect to a male standard of justification that is not because he sets a male standard of justification. It is because he sets no particular standard of justification.'[134] In other words, the reasonable person channels the standards of justification accepted in the societies in which it functions. In more egalitarian societies, the standard is construed in more egalitarian terms. In less egalitarian societies, the standard is construed in less egalitarian terms. When one studies, applies and, importantly, critiques the reasonable person, the dynamic character of this figure means that one must resist the temptation to reduce it to a particular set of characteristics derived from various precedents and historical pronouncements as to who the reasonable person may or may not be. One must, in other words, give the reasonable person a certain amount of space within which it can take on different qualities, depending on the circumstances.

This also means that one must take care not to describe the reasonable person in terms that risk rendering certain characteristics of a particular

[129] *R v Criminal Injuries Compensation Appeals Panel* [2000] PIQR Q361 (Queen's Bench Division) 366 (Munby J).

[130] *Re W (an Infant)* [1970] 2 QB 589 (Court of Appeal) 601 (Sachs LJ).

[131] *Sidaway v Board of Governors of the Bethlem Royal Hospital* [1985] AC 871 (House of Lords) 888–889 (Lord Scarman).

[132] *R v Blaue* [1975] 1 WLR 1411 (Court of Appeal) 1415 (Lawton LJ). During the case the question arose whether the refusal of the deceased, a Jehovah's Witness, to accept blood transfusion, which was necessary for the treatment of injuries incurred as a result of the defendant's attack, was 'unreasonable', thereby breaking the chain of causation between the defendant's acts and the deceased's death. The court held that the deceased's refusal did not break the chain of causation.

[133] Notable exceptions include the description of the reasonable man 'with the Chelsea tractor' (*Ann Gloag v Perth and Kinross Council and The Ramblers' Association* 2007 SCLR 530 (Sheriff Court (Tayside, Central and Fife)) 544 (Sheriff Fletcher)) or as the man 'who takes the magazine at home, and in the evening pushes the lawn mower in his shirt sleeves' (*Hall v Brooklands Auto Racing Club* [1933] 1 KB 205 (Court of Appeal) 224).

[134] Gardner (n 121), 568.

manifestation of the concept fossilised across time and space. An example of fossilisation is the still widespread description of the reasonable person as a man. As Wilhelm von Humboldt (1767–1835), the brother of Amelia Opie's friend, Alexander von Humboldt, observed, 'language is the formative organ of thought',[135] it is a 'guide to "social reality"'.[136] Thus, as discussed at the beginning of this section, referring to the reasonable person in male language and in male metaphors invites the judges to continue picturing a man when they apply the standard.[137] As a result, the maleness of the reasonable person persists in certain areas of the law long after 'the model from which the concept was once derived has disappeared'.[138] Indeed, it has been argued that the continued characterisation of the reasonable person as a man has meant that the standard 'has resisted alteration in accord with the emerging social reality of women, minority group members, and individuals not in the mainstream of middle-class values.'[139] Consequently, it is imperative to refer to the reasonable person in a manner that does not prejudicially affect the outcome of a judge's perspective-taking exercise. The risk of prejudice is of course significant, and by no means limited to the question of gender explored in this section. Describing the reasonable person as the man on the Clapham omnibus also excludes children,[140] the mentally disabled,[141] the physically disabled[142] – in short, most members of most minorities.

The standard's dynamic nature makes it challenging to prevent misusing the concept so as to exclude others. However, as established in Chapter 2 and argued towards the end of Section 3.2 here, if applied in accordance with its rationale, the reasonable person is, despite its dynamic nature, always committed at least to respecting the perspectives of others. This does not mean that invoking this figure always carries out the perspectives of others, but it ensures that other perspectives than the judge's own are, or should be, considered on equal terms. Judges who take the concept of the reasonable person seriously are therefore not at liberty to attribute to it any characteristics

135 W. von Humboldt, *On Language* (Michael Losonsky ed., Peter Heath trans., Cambridge University Press 1999) 54.

136 E. Sapir, 'The Status of Linguistics as a Science' (1929) 5 Language 207, 209. See also B.L. Whorf, 'Science and Linguistics', in J.B. Carroll (ed.), *Language, Thought, and Reality: Selected Writings of Benjamin Lee Whorf* (MIT Press 1956); A. Schaff, *Language and Cognition* (McGraw-Hill 1973) 29.

137 Collins (n 80), 322.

138 K.N. Llewellyn, 'A Realistic Jurisprudence: The Next Step' (1930) 30 Columbia Law Review 431, 454. It has rightly been pointed out, however, that semantic changes alone (i.e. from reasonable man to reasonable person to reasonable woman) do not necessarily alter the way in which courts and juries apply the standard: E.L. Shoenfelt, A.E. Maue and J. Nelson, 'Reasonable Person versus Reasonable Woman: Does It Matter?' (2002) 10 Journal of Gender, Social Policy & the Law 633.

139 D.A. Donovan and S.M. Wildman, 'Is the Reasonable Man Obsolete: A Critical Perspective on Self-Defense and Provocation' (1981) 14 Loyola of Los Angeles Law Review 435, 464.

140 For an overview, see Moran (n 53), ch 3.

141 For an overview, see ibid., ch 2.

142 *Cheshire West and Chester Council v P* [2012] PTSR 1447 (Court of Appeal) 1473 (Munby LJ).

they please.[143] The reasonable person may not stand for one particular standard of justification, but it stands for the position that, whatever standard one applies, it must be one ascertained through empathetic perspective taking. I will argue in the Conclusion that, if it is construed in this manner, the standard of the reasonable person can act as a bulwark against prejudicial, subjective assessments of the behaviour of others. But before I do so we must examine a period in the life of the reasonable person standard that has received little attention to date: the period of the British colonies. A look at how the reasonable person concept was understood and applied in the British colonies renders particularly visible the discriminatory potential of the standard, already identified and discussed in this chapter. But we will also see how the standard was able to facilitate empathetic judgment making in relatively heterogenous contexts.

[143] For that reason, any suggestion that 'the reasonable person is an abstraction whose characteristics are invented by judges' (J. Goudkamp and P. Cane, *Atiyah's Accidents, Compensation and the Law*, 9th ed., Cambridge University Press 2018, 29) must be treated with caution. It might be an accurate account of what judges do and have done, but it is a misleading account of the function that the reasonable person is meant to have, if applied in accordance with the concept's rationale.

4

The Reasonable Person in the Colonies

In 1856, the same year in which Baron Alderson was asked to determine whether the Birmingham Waterworks Company's management of the pipes in Woodcock Street had been negligent, the British explorer and missionary David Livingstone (1813–73) returned to Britain from an expedition to the Zambesi River. His aim was to tour the country to garner support for his next trip to Africa. Wherever he went, Livingstone shared with eager audiences vivid accounts of his various adventures on the continent between Cairo and the Cape of Good Hope. He also provided detailed reports of his efforts to preach the Gospel to the indigenous populations he encountered.[1] Incidentally, one of Livingstone's most forceful supporters was one of the 'great men' of Clapham whom we met in the previous chapter and will meet again here: Clapham-born Samuel Wilberforce (1805–73), Bishop of Oxford.[2] But it was at Cambridge, Baron Alderson's *alma mater*, that Livingstone's two-year lecture tour reached its climax.[3] Greeted by 'volley after volley of cheers',[4] Livingstone 'begged' his countrymen – who had flocked into a packed Senate House on 4 December 1857 – to direct their attention to Africa and to help him continue the work of bringing 'commerce and Christianity'[5] to the continent. Livingstone's plea was heeded. The Foreign Office decided to sponsor him, and by May 1858 he was back in Africa, leading an expedition to explore the Zambesi valley by boat. In late 1858, a set of whitewater rapids, the cataracts at Cabora Bassa, prevented his party from travelling further upstream. Thus he turned his attention to one of Zambezi's tributaries: the Shire River. This river, too, proved very challenging to navigate, but in October 1859 Livingstone was able to 'convey the information' that he had

[1] D. Livingstone, *Dr Livingstone's Cambridge Lectures* (W. Monk ed., Deighton, Bell, & Co 1858) 21.

[2] B. Stanley, 'Anglican Missionary Societies and Agencies in the Nineteenth Century' in R. Strong (ed.), *The Oxford History of Anglicanism*, vol. 3: *Partisan Anglicanism and Its Global Expansion, 1829–c.1914* (Oxford University Press 2017) 128.

[3] A.C. Ross, *David Livingstone: Mission and Empire* (Hambledon Continuum 2006) 121.

[4] Livingstone (n 1), 1. [5] Ibid., 24.

'traced the river Shiré up to its point of departure from the hitherto undiscovered Lake Nyinyesi or Nyassa'.[6]

Lake Nyasa (as the body of water came to be called), which Livingstone claimed to have discovered, had been known to Europeans for hundreds of years. It appeared on Dutch maps as early as 1610.[7] However, Livingstone's expedition certainly marked the beginning of British interest in the territory that was to take its name from this lake: Nyasaland. In the years that followed, different Scottish and English churches established missions in the area and a group of merchants founded the Africa Lakes Corporation, which sought to make Nyasaland accessible to European traders.[8] The British had answered Livingstone's call. They had followed him to Nyasaland. But they brought with them not only commerce and Christianity; they also brought their common law. By virtue of an 1891 notification issued by the Foreign Office in London, Nyasaland was placed 'under the Protection of Her Majesty the Queen'.[9] Henceforth the territory was governed by 'British law supplemented by local ordinances'.[10] This meant that English common law displaced most fields of local law. It also meant that the concept of the reasonable person had arrived in Nyasaland.

This chapter considers how and in what contexts the reasonable person standard was applied by selected colonial courts of the British Empire. Since the jurisdiction of colonial courts was most extensive in matters of criminal law, the discussion in this chapter will focus on criminal cases.[11] The key

[6] David Livingstone, letter of 15 October 1859 to the Earl of Malmesbury, written at Murchison's Cataract; in D. Livingstone, *Zambezi Expedition of David Livingstone, 1858–1863*, vol. 2 (J.P.R. Wallis ed., Chatto & Windus 1956) 332.

[7] T.J. Thompson, 'Lake Malawi, I Presume? David Livingstone, Maps and the "Discovery" of Lake Nyassa in 1859' (2013) 66 The Society of Malawi Journal 1, 1.

[8] Historical Section of the Foreign Office, *Nyasaland* (Historical Section of the Foreign Office 1920) 12–13; P. Devlin et al., 'Report of the Nyasaland Commission of Inquiry' (Colonial Office 1959) 8.

[9] Notification of 14 May 1894, issued by the Foreign Office in London concerning the British Protectorate over Nyasaland; in Historical Section of the Foreign Office (n 8), 84.

[10] Ibid., 19; F. von Benda-Beckmann, *Rechtspluralismus in Malawi: geschichtliche Entwicklung und heutige Problematik* (Weltforum Verlag 1970) 27. Note that it was not always uncontroversial whether the term 'British law' included Scottish and Irish law (ibid., 47).

[11] This chapter studies the reasonable person's role in British colonial law. It does not attempt to determine whether indigenous legal systems possessed equivalent concepts. In accordance with the argument I offered in Chapter 1, it is very likely that figures with functions similar to the common law's reasonable person can be found in most contexts. Whether establishing such equivalences is meaningful and, if it is, how one would go about it formed the subject of a famous debate that spanned multiple decades, between the legal anthropologists M. Gluckman (1911–75) and P.J. Bohannan (1920–2007). Compare M. Gluckman, *The Judicial Process Among the Barotse of Northern Rhodesia* (Manchester University Press 1955) ch. 3 and M. Gluckman, 'Concepts in the Comparative Study of Tribal Law', in L. Nader (ed.), *Concepts in the Comparative Study of Tribal Law* (University of California Press 1969) 354–5, 367–71 with P. Bohannan, *Justice and Judgment among the Tiv* (Oxford University Press 1968) 33–4 and P. Bohannan, 'Ethnography and Comparison in Legal Anthropology', in L. Nader (ed.), *Ethnography and Comparison in Legal Anthropology* (University of California Press 1969)

question here is whether the reasonable person imported from England remained English in substance – that is, whether this construct continued to resemble a man on the Clapham omnibus, or the courts tailored the standard to the specific circumstances before them. As Section 4.1 will show, there are many cases in which the reasonable person was equated with an Englishman. This suggests that the standard was static in nature. However, Section 4.2 in this chapter complicates the conclusion by introducing numerous cases and settings in which the standard was adapted to specific contexts – sometimes so successfully that local variants developed. Drawing together the first two sections, Section 4.3, the chapter's final part, considers the nexus between the standard's resemblance to the people to whom it is applied and the authority of law.

4.1 Jackson, Son of Frank

It was in 1956 that Jackson, son of Frank, heard that his older brother Edward had died. Without delay, Jackson travelled from Salisbury, the capital of Southern Rhodesia,[12] back to his native village in neighbouring Nyasaland.[13] It had been two years since he had last been home. Jackson was a young man, about twenty-five years old.[14] The death of his brother had been unexpected. After arrival in his village, Jackson asked his relatives why and how his brother had died. According to him, nobody wished to give him any answers. The elder of the family, Nthambile, one of Jackson's cousins, was particularly 'unpleasant'. She 'gave him no welcome' and refrained from preparing the ceremonial funeral beer, which is customarily brewed by the eldest family member on the occasion of a relative's passing.[15] After a few weeks, Jackson decided to take matters into his own hands. He acquired the materials needed for the funeral beer and prepared to brew it himself. This angered Nthambile. She sent for him and Jackson went to her house. Later, Jackson would report that Nthambile was 'rude' and 'offensive' during the conversation that ensued and that she was displeased that Jackson had interfered with the process of brewing the funeral beer. Jackson further alleges that Nthambile said to him: 'On account of your impertinence you will not see the sun to-day.'[16]

408–14. For an introduction to the debate, see A. Good, 'Folk Models and the Law' (2015) 47 The Journal of Legal Pluralism and Unofficial Law 423.

[12] Since 1953, Salisbury had also been the capital of the newly created Federation of Rhodesia and Nyasaland. Today the city is called Harare and is the capital of Zimbabwe.

[13] It is not entirely clear where Jackson's village would have been located. However, the fact that he belonged to the Amang-anja tribe suggests that Jackson came from southern Malawi; see T. Price, 'The Meaning of Mang'anja' (1963) 16 The Nyasaland Journal 74, 74–75.

[14] *Attorney-General for Nyasaland v Jackson* [1957] R & NLR 443 (Federal Supreme Court of Rhodesia and Nyasaland) 450 (Lewey FJ).

[15] Ibid., 450–1 (Lewey FJ). [16] Ibid., 451.

Nthambile's words affected Jackson greatly. He went home and 'brooded over them'. Eventually, he concluded that Nthambile had used witchcraft to curse him so that he would die 'before the day was over'.[17] He also concluded that Nthambile had caused his brother's death, with whom she did not get along. During a subsequent interrogation, Jackson stated: 'I then thought to myself that . . . the best thing was to go and kill her, because if I killed her before she prepared her magic she would not kill me.'[18] It was unclear whether Jackson thought that the spell had already been cast and could be lifted only by killing Nthambile or whether he was afraid that she would cast it later that day.[19] In any event, after about an hour, Jackson took his bow and arrow and returned to Nthambile's house. He encountered Nthambile in her garden, confronted her and asked whether what she had told him earlier was meant in earnest. Nthambile answered in the affirmative. According to the law reports, upon hearing this Jackson 'shot an arrow' into her abdomen, then 'took a hoe . . . and with it inflicted at least three injuries' on her head, 'which resulted in her death'.[20] Then Jackson hid his bow and arrow in a bush and surrendered himself to the police.

The question that subsequently arose was whether Jackson could be said to have acted in self-defence. Nyasaland's native courts lacked jurisdiction to hear cases concerning acts 'in consequence of which death is alleged to have occurred'.[21] Thus the matter was dealt with by courts of the British colonial administration: first by Nyasaland's High Court in Port Herald, and ultimately by the Supreme Court of the Federation of Rhodesia and Nyasaland in Salisbury. In Jackson's case, the three judges on the bench of the Federal Supreme Court held that the successful establishment of the defence required that the person alleging to have acted in self-defence 'genuinely and reasonably believed' his or her own life to be under threat.[22] In light of the facts, they determined that Jackson's belief that Nthambile's curse would kill him was genuine. However, they rejected the possibility that Jackson's belief was reasonable. According to the Supreme Court judges, no reasonable person could have entertained this belief. Although the opinions of the three Supreme Court judges differ slightly, they all reached this conclusion in essentially three steps.

First, they held that the applicable criminal law of Nyasaland was the criminal law of England. Indeed, section 18 of the Nyasaland Penal Code

[17] Ibid. [18] Ibid. [19] Ibid.

[20] *R v Jackson* [1956] R & NLR 666 (High Court of Nyasaland) 667.

[21] Acting Governor of Nyasaland (K.L. Hall), 'Ordinance No. 14 of 1933 (An Ordinance Relating to Native Courts)', article 11(a). The full text of the Native Courts Ordinance can be found in *Ordinances of the Nyasaland Protectorate for the Year Ended 31st December 1933*, vol. 20 (Government Printer 1934) 29–37.

[22] *Attorney-General for Nyasaland v Jackson* [1957] R & NLR 443 (n 14), 448 (Tredgold CJ). Chief Justice Tredgold (1899–1977) was the grandson of David Livingstone's brother-in-law, the missionary John Moffat (1835–1918).

stipulates that 'criminal responsibility for the use of force in the defence of person or property shall be determined according to the principles of English common law'.[23] Second, the Supreme Court judges held that the principles of English common law provide that the reasonableness of the belief of a person who claims to have acted in self-defence is determined in relation to an objective standard, namely the standard of 'the reasonable man'.[24] Third, they pronounced that the reasonable man is not just any man. He is certainly not 'a person with the upbringing and background of an African'.[25] Instead, the reasonable man is 'the man in the street in England'.[26] Since 'no reasonable person in England could have . . . believed that the curse would kill' Jackson,[27] Jackson's belief cannot have been reasonable. Thus the Supreme Court of Rhodesia and Nyasaland dismissed Jackson's defence and convicted him of murder.[28]

The image of the reasonable person that emerges from the Supreme Court's decision in *Jackson* is relatively static. It is also detached, both from the society in which the court that applies this image is embedded and from the parties summoned before the court – the parties to whom the standard is applied. The explicit manner in which the court defines the reasonable person in Nyasaland as the man in the street in England is unusual. The phenomenon itself, however, was a common occurrence in colonial courts during the twentieth century.

A fairly well known example of a court equating the reasonable person with an Englishman is *Mbombela*,[29] a 1933 case from the South African Appellate Division. In that case, two young boys alerted eighteen-year-old Dhumi Mbombela that they had spotted a 'small pair of feet'[30] behind a door while playing nearby. The boys and Mbombela feared that the small feet might belong to a *tikoloshe* – an evil spirit that appears in the form of a small man and whose gaze kills those who meet its eyes.[31] Mbombela took an axe, went to the place the boys had described and, without looking at the creature, hit it numerous times. Once he turned around to check what he had hit, Mbombela realised that the small feet belonged not to a *tikoloshe* but to his young nephew, who now laid dead before him.

In the trial that ensued, the court held that Mbombela's actions could not be excused by his mistake concerning the identity of the object of his violence.

[23] Penal Code 1946 (Nyasaland), chapter 88, in *The Laws of Nyasaland* vol. 2 (Government Printer 1946), section 18.

[24] *Attorney-General for Nyasaland v Jackson* [1957] R & NLR 443 (n 14), 448 (Tredgold CJ). See also ibid., 455 (Lewey FJ); ibid., 459 (Clayden FJ).

[25] Ibid., 448 (Tredgold CJ). [26] Ibid. [27] Ibid., 461 (Clayden FJ).

[28] The law reports do not disclose the sanction to which Jackson was sentenced.

[29] *R v Mbombela* 1933 AD 269 (Appellate Division (South Africa)).

[30] P. Lenta, 'The Tikoloshe and the Reasonable Man: Transgressing South African Legal Fictions' (2004) 16 Law and Literature 353–4.

[31] For a more detailed description of the characteristics of a *tikoloshe*, see J.B. Shephard, *Land of the Tikoloshe* (Longmans Green 1955) 81–2.

Applying a reasoning similar to the one we saw in *Jackson*, the South African judges held that Mbombela's mistake could excuse his actions only if it was the result of a genuine belief of killing a *tikoloshe* and if this belief could have been entertained by a reasonable man.[32] De Villiers JA (1894–1960) held that Mbombela's belief in the existence of the *tikoloshe* might have been genuine, but such a belief disclosed a lack of knowing 'what is known to all or most of the inhabitants of the state'.[33] And, since the Court will not regard 'superstition' as reasonable 'unless it is believed by the majority of reasonable people',[34] Mbombela's assumption that two small feet belonged to a *tikoloshe* was not the kind of assumption that a reasonable person could have made. Thus Mbombela's defence was dismissed.

It may look at first sight as if the court reached its verdict in *Mbombela* by applying a dynamic variant of the reasonable person that was not tied to a specific cultural context, but rather to the views of the majority of people in the society in which the court was embedded. This seems to distinguish *Mbombela* from *Jackson*, where the court explicitly invoked and applied the standards of a different, far-removed society. The parallel between *Jackson* and *Mbombela* becomes apparent, however, if one considers that the court could have reached the conclusion that most members of society did not believe in the existence of the *tikoloshe* only by discounting the views of South Africa's indigenous population, among which the belief in the *tikoloshe* was apparently widespread.[35] The court's implicit disregard, in *Mbombela*, for the views held by the majority can be contrasted with the court's explicit dismissal of the defendant's views in the Nigerian case of *Yaro Paki*.[36] In that case, a Nigerian third-generation Nigerian barber who had carried out a medical operation was convicted of manslaughter because his patient died as a result of an infection allegedly caused by the barber's failure to disinfect his medical instruments before the operation. Towards the end of his judgment, Bairamian J (1900–84) asked rhetorically: 'What would one think of a surgeon who operated without first sterilising his instruments. . .? The defendant has never, I am sure, heard the name of Lord Lister or has the slightest idea about the need for care to avoid infection.'[37] Lord Lister (1827–1912) was a British doctor considered one of the pioneers of antiseptic surgery. Ignorance is rarely a defence. But what is significant about the judgment in *Yaro Paki* is that the judge measured the defendant's conduct against a standard that, by the judge's own admission, the defendant had never heard of.[38]

32 *R v Mbombela* 1933 AD 269 (n 29), 272. 33 Ibid., 273. 34 Ibid., 270.

35 Lenta (n 30), 355. One must always be cautious with generalisations in this regard. It is evident, however, that the judges in *Mbombela* did not attempt to gather the views of 'all or most' inhabitants of the state, but rather assumed that their own views were representative of the general population's perspective.

36 *R v Yaro Paki and Another* (1955) 21 NLR 63 (Supreme Court of Nigeria). 37 Ibid., 66.

38 R.B. Seidman, 'Mens Rea and the Reasonable African: The Pre-Scientific World-View and Mistake of Fact' (1966) 15 The International and Comparative Law Quarterly 1135, 1151.

Although the colonial courts' disregard for the views of the local population ordinarily disadvantaged local defendants, there are a few cases where this attitude facilitated acquittals. In *Palamba*,[39] for example, the Court of Appeal for Eastern Africa acquitted a family father of murder on the basis of the court's dismissal of any evidence concerning the defendant's alleged use of witchcraft. Palamba, son of Fundikila, had suspected his wives and mother of having killed his eleven children by witchcraft. Embarking upon a trial by ordeal, he forced the women to drink Mwavi, a magical medicine that, in accordance with local popular belief, he expected to be deadly to a witch but harmless to an ordinary person. One of his wives, Wamlunda, and his mother died. During a subsequent trial, the court observed in passing that a murder conviction would require proof that Palamba intended to kill the women who died.[40] According to the evidence, however, Palamba intended to kill a person guilty of witchcraft. Since witchcraft 'does not exist',[41] the women who died could not have been guilty of it, and therefore Palamba could not have intended to kill them. Thus Palamba could not be guilty of murder; and he was acquitted. The court's reasoning in *Palamba* is not always coherent,[42] but this is a good example of the few cases where the courtroom encounter between a native defendant and a reasonable person construed as an English man did not disadvantage the former.[43]

So far we have considered cases concerning offences among members of the local communities – cases that British judges judged by means of the reasonable person standard. An additional dimension of the reasonable person's operation in the colonies is revealed when one looks at cases that involve relations not between native inhabitants among themselves, but between native inhabitants and colonisers. One instructive example is the 1961 decision of the High Court of Southern Rhodesia in *Mawema*.[44] In that case the defendant, Michael Mawema (1928–2000),[45] was charged, among other

[39] *R v Palamba s/o Fundikila, Kamumbi s/o Sikulu* (1947) 14 EACA 96 (Court of Appeal for Eastern Africa).

[40] The remarks of Sir Graham Paul CJ were made *obiter dictum*, since the court determined that there was no evidence to suggest that Mwavi was a poisonous substance, so that not even the *actus reus* of murder could be established.

[41] *Palamba* (n 39), 98 (Sir Graham Paul CJ).

[42] For the purposes of assessing Palamba's intention, the court accepts, for instance, that there could be a magical substance like Mwavi, which is triggered by witchcraft, but at the next step along this very line of reasoning the court is not prepared to accept that witches themselves exist.

[43] However, one should note that, even though the acquittal of a person such as Palamba might have benefitted Palamba himself, such an acquittal was probably not in the interest of the local community.

[44] *Mawema v R* [1961] R & NLR 655 (High Court of Southern Rhodesia) 656.

[45] Mawema was apparently the first person to use the word 'Zimbabwe' to refer to Rhodesia: J. Fontein, *The Silence of Great Zimbabwe: Contested Landscapes and the Power of Heritage* (Routledge 2016) 119.

things, with promoting 'hostility' between different sections of society.[46] The charge related to a speech that Mawema had delivered on 22 May 1960. In that speech he accused Europeans of having killed 'one thousand Mashonas' in 1896 just because the Mashona (the inhabitants of Northern Zimbabwe) were not willing to refer to the Europeans as superiors or masters ('Nkosi').[47] In order to determine whether this statement promoted hostility between different sections of society, the court referred[48] to the *Sutherland* case of the South African Transvaal Provincial Division.[49] In the *Sutherland* case, which concerned the interpretation of a section similar to the one in *Mawema*, Murray J (1888–1976) had stated that a person could not be found to 'have had as his purpose the promotion of hostility' if there was 'a reasonable possibility (not necessarily a probability) that his object was in truth the amelioration of conditions and the eradication of what he honestly considered to be an evil'.[50] Referring to Samuel Wilberforce of Clapham, Murray J continued:

> Presumably a Samuel Wilberforce inveighing against the evils of slavery in his endeavours to secure its abolition could scarcely have been said to have deliberately purposed to create hostility between slave and slave owner, whatever feelings might have been aroused in the minds of his listeners by his condemnation of the evils of slavery. Obviously, of course, the language uttered or the actions employed in each case must be taken into consideration, for if they disclosed such violence, such prejudice, such recklessness that a reasonable man could only infer that the individual's true objective was the promotion of hostile feelings, the individual's protestation of another purpose would be rejected and he would rightly be convicted of an offence.[51]

In *Mawema*, Lewis J (1917–?) accepted this test and concluded that a reasonable man could only infer from Mawema's statement that his true objective was the promotion of hostile feelings. He reached this conclusion on the grounds that Mawema's speech 'gross[ly] distort[ed]' the 'established history of this Colony . . . of which the Court is entitled to take judicial notice'.[52] While Lewis J accepted that a number of Africans were killed by Europeans in 1896, he made the point that this happened only

> as a result of the surrounding, by Africans, of a small European community at the Alice Mine at Mazoe, and in the course of the rescue of those Europeans and their conveyance back to the laager at Salisbury by the Mazoe patrol, which beat off attacks by armed Africans on the way.[53]

[46] *Mawema v R* [1961] R & NLR 655 (n 44), 660 (Lewis J). The provision in question was section 22(1)(a) of the Public Order Act 1955 (Southern Rhodesia).
[47] *Mawema v R* [1961] R & NLR 655 (n 44), 656. [48] Ibid., 663 (Lewis J).
[49] *R v Sutherland et al.* 1950 (4) SA 66 (T) (Transvaal Provincial Division).
[50] Ibid., 71 (Murray J) . [51] Ibid.
[52] *Mawema v R* [1961] R & NLR 655 (n 44) 664–5 (Lewis J). [53] Ibid., 664.

Noting that Mawema was 'a man of some education', Lewis J held that it is 'beyond the bounds of reasonable possibility' that Mawema would have believed that '1,000 Africans were deliberately slaughtered by the Europeans';[54] Mawema was therefore rightly convicted of having intended to promote hostility.[55]

This is not the place to critique the reasoning of the court in *Mawema* – a reasoning that appears to have ignored the first element of the *Sutherland* test (whether the defendant's object 'was in truth the amelioration of conditions and the eradication of what he honestly considered to be an evil'). Nor is it the place to offer an assessment of what really happened during what the British called the 1896 Mashona rebellion. For the purposes of illustrating how the reasonable person construed as an Englishman functioned in cases like *Mawema*, it suffices to point out that there are of course numerous counter-narratives of the 1896 events. Such narratives would for instance object to a description of the territory inhabited by the Mashona as a 'colony'. Some counternarratives regarded the Europeans as being 'fond of bullying'[56] and generally deemed their arrival as a source of 'unprecedented calamities'.[57] Europeans were reported 'to beat people as much as they liked', and the British Native Commissioner Henry Hawken Pollard (1868–96) had a 'reputation for flogging indiscriminately'.[58] From the point of view of many Mashona, the clashes of 1896 were a response to 'cruelty and oppression'.[59] Even contemporary British observers brought news of arbitrary executions carried out by British officials[60] and concluded that the treatment of the Mashona before the clashes of 1896 had converted them 'from a people who welcomed us . . . into a people who have dared death in its most abhorrent form in the hope of shaking off our rule'.[61] Again, the aim is not to offer an assessment of the events of 1896. The aim is merely to show that Lewis J's conclusion in *Mawema* – that no reasonable person could think that colonial forces could engage in deliberate and arbitrary violence – presupposes that the reasonable person in question resembles colonial officials. This equation of the reasonable man with an Englishman is particularly problematic in cases such as *Mawema* by comparison with cases such as *Jackson* or *Mbombela*, since the concept here in *Mawema* amplifies the views and preferences of one party to the proceedings, and does so at the expense of the other.

Some have argued that the colonial courts' equation of the reasonable person with an Englishman and the legal analyses in cases like *Jackson*,

[54] Ibid., 664–5. [55] Ibid.

[56] C.G. Chivanda, 'The Mashona Rebellion in Oral Tradition: Mazoe District' (University College of Rhodesia 1966) 6.

[57] Ibid. [58] Ibid., 7. [59] Ibid.

[60] Letter of 30 September 1896, written in Salisbury by Reverend John White, a Wesleyan missionary, and addressed to the editor of the Methodist Times; in H.C. Thomson, *Rhodesia and Its Government* (London, Smith, Elder & Co 1898) 232–40.

[61] H.C. Thomson, *Rhodesia and Its Government* (London, Smith, Elder & Co 1898) 230.

Mbombela or *Mawema* are representative of the way in which colonial courts in Africa have used the concept of the reasonable person in general.[62] And indeed, one can find the *Jackson* reasoning in many judgments from other colonial African jurisdictions, for example in decisions from the West African Appeals Court,[63] the Nigerian Supreme Court,[64] the High Court of Swaziland,[65] or the East African Appeals Court.[66] A similar image of the reasonable person emerges also from the law reports of British colonial jurisdictions beyond Africa, for instance India and Pakistan,[67] Hong Kong,[68] or Papua New Guinea.[69] Thus one could conclude that the concept of the reasonable person inherently and necessarily favoured the views of the British colonial administration and, consequently, that the concept does not actually facilitate empathetic judgment making – or at least fails to do so in inter-cultural settings.[70] This conclusion is not unwarranted. But it is only one part of the reasonable person's story in the colonies. The next section will show that there are numerous cases in which the concept of the reasonable person aided the efforts of colonial courts to engage in empathetic judgment making. The discussion of cases where colonial courts did not define the reasonable person as an Englishman is not meant to relativise the impact or significance of cases such as *Jackson*. On the contrary, the fact that there were colonial courts that managed to engage in empathetic judgment making emphasises the discriminatory and often racist nature of cases such as *Jackson*. What the contrast between this first and the second section will show, however, is that the outcomes in cases like *Jackson* are not attributable to the concept of the reasonable person itself, but rather to the way in which those charged with applying the standard applied it.

4.2 The Man on the Molue Bus

In the first section we encountered numerous cases where British colonial courts defined the reasonable person exclusively as an English man. The

62 Seidman (n 38), 1141–2.

63 See e.g. *Muhammedu Gadam v R* (1954) 14 WACA 442 (West African Court of Appeal).

64 See e.g. *R v Yaro Paki and Another* (1955) 21 NLR 63 (n 36).

65 See e.g. *R v Gija Dhlamini* [1940] HCTLR 33 (High Court of Swaziland) 34.

66 See e.g. *R v Akope s/o Karound et al.* (1947) 14 EACA 105 (Court of Appeal for Eastern Africa).

67 B. Brown, 'The "Ordinary Man" in Provocation: Anglo-Saxon Attitudes and "Unreasonable Non-Englishmen"' (1964) 13 The International and Comparative Law Quarterly 203, 214.

68 S.W. Man and C.Y. Wai, 'Whose Rule of Law? Rethinking Post-Colonial Legal Culture in Hong Kong' (1998) 7 Social & Legal Studies 147. See also J. Barrett, 'Counter-Conduct and Its Intra-Modern Limits' (2020) 34 Global Society 260.

69 R.S. O'Regan, 'Ordinary Men and Provocation in Papua and New Guinea' (1972) 21 The International and Comparative Law Quarterly 551; J.F. Hookey, 'The "Clapham Omnibus" in Papua New Guinea'. in B.J. Brown (ed.), *Fashion of Law in New Guinea* (Butterworths 1968).

70 See Folúkẹ́ Adébísí's discussion of the European colonisers' concept of the ideal subject of law, which is explicitly construed in discriminatory and racist terms: F. Adébísí, *Decolonisation and Legal Knowledge: Reflections on Power and Possibility* (Bristol University Press 2023) 76–8.

second section complicates these findings by introducing cases in which the standard of the reasonable person was not static but was more dynamically adapted to the situation and persons at hand. The section focuses on cases where the courts adapted the standard to local circumstances in an implicit manner. Towards the end, however, we will also encounter cases where the colonial courts addressed the identity of the reasonable person explicitly and, at times, even replaced the reasonable person with novel characters.

With respect to implicit adaptations of the reasonable person standard by colonial courts, the case of Jackson, son of Frank, is once more a suitable point of departure. As we have seen, the judges of the Federal Supreme Court held that Jackson's conduct had to be compared to the conduct of a reasonable person construed as a man on the street, in England. But the only reason why the Federal Supreme Court of Rhodesia and Nyasaland heard the case was that the Attorney General of Nyasaland had appealed against the first instance decision in *Jackson* by the Nyasaland High Court in Port Herald (now Nsanje). That first instance decision deserves some attention, because the High Court's analysis differs significantly from that of the Federal Supreme Court. Concerning the question whether Jackson could be said to have acted in self-defence, the High Court's Chief Justice, Thomas Spenser-Wilkinson (1899–1982), applied the same test as the Federal Supreme Court, namely whether Jackson 'both genuinely and reasonably in all the circumstances believed that his own death was imminent'.[71] However, contrary to the Federal Supreme Court, Spenser-Wilkinson CJ held that Jackson's belief that his life was threatened by an 'assault of witchcraft' was not only genuine but also reasonable.

In reaching this conclusion, Spenser-Wilkinson relied on the testimony of three native assessors. Assessors were consulted by the British courts in cases where the defendant was African and advice could be needed on matters of customary law.[72] The assessors were to be 'treated as reasonable and honest men'.[73] They did not, however, participate in the judgment-making process itself.[74] In Jackson's case, the assessors agreed that Nthambile had employed witchcraft and that her words should be interpreted to mean 'I will kill you'.[75] One of the assessors reportedly said: 'the interpretation, "I will kill you", here in our home among the Amang'anja is believed, because once it is said people really die'. Another assessor remarked:

[71] *R v Jackson* [1956] R & NLR 666 (n 20) 671 (Spenser-Wilkinson CJ).

[72] Benda-Beckmann (n 10), 42. On the role of assessors in East African British colonial courts more generally, see J. Gray, 'Opinions of Assessors in Criminal Trials in East Africa as to Native Custom' (1958) 2 Journal of African Law 5. For an illustration of the kind of questions courts would put to assessors and the manner in which such interviews were conducted, see *Greyson v R* [1961] R & NLR 337 (Federal Supreme Court of Rhodesia and Nyasaland) 345 (Briggs FJ).

[73] Gray (n 72), 17.

[74] Benda-Beckmann (n 10), 40.

[75] *R v Jackson* [1956] R & NLR 666 (n 20), 667.

> According to the Amang'anja custom I think that if she died at the hands of the accused it will be said that it was her words which killed her. From our ancestors among the Amang-anja people, if such a death occurred there was no case at all.[76]

The Chief Justice accepted this interpretation. Accordingly, he concluded that Nthambile was not an 'entirely innocent and unoffending person',[77] that she was 'the very cause of the trouble'[78] and that she had, in any event, violated section 6 of the Nyasaland Witchcraft Ordinance, which prohibited pretending to exercise the power of witchcraft.[79] It was immaterial from the Chief Justice's point of view that the threat might have been metaphysical rather than physical in nature.[80] If Jackson believed in the necessity of killing Nthambile in order to preserve his own life, in light of the fact that the 'nearest witchdoctor who could prevent the spell was three days' journey distant',[81] and if the assessors shared Jackson's view, then, according to Spenser-Wilkinson CJ, Jackson's belief was reasonable and the defence of self-defence must succeed. For this reason, Spenser-Wilkinson CJ handed down a judgment in favour of Jackson. This judgment subsequently triggered the appeal of Nyasaland's Attorney General. While the Federal Supreme Court set the High Court's judgment aside, the first instance decision is still relevant, since it shows that the British courts' conventional association of the reasonable person with an Englishman was not a necessity: the concept, aided by the opinions of local assessors, was in principle capable of facilitating empathetic judgment making that took the particular circumstances of particular defendants and situations into account. And yet, the High Court's decision in *Jackson* notwithstanding, in most cases of self-defence the British colonial courts chose to equate the reasonable person with an Englishman.

There is, however, a cluster of cases in which even the judges of the Federal Supreme Court of Rhodesia and Nyasaland accepted that the substantive standard of the reasonable person was not that of an Englishman but that of an ordinary member of the community in which a given court found itself. This cluster of cases concerns the defence of provocation. Section 199 of the 1946 Penal Code of Nyasaland provided that 'provocation'

> means . . . any wrongful act or insult of such a nature as to be likely, when done to an . . . ordinary person of the community to which the accused belongs . . . to deprive him of the power of self-control.[82]

[76] *Attorney-General for Nyasaland v Jackson* [1957] R & NLR 443 (n 14), 459.

[77] *R v Jackson* [1956] R & NLR 666 (n 20), 670 (Spenser-Wilkinson CJ). [78] Ibid.

[79] Witchcraft Ordinance 1911 (Nyasaland), Chapter 131, in *The Laws of Nyasaland*, vol. 2 (Government Printer 1946) (n 23), section 6.

[80] *R v Jackson* [1956] R & NLR 666 (n 20), 671 (Spenser-Wilkinson CJ).

[81] Ibid., 670 (Spenser-Wilkinson CJ) .

[82] 'Penal Code (Nyasaland), Chapter 88, in *The Laws of Nyasaland*, vol. 2 (Government Printer 1946) (n 23), section 199.

Thus, while, at least according to the last instance decision in *Jackson*, self-defence was assessed in relation to an external standard removed from the situation at hand, in provocation cases judges were authorised by statute to defer to the standards that prevailed in the community to which the accused belonged. Note that the test for provocation remained objective by being linked to 'a reasonable man's reaction to the provocation received'.[83] But, unlike in self-defence cases such as *Jackson*, in provocation cases the reasonable man was a member of the accused's community. The 1959 case *Bureke* from the Federal Supreme Court of Rhodesia and Nyasaland illustrates well how the defence of provocation operated. In *Bureke*, the accused had killed his wife, Ethel. He had suspected that she had left him for another man. Two days after Ethel left him, Bureke went to her place of work and asked her to return to him. When Ethel refused, Bureke first 'slapped her a blow with the open hand' and then 'produced a knife and stabbed her'.[84] Ethel's wounds indicated a 'wild and random' attack.[85] However, at trial, Bureke conceded that the attack had not been random but that he had intended to kill his wife.[86] On the basis of the evidence before him, Briggs FJ (1902–83) concluded that the defence of provocation could not succeed because Bureke had not lost his self-control and that, even if he had, the attack 'went far beyond anything which a reasonable man of the Appellant's community might have been expected to do'.[87] Consequently Bureke's murder conviction was upheld.

A few years earlier, the Privy Council, hearing a case from the West African Court of Appeal, had adopted the same approach. In *Kwaku Mensah*,[88] Lord Goddard (1877–1971) held that the question whether or not the defendant in the case, a 'West African villager', had been provoked by a stab wound allegedly inflicted upon the defendant by the deceased had to be considered with reference to the conduct of an 'ordinary person'. In *Kwaku Mensah*, the ordinary person was 'the ordinary West African villager'.[89] Since British judges might not have been familiar with the conduct of ordinary West African villagers, Lord Goddard pointed out that 'the knowledge and common sense of a local jury are invaluable'[90] for the purposes of identifying the substance of that standard.

Even in cases of witchcraft, where British courts otherwise tended to be particularly disinclined to defer to local customs, the reasonable person could take on features of ordinary members of the community. In *Fabiano*,[91] the Court of Appeal for Eastern Africa held that local beliefs and attitudes towards witchcraft could be taken into account when the defence of provocation was

[83] *Bureke v R* [1959] (2) R & NLR 353 (Federal Supreme Court of Rhodesia and Nyasaland) 357 (Briggs FJ).

[84] Ibid., 357. [85] Ibid., 356. [86] Ibid. [87] Ibid., 358 (Briggs FJ).

[88] *Kwaku Mensah v The King* [1946] AC 83 (Privy Council) 93 (Lord Goddard). [89] Ibid.

[90] Ibid.

[91] *R v Fabiano Kinene s/o Mukye, Seperiano Kiwanuka s/o Kintu, Albert Iseja s/o Kintu* (1941) 8 EACA 96 (Court of Appeal for Eastern Africa).

invoked. Three defendants saw a person whom they believed to be a wizard 'crawling about naked in their compound'.[92] They suspected the person of having orchestrated the death of many of their family members and killed him. The court held that, if the victim

> was performing in the actual presence of the accused some act which the accused did genuinely believe, and which an ordinary person of the community to which the accused belongs would genuinely believe, to be an act of witchcraft against him or another person . . . he might be angered to such an extent as to be deprived of the power of self-control and induced to assault the person doing the act of witchcraft.[93]

In such a situation, the defence of provocation would be open to an accused. Applying this test to the facts in *Fabiano*, Sir Joseph Sheridan CJ (1882–1964) concluded that an ordinary person of the community to which the three defendants belonged could have acted in a similar manner. Consequently he substituted the murder convictions of a lower court with convictions of manslaughter.[94] Similarly, in *Agumagu Nwaoke*,[95] the West African Court of Appeal admitted that, in principle, a reasonable person could be frightened by witchcraft to such an extent that they would take their own life to escape it. In *Agumagu*, a husband was disappointed that his wife Nwoacha had left him. Thus he 'brought a "Juju" called "Onye Uku," pointed it towards' his wife and uttered 'this juju will kill you'.[96] The words of the defendant affected Nwoacha greatly. Six days after he had brought the juju, an item infused with magic, Nwoacha hanged herself and died. Acquitting the defendant, the court held that there was no evidence that the juju could have killed her and that the wife's act of hanging herself broke the chain of causation. Taking into account Nwoacha's belief in witchcraft, however, the court did remark that her death could have been a reasonably likely consequence of the defendant's spell, if

> the accused had locked the woman in an upstairs room with the juju and the threat that if she remained in the room with the juju it would kill her and to escape that threat of death she had fatally jumped in fear out of the window.[97]

Thus, the judges of the West African Court of Appeal allowed for the possibility that a reasonable person in the position of Nwoacha could have feared the juju to such an extent that they would have taken their own life.

Apart from cases concerning the defence of provocation, implicit variants of the reasonable person also appeared in actions that could be contrasted with the decision of *Mawema*[98] discussed earlier. In *Nyandoro*,[99] the High Court of Southern Rhodesia – the same court that had heard *Mawema* – considered a reasonable person's views of the British colonial administration. In the case,

[92] Ibid., 100. [93] Ibid., 101 (Sir Joseph Sheridan CJ). [94] Ibid., 102.
[95] *R v Agumagu Nwaoke* (1939) 5 WACA 120 (West African Court of Appeal). [96] Ibid., 120.
[97] Ibid., 121. [98] *Mawema v R* [1961] R & NLR 655 (n 44).
[99] *R v Nyandoro* [1958] R & NLR 932 (High Court of Southern Rhodesia).

George Bodzo Nyandoro (1926–94) was charged with having intended to 'promote feelings of hostility between African members of the community . . . and European members', in violation of the same provision[100] that had been at issue in *Mawema*. It was alleged that, during a public meeting held on 25 May 1958, Nyandoro had made this declaration:

> African people were like an elephant being beaten or driven by a small man, the European. The elephant did not realise that he had the power to overcome the smaller man, and that the African people . . . now realised that they had the power to overcome the European.[101]

Nyandoro was also accused of having said

> that Europeans used the African as cows to be milked, that the Native Commissioners and the Township Superintendent were the herdboys of the Europeans, and that African members of the police force received unfair treatment compared with European members.[102]

While the prosecution alleged that Nyandoro had intended to promote hostility through these words, Nyandoro himself claimed that he 'was speaking figuratively in order to explain to the relatively uneducated people he was addressing that with universal adult suffrage the greater political power would rest with Africans'.[103] Nyandoro also explained that the reference to milking was intended to 'illustrate the low wages received by Africans in relation especially to the high rents they had to pay, and also to the long hours they had to work'.[104]

The judge in *Nyandoro*, Hathorn J (1908–67), had 'no doubt that many, if not all' of Nyandoro's remarks were likely to, and probably did, promote racial hostility. But he noted Nyandoro's 'genuinely held political views', in contrast with the situation in *Mawema*, and, citing *Sutherland*'s test,[105] concluded that the prosecution had failed to eliminate 'the reasonable possibility' that the defendant was pursuing political interests rather than promoting feelings of hostility.[106] Accordingly, Nyandoro was acquitted of this charge.[107] Notably, Hathorn J found for the prosecution and against Nyandoro with respect to a charge that Nyandoro had promoted feelings of hostility among members of the community when he claimed that Europeans had deliberately killed one of Nyandoro's political allies, since Nyandoro must have known that the person in question died as a result of medical complications from a brain

[100] Public Order Act 1955 (Southern Rhodesia) (n 46), section 22(1)(a).

[101] *R v Nyandoro* [1958] R & NLR 932 (n 99) 937. [102] Ibid., 938. [103] Ibid. [104] Ibid.

[105] Indeed, *Sutherland's Case* (*R v Sutherland et al.* 1950 (4) SA 66 (T) (n 49)) could itself be an example of the dynamic application of the reasonable person standard. However, the case might be an imperfect counterpart to *Mawema* since in *Sutherland's Case* a European judge, Murray J, assessed the conduct of three established European defendants – Sutherland, Hughes, and Cross.

[106] *R v Nyandoro* [1958] R & NLR 932 (n 99) 938. [107] Ibid., 939.

operation.[108] Thus, deferring to local circumstances when applying the standard does not necessarily result in a defendant's acquittal. Yet cases like *Nyandoro* show that the image of the reasonable person remained dynamic: the reasonable person in the colonial courts of Africa and beyond[109] did at times manifest itself in the form of an Englishman and sometimes in the form of a member of the local community.

As we have seen thus far, ordinarily colonial courts did not discuss the exact identity of the reasonable person explicitly. But as mentioned at the beginning of this section, there are a few cases where judges consciously and explicitly addressed the challenge of transferring a concept that emerged in the context of tort law in early nineteenth-century Birmingham to (normally criminal) colonial jurisdictions. One such case is the 1958 decision of the Sudanese Court of Criminal Appeals in *El Baleila Balla*.[110] The events giving rise to the proceedings took place on 3 March 1957. On that day, at 3.30 p.m., Sudan Railways Train No. 94 was travelling from Kosti to the town of Rabak. As the train approached the track's kilometre 376,

> some Arabs were driving their cows across the railway line from east to west. At that moment the said train emerged from the curve and ran over the animals. It waded through killing them right and left.[111]

The train came to a hold. Having witnessed the death of their cows, six or seven of the herdsmen ran towards the locomotive, in search of the train's driver. Eventually they found him. After a brief argument, they 'speared and stabbed him to death'.[112] At trial, one of the accused invoked the defence of provocation based on a provision[113] that was modelled on Indian criminal law, which in turn derived from English criminal law.[114] The first instance judge rejected this argument by making the following analogy:

> if 'A' was driving his brand new Cadillac car, and Deceased, a driver of a lorry, accidentally collides with it and destroys it, are we to give 'A' the benefit of provocation, if he loses his self-control and kills Deceased? Of course we should not. We believe that the position of 'A' in this case is not very much different from that of the owner of the Cadillac.[115]

[108] Ibid., 939, 941.

[109] For a discussion of provocation cases heard by the Rangoon and Sind High Courts, for instance, see Brown (n 67), 215. An exemplary case from Rangoon is *Nga Paw Yin v Emperor* AIR (1936) Rang 40 (Rangoon High Court). Marsack discusses provocation in the colonial jurisdiction of Western Samoa: C.C. Marsack, 'Provocation in Trials for Murder' [1959] Criminal Law Review 697.

[110] *Sudan Government v El Baleila Balla Baleila and Others* 1958 SLJR 12 (Court of Criminal Appeal of Sudan).

[111] Ibid., [2]. [112] Ibid., [2]. [113] Section 249(1)(1) of the Sudan Penal Code.

[114] W.L. Twining, 'Normative and Legal Pluralism: A Global Perspective' (2010) 20 Duke Journal of Comparative & International Law 473, 490.

[115] *Sudan Government v El Baleila Balla Baleila and Others* 1958 SLJR 12 (n 110) [5].

On appeal, Chief Justice Abu Rannat (1902–77) disagreed with this analogy. He remarked that 'the "reasonable man" referred to in the textbooks is the man who normally leads such life in the locality and is of the same standard as others'.[116] In *Baleila*, the reasonable person to refer to would thus be not an ordinary owner of a brand-new Cadillac. Rather, the test would have to be whether 'an ordinary Arab' of the standard of the accused herdsman 'would be provoked or not'.[117] Applying this test, Abu Rannat CJ concluded that a reasonable man in the position of the accused herdsman would be 'highly provoked', since for him the killed cattle were the foundation of his family's livelihood.[118] Accordingly, Abu Rannat CJ accepted the defence of provocation and substituted the murder conviction with a conviction of culpable homicide.

An explicit discussion of the identity of the reasonable person in colonial settings can also be found in the Sind High Court's 1938 judgment in *Ghulam Mustafa Gahno*.[119] In the case, the defendant had killed his wife in response to her showing him a 'booja'. According to the law report, a 'booja' was a gesture of severe contempt in the community of which both the defendant and the deceased formed part.[120] At trial, the defendant sought to invoke the defence of provocation, since he claimed that the gesture caused him to lose his self-control. The first instance judge rejected the defendant's claim. Relying on an English King's Bench decision, he held that the gesture of booja was not of a nature to cause a reasonable man to lose his self-control. This reasoning (though not the conclusion) was criticised by Davis CJ (1890–1964), who heard the appeal. Davis CJ remarked that the English authority relied upon by the lower court was 'dealing presumably with Englishmen or some people like them'. The case

> was not dealing with Baluchis nor do we think that judgment was intended to lay down that what is grave and sudden provocation to a Baluchi is grave and sudden provocation to an Englishmen or vice versa. In short the 'reasonable man' always a somewhat ideal figure, is not a person of identical habits, manners and feelings wherever he may be. We think the generality of the words used in the judgment necessarily imply some qualification. The 'reasonable man' is the normal man of the same class or community as that to which the accused belongs.[121]

Davis CJ was of the view that the meaning of provocation was different 'among different peoples in different countries at different times'.[122] Consequently, the identity of the reasonable person also had to differ. Depending on context, the reasonable person can be 'the ordinary normal Baluchi, when dealing with Baluchis and the ordinary normal Englishman

116 Ibid. 117 Ibid., [6]. 118 Ibid.
119 *Ghulam Mustafa Gahno v Emperor* 1939 AIR Sind 182 (Sind High Court). 120 Ibid., 183.
121 Ibid., 183 (Davis CJ). 122 Ibid., 184 (Davis CJ).

when dealing with the English'.[123] Applying this test to the defendant in *Ghulam Mustafa Gahno*, Davis CJ concluded – with reference, inter alia, to witness statements from persons in the defendant's community – that the booja was not the sort of provocation that could 'deprive an ordinary reasonable man of the class or community to which the accused belonged of the power of self-control'.[124]

A similar view also informed the Australian decision of Kriewaldt J (1900–60) in *Muddarubba*[125] – the last court case we examine before turning to outright readaptations of the reasonable person. The facts of *Muddarubba* are similar to those of *Ghulam Mustafa Gahno*. The defendant, a Pitjantjatjara man, had killed his wife, a Pitjantjatjara woman, with a spear, in response to her having seriously insulted him 'by gestures and words'.[126] Like the defendant in *Ghulam Mustafa Gahno*, the defendant in *Muddarubba*, too, argued that his wife's conduct had provoked him and that he had subsequently lost his self-control. When instructing the jury in that case, Kriewaldt J noted that, when assessing whether a reasonable person would have been provoked by the conduct of the deceased, 'the same rules apply in the trial of a white person as in the trial of a native'.[127] Then, however, Kriewaldt J proceeded to opine that he disagreed with that principle. He argued as follows:

> matters regarded as sufficient provocation a century ago ... in white communities ... would not be regarded as sufficient today. This suggests the standard is not a fixed and unchanging standard, it leaves it open, and I think properly so, to regard the Pitjinjara tribe as a separate community for the purposes of considering the reaction of the average man ... I may be wrong but until put right by a higher court I shall continue to tell juries that the members of the Pitjinjara tribe are to be considered as a separate community for the purposes of the rules relating to provocation. I shall not apply to them the standard applied to the white citizens of the Northern Territory.[128]

Thus, Kriewaldt J instructed the jury to consider whether 'the average member of the Pitjinjara tribe ... would have retaliated to the words and action of the woman by spearing her'.[129] He noted that the word used by the deceased (*karlu*) was a 'serious insult', but the jury had to decide whether 'it was sufficiently serious to cause the person to whom it was used to retaliate by throwing a spear'.[130] The jury accepted the defence of the defendant and returned a verdict of manslaughter.

Two of the most explicit judicial engagements with the question of the transferability of the man on the Clapham omnibus to the colonies come

[123] Ibid. [124] Ibid.

[125] *R v Aboriginal Muddarubba* [1956] (1) NTJ 317 (Supreme Court of the Northern Territory of Australia).

[126] Ibid., 317. [127] Ibid., 322 (Kriewaldt J). [128] Ibid., 322 (Kriewaldt J). [129] Ibid.

[130] Ibid.

respectively from Papua New Guinea and from Nigeria. In *Rumints-Gorok*,[131] a 1963 decision from the Supreme Court of Justice in Papua New Guinea, the defendant had suspected his wife of having commenced relations with another man. He confronted her about it and offered to forgive her if she returned to him. She refused. The defendant then grabbed her and struck her with an axe, with fatal consequences. At trial, the defendant pleaded the defence of provocation. The question that arose before the Supreme Court was whether the adultery was an act 'which if done to an ordinary man would have caused him to lose the power of self control and assault the person concerned'.[132] In considering this question, Smithers J (1903–94) observed that, 'in the search for the reasonable man in this Territory, the man in the lap lap takes the place of the man on the Clapham omnibus'.[133] Thus, 'for the exemplification of the ordinary man one must take the ordinary native living the rural life of low standard led by the Accused and his relatives and similar lines'.[134] Having explicitly replaced the reasonable person modelled after the man on the Clapham omnibus with one in the image of the man in the lap-lap (a Papuan waistcloth), Smithers J held that 'the commission of adultery in the circumstances of this case' could 'cause an ordinary native to be deprived of the power of self control and induce him to assault the woman'.[135] Nonetheless, the defendant was convicted because Smithers J determined that the defendant had not actually lost his self-control, as the killing resembled 'the execution of a judgment deliberately made'.[136]

With the exception of *Mawema* and *Nyandoro*, all the cases discussed in this section are focused on the use of the concept of the reasonable person in criminal law. Before turning to a more general appraisal of the role of this concept in the broader colonial context, let us look at a relatively recent civil decision from the High Court of Lagos in Nigeria: this decision is remarkable for the judge's explicit attempt to craft a Nigerian variant[137] of the reasonable person, hitherto defined as the man on the Clapham omnibus.[138] In the

[131] *R v Rumints-Gorok* [1963] PNGLR 81 (Supreme Court of Justice (Papua New Guinea)). For commentary on the case, see also L.C. Green, '"Civilized" Law and "Primitive" Peoples' (1975) 13 Osgoode Hall Law Journal 233, 242.

[132] *R v Rumints-Gorok* [1963] PNGLR 81 (n 131) 82 (Smithers J). [133] Ibid., 83. [134] Ibid.

[135] Ibid. [136] Ibid.

[137] The local variants crafted by British colonial courts, which represent adaptations of the English standard to local circumstances, must be distinguished from local anthropomorphised standards that predate the advent of the colonial administrations. Paul Bohannan offers the *or u fan kwagh* of the Nigerian Tiv as an example of such an embedded local standard. The *or u fan kwagh* is a man 'who knows things', 'is well versed in Tiv custom and belief', and 'governs his external life according to the standards of propriety compatible with such custom and belief'. See Bohannan (n 11), 33.

[138] For another example, see the speech of Lady Justice Njoki S. Ndungu of Kenya, who suggested that in Kenya the man on the Clampham omnibus has been replaced by the concept of the Wanjiku: N.S. Ndungu, *Key Note Address (Law, Justice and Development Week 2015)* (World Bank 2015) 3, 4. https://thedocs.worldbank.org/en/doc/611001447980399421-0260022015/original/KeynotebyJusticeNjokiNdunguLawJusticeandDevelopmentWeek2015.pdf

1990 case of *Sola Kuti v Vanguard Media Ltd*,[139] the owner of a hotel in Lagos claimed that an article published on 20 May 1987 by the Nigerian daily newspaper *Vanguard* defamed the hotel. The article in question had alleged that the hotel's backyard was a 'den of robbers', that stolen goods were stored in the hotel,[140] and that the hotel's owner was a 'baron of teenage armed robbers'.[141] At trial it was established that the allegations were false.[142] The question that arose was whether a reasonable man who read the article would 'be likely to understand it in a libellous sense'.[143] Onalaja J (1933–2017) began considering this question by noting that the reasonable person of Nigeria is 'no longer the man on the Clapham Omnibus'.[144] Onalaja J then cited a lengthy excerpt from a Nigerian precedent[145] in which the judge, Eso JSC (1925–2012), observed that the reasonable person in Nigeria could be

> a peasant housewife, shopping for meal in Sandgrouse, and not the wife of an executive, shopping for her grocery in Moloney Supermarket; he may be the ordinary worker in the Kano Native City, living on his 'Tuwo', and not the Senior Assistant Secretary cruising in his officially produced air-conditioned Peugeot 505 SR to his air-conditioned office; or she is the plain woman in Okrika dress and not the voile-laced fashion enthusiast.[146]

Onalaja J approved of this account, but specified it still further, for the purposes of the case before him. Thus he pronounced:

> I put the reasonable ordinary man as the man who commutes between Agege, Ipaja, Iju in Molue Bus or Agege Danfo Bus to Apapa or Central Lagos and relish his Boli (roasted plantain) with ground nut especially in the middle of the month or toward the month end when he is at his lowest ebb financially.[147]

According to Onalaja J, the reasonable person, thus defined, would presumably understand the newspaper article published by Vanguard Media in a libellous sense. The plaintiff's suit succeeded.

By comparison with the cases encountered in the first section, the ones discussed in this second section show that there were colonial (and, later, postcolonial) courts and judges who did not simply transplant into their jurisdictions the reasonable person construed as an Englishman, but made an effort to adapt the standard, often implicitly, sometimes explicitly, to the specific circumstances they encountered. As acknowledged earlier, this finding is not meant to trivialise the discriminatory effects of the application of the reasonable person standard in the colonial setting (and beyond). Rather, it

139 *Sola Kuti v Vanguard Media Ltd* [1991] 2 CCHCJ 185 (High Court of Lagos State).
140 Ibid., 188. 141 Ibid., 191. 142 Ibid., 205. 143 Ibid., 202. 144 Ibid., 203.
145 *Prince Yahaya Adigun et al. v The Attorney General of Oyo State et al.* (1987) All NLR 111 (Supreme Court of Nigeria).
146 *Prince Yahaya Adigun et al. v The Attorney General of Oyo State et al.* (1987) All NLR 111 (Supreme Court of Nigeria) [48]. Quoted (with stylistic modifications) by M.O. Onalaja J in *Sola Kuti v Vanguard Media Ltd* [1991] 2 CCHCJ 185 (n 139), 203–4.
147 Ibid., 204 (Onalaja J).

shows that the standard can facilitate the process of making accurate judgments through empathetic perspective taking only if the judges involved apply it in accordance with its rationale.

4.3 Sir David Maxwell Fyfe

On 1 July 1955, the Lord High Chancellor of Great Britain, Sir David Maxwell Fyfe (1900–67), delivered a speech in Salisbury, Southern Rhodesia, on the occasion of the opening of the Federal Supreme Court of Rhodesia and Nyasaland.[148] In this speech the Lord High Chancellor identified the standard of the reasonable man as one of law's most important elements. Addressing the judges of the newly established court, he said:

> I think it is of vital importance that we should keep as our standard of duty and care that of the reasonable man – the ordinary prudent person. Such a standard in a country's law is, I believe, reflected in the tolerance and understanding of its people.[149]

To many judges who were present, Sir David Maxwell Fyfe's plea for the standard of the reasonable person must have seemed to state the obvious. As we have seen, the figure of the reasonable man appeared in colonial courts both within and beyond Rhodesia and Nyasaland on a regular basis. But, as the first two sections established, it did so in quite different, nearly contradictory shapes. The first section focused on cases in which colonial courts transplanted the reasonable man into their local jurisdictions, in the form of the literal man on the Clapham omnibus. In these cases, the judges essentially equated the perspective of the reasonable person with their own,[150] and legal objectivity with Englishness.[151] As a result, the judges in cases like *Jackson*, *Mawema*, or *Mbombela* suffered from what one postcolonial court has described as 'an Olympian detachment from reality'.[152] In light of the cases considered in the first section, it is not surprising that some have argued that the concept of the reasonable person was used as a tool for obliterating 'the subjectivity of the (colonized) accused'[153] and, more generally, that the

[148] A brief recording of the ceremony is available at https://www.britishpathe.com/asset/251535.

[149] D. Maxwell Fyfe, 'Speech by the Lord High Chancellor of Great Britain (1 July 1955)' [1956] Rhodesia and Nyasaland Law Reports ii, iii.

[150] Lenta (n 30), 355, 359.

[151] H. Corder, *Judges at Work: The Role and Attitudes of the South African Appellate Judiciary, 1910–1950* (Juta 1984) 237. See also S.K.B. Asante, 'Over a Hundred Years of a National Legal System in Ghana' (1987) 31 Journal of African Law 70, 77–8. An extreme example of this attitude is the observation of a British colonial district commissioner in Kenya that 'in Kenya the Man in the Clapham Omnibus did not exist'. See C.C. Trench, *Men Who Ruled Kenya: The Kenya Administration, 1892–1963* (I.B. Tauris 1993) 120 (quoting R.A. Wilkinson).

[152] *Mapeto Chitewera Nyuzi and Lackson Kudemera v The Republic*, Cr App 331 of 1966, MHC cited by Benda-Beckmann (n 10), 132.

[153] Lenta (n 30), 355.

standard tended to favour the privileged.[154] However, the judgments presented in the first section can be contrasted with the views of more 'sensitive' judges[155] featured in the second, who attempted to adapt the standard to the persons and situations before them. These judges let themselves be guided by the 'common sense' of 'local' juries[156] and by the opinions of assessors who could 'speak with experience and knowledge about the probable reactions' of members of their community.[157]

Both manifestations of the reasonable person are undoubtedly part of the concept's life. Yet they do not realise its potential in equal amounts. In fact it could be argued that the cases in the first section defeat the very rationale of the concept, while those in the second give effect to it in an exemplary manner.

With respect to the former, we have seen in Chapters 2 and 3 that a key feature of the concept of the reasonable person is its relatability. The image of this person as a man on the Clapham omnibus was able to communicate ideas of right and wrong effectively because it invoked notions familiar to the people to whom the standard was addressed. This was not so when colonial courts sought to implant the literal figure of the man on the Clapham omnibus into their jurisdictions. As Eso JSC pointed out in *Prince Yahaya Adigun*,[158]

> It is not in vain that English law invented the standards of the man in Clapham Omnibus in describing the ordinary reasonable citizen. But then, except one has been to England, and appreciated the man that goes to work in an Omnibus in Clapham area in London as against the executive who drives in his Rolls Royce in Mayfair, the phrase 'Clapham Omnibus' is completely lost to him.[159]

A reasonable person thus construed not only lacked relatability but also restricted the ability of ordinary people to lead autonomous lives. As Sir David Maxwell Fyfe pointed out during his 1955 speech in Southern Rhodesia, the ability to lead autonomous lives presupposes that 'people … know what is forbidden and why'.[160] This is not the case when defendants in cases like *Jackson*, *Mbombela*, or *Yaro Paki* are convicted without understanding why their conduct violated a norm, since the norm in question does not originate from their own society and since their conduct is measured not against that of a person who belongs to their community but against 'the

154 D.A. Donovan and S.M. Wildman, 'Is the Reasonable Man Obsolete? A Critical Perspective on Self-Defense and Provocation' (1981) 14 Loyola of Los Angeles Law Review 435, 436–7. See also M. Moran, *Rethinking the Reasonable Person: An Egalitarian Reconstruction of the Objective Standard* (Oxford University Press 2003) 210.

155 W.L. Twining, 'Introduction' (1973) 17 Journal of African Law 1, 1.

156 *Kwaku Mensah v The King* [1946] AC 83 (n 88), 93 (Lord Goddard).

157 *Chasiyana v R* [1959] (1) R & NLR 87 (Federal Supreme Court of Rhodesia and Nyasaland) 91-92 (Briggs FJ).

158 *Prince Yahaya Adigun et al. v The Attorney General of Oyo State et al.* (1987) All NLR 111 (n 145).

159 Ibid., [45].

160 Maxwell Fyfe (n 149), ii.

image of a man who may be playing darts or shivering in a bus queue some seven thousand miles away'.[161] Moreover, if legal subjects cannot know what is forbidden and why, legal norms gradually lose their deterrent effect, particularly in criminal law, and their action-guiding character in general.[162] This insight already informed Blackstone's observation that 'colonists carry with them only so much of the English law, as is applicable to their own situation and the condition of an infant colony'.[163] Lord Denning, too, advocated a considered and restrictive extension of the common law to the colonies. In a decision from 1955, he noted that the common law has

> many principles of manifest justice and good sense which can be applied with advantage to peoples of every race and colour all the world over: but ... common law cannot fulfil this role except with considerable qualifications.[164]

Only if these qualifications are undertaken, Denning continued, will the people in 'these far-off lands ... have a law which they understand and which they will respect'.[165] The problem with the cases discussed in the first section is that the judges did not tailor the concept of the reasonable man to the contexts before them. The 'flexible, even amorphous'[166] principle of the reasonable man that can formally be 'stated in identical terms, but produce different results in different circumstances'[167] was transformed into a rigid, static and 'cultureless'[168] norm, which claimed to represent objective truth.[169] Indeed, in *Jackson*, Tredgold CJ insisted that the reasonable person standard must embody 'one norm' only and that this norm 'cannot ... be varied in any

[161] Brown (n 67), 217. For an in-depth discussion of *mens rea* in British colonial courts, see Seidman (n 38).

[162] See also A. Kenny, *Freewill and Responsibility* (Routledge 1978) 20.

[163] W. Blackstone, *Commentaries on the Laws of England*, vol. 1 (Clarendon 1768) 107. William Blackstone appears to have added this qualification to the 1768 edition of his *Commentaries*, since the passage cited here does not exist in the first edition; see W. Blackstone, *Commentaries on the Laws of England*, vol. 1 (Clarendon 1765) 105.

[164] *Nyali Ltd v Attorney-General* [1956] 1 QB 1 (Court of Appeal) 16–17.

[165] Ibid. See also, Asante (n 151), 72; A.N. Allott, 'The Authority of English Decisions in Colonial Courts' (1957) 1 Journal of African Law 23, 39. Similarly, the Norwegian sociologist Vilhelm Aubert (1922–88) noted that the concept of the reasonable person might be transferable to contexts beyond the British common law, but the concept's 'application' 'to a non-Western society might fail' if the standard is imbued with the 'specific implications' that it has in Western systems. See the memo sent by Vilhelm Aubert to Laura Nader and cited by her in L. Nader, 'Introduction', in L. Nader (ed.), *Ethnography and Comparison in Legal Anthropology* (University of California Press 1969) 3.

[166] J. Cottrell, 'The Functions of the Law of Torts in Africa' (1987) 31 Journal of African Law 161, 163.

[167] Twining (n 155), 1.

[168] R. Martin, 'A Feminist View of the Reasonable Man: An Alternative Approach to Liability in Negligence for Personal Injury' (1994) 23 Anglo-American Law Review 334, 343.

[169] Ironically, in some contexts the identification of the reasonable man with the colonial administrators appears to have become so pronounced that the term was used as a shorthand for corrupt British officials; see W.B. Modisane, *Blame Me on History* (Donker 1986) 35.

way by the eccentricities of the particular individual who is on trial'.[170] Otherwise, he said, the concept of the reasonable person would be deprived of any content.[171] But the cases discussed in the second section clearly show that this does not happen when judges calibrate the standard carefully and consciously, in light of the circumstances that confront them. And, depending on the case, this could mean that the standard would take into account certain features of a particular person.

Towards the end of the 1999 South African movie *A Reasonable Man*,[172] the protagonist, Sean Raine – a lawyer representing a defendant who killed a young child in circumstances similar to those at issue in *Mbombela* – turns to the jury and asks:

> Who in a multicultural society is a reasonable man? Is he urban or rural? Is he a person of Western education, of Judeo-Christian beliefs, or is he perhaps a person from a kraal, with a deep faith in his ancestors and a genuine fear of the tikoloshe?[173]

It is difficult to answer the lawyer's question in the abstract. Depending on context, any or none of the people Sean Raine mentions could reflect a reasonable person's perspective. At one end of the spectrum, one finds cases concerning conduct that speaks for itself regardless of the perspective one might adopt. These are cases in which cultural, subjective and individual factors do not condition the outcome; no matter how you model the reasonable person, the analysis yields the same result. The Malawi Supreme Court decision in *Cummings Kholiyo*[174] is an example. In that case, the defendants had abducted a night watchman and pushed a piece of rag into his mouth to silence him. The watchman subsequently died of asphyxiation. While the court found that the defendants did not intend to kill the watchman, Southwold P held that

> any reasonable man, from a village in Bangwe or elsewhere in Malawi or from anywhere in the world, from Clapham or elsewhere, must contemplate if he put this particular gag into a person's mouth that death or grievous harm would probably result.[175]

In other words, anyone – a person from Clapham, a man in a lap-lap, a man on the Molue bus (Figure 4.1), or someone from a village in Bangwe – would have realised that preventing the watchman from breathing would cause his

170 *Attorney-General for Nyasaland v Jackson* [1957] R & NLR 443 (n 14), 448–9 (Tredgold CJ). In *Mbombela*, De Villiers JA expressed exactly the same view: *R v Mbombela* 1933 AD 269 (n 29) 272 (De Villiers JA).

171 *Attorney-General for Nyasaland v Jackson* [1957] R & NLR 443 (n 14), 448–9 (Tredgold CJ).

172 *A Reasonable Man* (dir. G. Hood, Pandora Cinema 1999).

173 Ibid., minute 1:28:00. For a legal commentary of the film, see Lenta (n 30).

174 *Cummings Kholiyo and Fernande Mablesi v R* (1966) 10 JAL 63 (Supreme Court of Malawi).

175 Ibid., 64 (Southwold P).

Figure 4.1 A Molue bus on Agege Motor Road in Oshodi, Lagos. Judge Onalaja likened the reasonable man in Nigeria to a commuter on this type of vehicle.
Credits: Bolaji Alonge 2018

death. These types of cases do not require an extensive degree of deference to the particular persons before the court. At the other end of the spectrum, one finds cases that engage types of conduct that can be understood only by taking into account the defendant and the unique circumstances of the situation. Examples include the witchcraft cases *Jackson* or *Fabiano*, considered earlier. In *Ghulam Mustafa Gahno*, too, the judge's deference to the contextual meaning of the term 'booja' was the only way to reach an accurate appreciation of whether this expression could cause a member of the local community to lose self-control. Cases at this end of the spectrum are nowadays ordinarily discussed by commentators with respect to the concept of a cultural defence[176] – the possibility, allowed in some jurisdictions, to invoke a defendant's cultural background in defence of a practice otherwise deemed unlawful.

For our purposes, it is enough to note in this regard that an adequate understanding and application of the standard of the reasonable person presupposes that this standard does not resemble too closely either that of the judges (as it did in the cases discussed in Section 4.1) or that of the persons whose conduct it assesses (as it would if one deferred entirely to such a person's views). In both cases, the law loses its authority. In the first scenario, this happens because a law detached from the reality to which it should relate renders itself irrelevant. Going even further, Gustav Radbruch (1878–1949)

[176] For an overview of the contemporary discussion of the concept, see M.-C. Foblets and A.D. Renteln (eds), *Multicultural Jurisprudence: Comparative Perspectives on the Cultural Defense* (Bloomsbury Publishing 2009); W. Kymlicka, C. Lernestedt and M. Matravers, *Criminal Law and Cultural Diversity* (Oxford University Press 2014).

argued that a discrepancy between law's image of the human and the actual, empirical humans of a legal system must sooner or later lead to the downfall of the legal system.[177] The ultimate collapse of most colonial jurisdictions in the second half of the twentieth century lends support to Radbruch's thesis. Nyasaland, for instance, gained independence and renamed itself Malawi six years after the decision in *Jackson* was handed down. Malawi's newly established courts rejected the *Jackson* rationale within the first year of Malawi's independence.[178]

Law also loses its authority when it mirrors the perspective of persons whose conduct is at issue because it is incapable of being action-guiding, lacking any normative force. Finding the balance between these opposites can be a challenging task, especially in an empathy-deprived context such as that created by colonialism. Champions of the sentimental Enlightenment, for example David Hume, assumed that the balance between subjectivity and objectivity and between the judge's perspective and that of the person judged could be determined by reference to certain universal norms. Baron Alderson, too, believed that there is 'one humanity' shared by 'all the various races of men on the earth . . . whatever may be their religion, government, manners, progress in arts or sciences, and the like'.[179] Others doubt that it is possible to find norms and principles that all the members of our increasingly diverse societies can accept; and on this basis they question the utility of a reasonable person concept in heterogenous settings.[180] Ultimately such views are informed by the concern that it is difficult, if not impossible, for one person to understand another accurately, especially when the two differ in social status, ethnicity, nationality, educational background, and so on. No doubt the assumption of another's perspective can rarely be more than an approximation of that other's true perspective. For this reason, human judg(e)ments are bound to be imperfect, risking misunderstanding or misinterpreting the behaviour of others. But, unless one were to question the human administration of justice and the human institution of law, judging others on the basis of imperfect assumptions is inevitable. As the cases in Section 4.2 sought to show, the concept of the reasonable person, when used in accordance with its rationale, can help enhance the accuracy of judgments by reminding judges that theirs is only one of many perspectives. As we will see in the next chapter, this reminder is of particular importance when the reasonable person wanders into a battlefield.

177 G. Radbruch, 'Law's Image of the Human' (2020) 40 Oxford Journal of Legal Studies 667, 674.

178 See the judgment of Malawi's Supreme Court of Appeal (and of the High Court of Malawi to which the judgment refers) in *Lufazema v The Republic* (1967) 4 ALR Mal 415, (1979) 53 ILR 178 (Supreme Court of Appeal of Malawi) 179.

179 C. Alderson, *Selections from the Charges and Other Detached Papers of Baron Alderson* (J.W. Parker & Son 1858) 145–6.

180 Seidman (n 38), 1164; Brown (n 67), 212–13.

5

The Reasonable Person on the Battlefield

A few years before Sir David Maxwell Fyfe travelled to Southern Rhodesia to attend the opening of the Federal Supreme Court in Salisbury, he served as the Deputy Chief British Prosecutor before the International Military Tribunal at Nuremberg. The Nuremberg Tribunal's main task was to assess to what extent twenty-four prominent figures of Nazi Germany – including Hermann Göring (1893–1946) and Rudolf Hess (1894–1987) – were guilty of crimes against peace, war crimes, and crimes against humanity. Apart from passing judgment on these twenty-four men, the Tribunal was also asked to declare whether seven Nazi organisations, which included the Gestapo and the SS, were 'criminal organizations'.[1] If they were, individual members of those organisations could be prosecuted for the crime of having belonged to them.[2] At trial, the question arose as to how the term 'criminal organization' should be understood, since the Charter that had established the International Military Tribunal did not define it. The meaning of this term was of some significance. After all, members of organisations that the Tribunal declared to be criminal could be 'punished for that crime by death'.[3] Accordingly, the members of the Tribunal invited submissions from the prosecutors and the defence counsel concerning the term's meaning.[4] Sir David's answer, on 28 February 1946, to the Tribunal's question is one of the first, if not the first, documented reference to the figure of the reasonable man in international law.[5] Sir David said that one factor that indicates that an organisation is a criminal one is the following:

[1] Charter of the International Military Tribunal at Nuremberg, annexed to the Agreement for the Prosecution and Punishment of the Major War Criminals of the European Axis (1945) 82 UNTS 280, article 9.

[2] Ibid., article 10.

[3] *Nazi Conspiracy and Aggression (Opinion and Judgment)* (Office of United States Chief Counsel for Prosecution of Axis Criminality 1947) 85.

[4] International Military Tribunal at Nuremberg, *Trial of the Major War Criminals before the International Military Tribunal (Proceedings 20 February 1946–7 March 1946)*, vol. 8 (International Military Tribunal at Nuremberg 1947) 353, 367 (28 February 1946, Jackson J).

[5] An audio recording of this passage of Sir David's submission is available in *Nuremberg Trial Day 70 (1946): Sir David Maxwell-Fyfe: Criminal Organizations* (1946), https://www.youtube.com/watch?v=mzJvtj6odwI.

> The criminal aims or methods of the organization must have been of such a character that a reasonable man would have constructive knowledge of the organization which he was joining; that is, that he ought to have known what type of organization he was joining.[6]

Later that same day, Sir David specified that the relevant question was whether 'a reasonable person in the position of a member' ought 'to have known'[7] of the crimes committed by the organisation or its members. With respect to the SS, for instance, Sir David observed:

> the crimes of the SS were committed, first, on such a vast scale, and, secondly, over such a vast area that the criminal aims and methods of the SS, which have staggered humanity since this Trial opened, must have been known to its members.[8]

The counsel for the defendant organisations criticised the test proposed by Sir David. Dr Egon Kubuschok (1902–81), appearing for the Cabinet of the Reich, objected that the reasonable person test is too broad, since it would include 'those members who did not possess the aforementioned knowledge and who are therefore innocent'.[9] In light of the serious nature of the crimes involved, he said, the prosecution should establish a person's actual, not constructive, knowledge of the criminal activities of an organisation.[10] Dr Martin Löffler (1905–87), who represented the paramilitary wing of the Nazi Party (SA), remarked that he knew 'of no system of penal law in any modern civilized state' that would expose persons to the risk of a death sentence that was based on negligence, that is, on an objective reasonable person test alone.[11] Dr Löffler intimated that Sir David's invocation of the reasonable person standard might be attributable to a peculiarity of 'Anglo-Saxon and other foreign legal systems'.[12]

The Tribunal itself was also sceptical of Sir David's test. The judges were particularly concerned that Sir David and the Chief US Prosecutor, Robert H. Jackson (1892–1954), appeared to suggest that their test was an irrebuttable presumption – that is, that they seemed unwilling to accept that there could have been individuals who did not know, constructively or otherwise, of the criminal activities of the organisations they had joined.[13] Ultimately the

[6] International Military Tribunal at Nuremberg (n 4), 378 (28 February 1946, Sir David Maxwell Fyfe). Chief US Prosecutor Robert H. Jackson had put forward a similar test, but without referring to the reasonable person: 'The criminal aims or methods of the organization must have been of such a character that its membership in general may properly be charged with knowledge of them', ibid., 381 (28 February 1946, Jackson J). See also ibid., 439–49 (1 March 1946, Jackson J).

[7] International Military Tribunal at Nuremberg (n 4), 458 (1 March 1946, Sir David Maxwell Fyfe).

[8] Ibid., 381 (1 March 1946, Sir David Maxwell Fyfe).

[9] Ibid., 394 (28 February 1946, Dr Kubuschok).

[10] Ibid., 394 (28 February 1946, Dr Kuboschok).

[11] Ibid., 412 (1 March 1946, Dr Löffler).

[12] Ibid., 412 (1 March 1946).

[13] Ibid., 444–9 (1 March 1946, Jackson J).

Tribunal rejected Sir David's test and ruled that the declaration that any of the seven entities on trial was a criminal organisation would 'exclude persons who had no knowledge of the criminal purposes or acts of the organization'.[14] This could have been the beginning of the end for the reasonable person concept's foray into international law. Before long, however, the figure resurfaced in the same court room, in a manner that was meant to make a long-lasting impact on the international law of armed conflict.

This chapter commences by retracing how, beginning in Nuremberg, the reasonable person entered the battlefield in the form of the reasonable military commander (Section 5.1). Next it explores two challenges that confront the concept of the reasonable person on the battlefield and beyond. The first challenge is that it is easier to empathise with people close to us. In the theatre of war, this raises the question whether the reasonable person, when acting as a reasonable military commander, can meaningfully balance the interests of civilians on opposite sides of the front line (Section 5.2). The second challenge, addressed in Section 5.3, is that it is more difficult for powerful people such as military commanders (or judges) to adopt the perspective of others and to empathise with them.

5.1 Lothar Rendulic

When the German Wehrmacht left the Norwegian town of Hammerfest on 10 February 1945, the cemetery chapel was the only building left standing (see Figure 5.1). Having forcibly evacuated the town's inhabitants, the Wehrmacht burned their homes to the ground and destroyed their hospitals and schools, the waterworks, the power station, every shop and every factory. Foundations that survived the fires were blown up. Bridges were blasted, electricity cables were cut, telegraph posts capped. As the German forces left the town, they mined the ruins.[15] The destruction was later described as being 'as complete as an efficient army could do it'.[16] Hammerfest was just one of many towns in Finnmark – the part of Northern Norway that bordered the Soviet Union – that the German forces destroyed in the winter of 1944–5. Confronted with

[14] *Nazi Conspiracy and Aggression (Opinion and Judgment)* (n 3), 86. Subsequently the Tribunal followed this approach with respect to the leadership corps of the NSDAP, the Gestapo and the SD, and the SS (ibid., 91, 97, 102).

[15] For a comprehensive account of Hammerfest's destruction, see the report 'The Devastation of Hammerfest after the Compulsory Evacuation of the Population at the Beginning of the Month of November 1944' dated 20 April 1945, by the city's engineer, Johannes Kummeneje. Excerpts of the report were cited by the prosecution during the Hostage Case; see US Nuremberg Tribunal, 'Transcript for NMT7: Hostage Case' 2761–9 (27 August 1947), https://nuremberg.law.harvard.edu.

[16] *United States v Wilhelm List et al. = Hostage Case*, Judgment of 19 February 1948, in Trials of War Criminals before the Nuernberg Military Tribunals under Control Council Law No. 10, vol. 11 (1950) 1296.

Figure 5.1 In 1944–5 the German Wehrmacht burned the Norwegian town of Hammerfest to the ground.
Credits: Bjarne Lous Mohr / Museene for kystkultur og gjenreisning IKS

the threat of quickly advancing Soviet troops in the north of Norway, the Wehrmacht was retreating and attempted to slow down the Soviets by pursuing a scorched earth policy. Implementing a decision by Adolf Hitler (1889–1945), Alfred Jodl (1890–1946), the Chief of the Operations Staff of the German Armed Forces High Command (Oberkommando der Wehrmacht), had decreed that 'the entire Norwegian population east of the fjord of Lyngen' had to be 'evacuated by force':

> all homes are to be burned down or destroyed . . . Only by this method can it be prevented that the Russians with strong forces, and aided by these homes and the people familiar with the terrain, follow our withdrawal operations during this winter and shortly appear in front of our position in Lyngen. This is not the place for sympathy for the civilian population.[17]

The decree was addressed to the chief of the German forces in Northern Norway, Dr Lothar Rendulic (1887–1971). Rendulic, in turn, instructed his troops to carry out the order 'ruthlessly'. He reiterated that '[p]ity for the

[17] A. Jodl, 'Teletype, Dated 28 October 1944, from Chief of the Operations Staff of the German Armed Forces High Command to Armed Forces Commander in Chief, Norway Concerning the Evacuation of Northern Norway'. Reproduced as document 754-PS in *Hostage Case* (n 16), 836.

civilian population is out of place'[18] and that 'no shelter or means of existence of any kind'[19] were to be left for the advancing Russian troops. The subsequent actions by the German armed forces resulted not only in the destruction of towns such as Hammerfest. They also led to the complete devastation of remote fishing villages and settlements in the interior of Norway. In early December 1944, the destruction of Finnmark being well under way, Rendulic received the news that Soviet troops were withdrawing from the northern front and were no longer expected to advance further into Northern Norway.[20]

After the end of the war, Rendulic appeared as a defendant before the US Military Tribunal at Nuremberg, which was located in the same court building as the International Military Tribunal before it. In what came to be known as 'the Hostage Case',[21] the US prosecutors charged him, among other things, with 'wanton destruction of private and public property in the province of Finmark, Norway, during the retreat of the 20th Mountain Army commanded by him'.[22]

The applicable legal norm was article 23(g) of the 1907 Hague Convention (IV) Respecting the Laws and Customs of War on Land.[23] According to this provision, it is forbidden to 'destroy or seize the enemy's property, unless such destruction or seizure be imperatively demanded by the necessities of war'.[24] Rendulic argued in his defence that the scorched earth policy he had carried out in towns such as Hammerfest was demanded by the necessities of war – in other words, his actions were mandated by 'military necessity'.[25]

The Tribunal accepted that 'the destruction of public and private property by retreating military forces which would give aid and comfort to the enemy may constitute a situation coming within the exceptions contained in Article 23g'.[26] The key point of contention concerned the definition of 'military necessity' and the extent to which this concept was informed by a commander's own assessment. In Rendulic's case, it was clear from the evidence presented to the Tribunal that 'there was no military necessity' for the

[18] L. Rendulic, 'Teletype from 20th (Mountain) Army to Subordinate Units Concerning the Evacuation of Northern Norway'. Reproduced as document NOKW-086 in *Hostage Case* (n 16), 1114–17.

[19] Rendulic (n 18). Reproduced as document NOKW-086 in *Hostage Case* (n 16), 1117.

[20] Rendulic's testimony, reproduced by US Nuremberg Tribunal (n 15), 5542 (31 October 1947).

[21] According to the Tribunal's own law report, the case was so called because 'the greater part of the trial was concerned with alleged hostage or reprisal actions of one kind or another': Hostage Case (n 16), 759. The official designation of the case is, however, *United States of America vs. Wilhelm List, et al.* (Case No. 7).

[22] Ibid., 1295.

[23] Hague Convention (IV) Respecting the Laws and Customs of War on Land and Its Annex: Regulations Concerning the Laws and Customs of War on Land (1907) 3 Martens (3d) 504.

[24] Ibid., article 23(g).

[25] *Hostage Case* (n 16), 1295. See also Rendulic's testimony, reproduced in US Nuremberg Tribunal (n 15), 5536 (30 October 1947).

[26] *Hostage Case* (n 16), 1296.

'destruction and devastation' of Finnmark, since the Soviet troops 'did not follow up the retreat' of the German forces 'to the extent anticipated'.[27] Retrospectively, Rendulic himself acknowledged that the scorched earth policy was unjustified. But, he argued, at the time when he gave the order to destroy Finnmark, he believed that these actions were necessary for hindering the Soviet advances.[28]

The Tribunal agreed with Rendulic that it was asked to consider 'the situation as it appeared to the defendant at the time', not to assess it retrospectively.[29] The question, the Tribunal said, is whether the defendant 'acted within the limits of honest judgment' in light of the knowledge and conditions available to him at the time when the decision was made.[30] If the defendant's decision fell within the limits of an honest judgement, the action taken as a consequence of that decision was not unlawful.[31] This applied even to decisions based on mistaken assumptions – such as that of Rendulic about the Soviet troops' anticipated advance, which did not occur. Applying the test to Rendulic, the Tribunal determined that, in light of the information available to Rendulic in November 1944, he could 'honestly conclude that urgent military necessity warranted'[32] the adoption of a scorched earth policy. Thus Rendulic was acquitted of that particular charge.[33] Although the Tribunal did not explicitly refer to the 'reasonable person' when discussing Rendulic's conduct in Finnmark (it does so, however, when evaluating whether Rendulic passed on Adolf Hitler's 'clearly unlawful' orders on the Eastern Front),[34] the passage of this judgment, which concerns the limits of honest judgement, is frequently cited[35] as one of the first manifestations of the reasonable person in the shape of the 'reasonable military commander'.

In the course of the seventy-five years that have passed since the US Military Tribunal delivered its judgments at Nuremberg, the concept of the reasonable military commander has become an established standard for assessing the conduct of military personnel in times of war. Most frequently, this standard is used to evaluate a commander's assessment of the proportionality of an attack – that is, to evaluate whether a commander struck a reasonable balance

[27] Ibid.

[28] US Nuremberg Tribunal (n 15), 5345 (31 October 1947). See also Lothar Rendulic, *Soldat in stürzenden Reichen* (Damm Verlag 1965) 374.

[29] *Hostage Case* (n 16), 1296. [30] Ibid., 1297. [31] Ibid., 1296. [32] Ibid., 1297.

[33] But Rendulic was convicted on counts one, three and four, which related respectively to 'murder of hundreds of thousands of civilians', to 'drafting, distribution, and execution of illegal orders', and to 'murder, torture, and systematic terrorization, imprisonment in concentration camps, forced labor' of civilians, ibid., 1233–4.

[34] Ibid., 1294.

[35] S.R. Johansen, *The Military Commander's Necessity: The Law of Armed Conflict and Its Limits* (Cambridge University Press 2019) 77; J.J. Merriam, 'Affirmative Target Identification: Operationalizing the Principle of Distinction for U.S. Warfighters' (2016) 56 Virginia Journal of International Law 83, 111–112; B. Clarke, 'Proportionality in Armed Conflicts: A Principle in Need of Clarification?' (2012) 3 Journal of International Humanitarian Legal Studies 73, 78.

between the anticipated military advantage of a given operation and the expected civilian casualties and damage to civilian property that the operation entails. A US Air Force manual specifies, for example, that 'final determination of whether a specific attack is proportional is the sole responsibility of the air commander', who is expected to meet the reasonable military commander standard.[36] The Israeli Government has stated that a 'core question' when 'assessing a commander's decision to attack' is 'whether a reasonable commander could have reached a similar conclusion'.[37] A Canadian military manual stipulates that targeting decisions are evaluated against 'what a reasonable person would have done in the circumstances'.[38] An embedded legal advisor to NATO's Operation Allied Force described his job as voicing 'concerns when the assumptions being made' by military commanders – for example about 'weapon effectiveness, absence or presence of people, impact on the enemy' – went 'beyond the reasonable person standard'.[39] The United Nations[40] and non-governmental organisations such as the International Law Association[41] and Human Rights Watch[42] endorsed the standard. In judicial practice, both domestic and international courts have referred to it. In the domestic context, Israeli courts have repeatedly applied the reasonable military commander standard when assessing whether a military commander could demolish the homes that belonged to relatives of persons convicted of criminal acts,[43] for example, or was entitled to propose that the wall that separates the occupied Palestinian territories from Israel be constructed in a manner that would prevent Palestinians from accessing their agricultural land.[44] At the international level, the International Criminal Court and the

36 USAF JAG Department, *Air Force Operations and the Law* (3rd ed., United States Air Force 2014) 19.

37 Ministry of Foreign Affairs (Israel), 'The Operation in Gaza: Factual and Legal Aspects' (2019) [125].

38 Office of the Judge Advocate General (Canada), 'Joint Doctrine Manual, Law of Armed Conflict at the Tactical and Operational Levels, B-GJ-005–104/FP-021' [418(3)]. For an overview of state practice in this area, see the International Humanitarian Law Database of the International Committee of the Red Cross, https://ihl-databases.icrc.org.

39 T. Montgomery, 'Legal Perspective from the EUCOM Targeting Cell', in A.E. Wall (ed.), *Legal and Ethical Lessons of NATO's Kosovo Campaign*, vol. 78 (Naval War College 2002) 189.

40 Human Rights Council, 'Human Rights in Palestine and Other Occupied Arab Territories: Report of the United Nations Fact-Finding Mission on the Gaza Conflict, UN DOC A/HRC/12/48' [42, 700, 1922].

41 International Law Association's Study Group on the Conduct of Hostilities in the 21st Century, 'The Conduct of Hostilities and International Humanitarian Law: Challenges of 21st Century Warfare' (2017) 93 International Law Studies 322, 369.

42 Human Rights Watch, 'Making the Case: The Dangers of Killer Robots and the Need for a Preemptive Ban' (2016) 7, https://www.hrw.org/sites/default/files/report_pdf/arms1216_web.pdf.

43 *Hamri v Commander of the Judea and Samaria* [1982] HCJ 361/82, 1984 (1) Palestine Yearbook of International Law 129 (The Supreme Court of Israel sitting as High Court of Justice) 133.

44 *Beit Sourik Village Council v The Government of Israel et al.* [2004] HCJ 2056/04 (The Supreme Court of Israel sitting as High Court of Justice) [46]. See also *Public Committee against Torture*

International Criminal Tribunal for the Former Yugoslavia (ICTY) have respectively applied the standard to cases involving, inter alia, North Korea's shelling in 2010 of a South Korean island – an event that produced civilian casualties[45] – and the killing of thousands of civilians during the siege of Sarajevo in 1992.[46]

In contemporary discussions, the standard is commonly attributed to the ICTY's 2000 report concerning NATO's bombing campaign against the Federal Republic of Yugoslavia.[47] The authors of the report stipulated that the balance between 'the relative values to be assigned to the military advantage gained' as a result of a given military operation and 'the injury to non-combatants and or the damage to civilian objects' should be struck with reference to the view of 'the reasonable military commander'.[48] The authors of the report were meant to be anonymous. However, the passage that proposes the standard of the reasonable military commander is an (unattributed) verbatim reproduction of parts of an article authored by William J. Fenrick.[49] Hence it is likely that it was Fenrick, a Canadian military lawyer and self-identified member of the group of experts who produced the report,[50] who inserted the reference to the reasonable person standard into the ICTY report.[51] This is not in itself remarkable, but it is noteworthy that, after Sir David's reference to the standard in 1946, the standard's prominent

in Israel and Palestinian Society for the Protection of Human Rights and the Environment v The Government of Israel et al. [2006] HCJ 769/02 (The Supreme Court of Israel sitting as High Court of Justice) [57]. For a reference to the standard of the reasonable person when assessing the conduct of military personnel in the United States, see e.g. *United States v Carr* 25 F Cas 306, 1 Woods 480 (1872) (Circuit Court for the Southern District of Georgia) 308-309 (Woods, Circuit Judge).

45 Office of the Prosecutor of the International Criminal Court, 'Situation in the Republic of Korea (Article 5 Report)' (International Criminal Court 2014) [26], [75], [81].

46 *Prosecutor v Stanislav Galić* (Judgment and Opinion) Case No IT-98-29-T, TC I (International Criminal Tribunal for the Former Yugoslavia) [55, 58, 719].

47 ICTY Review Committee, 'Final Report to the Prosecutor by the Committee Established to Review the NATO Bombing Campaign against the Federal Republic of Yugoslavia' (2000). The authors of this report are at times credited with having created the standard of the reasonable military commander; see I. Henderson and K. Reece, 'Proportionality under International Humanitarian Law: The "Reasonable Military Commander" Standard and Reverberating Effects' (2018) 51 Vanderbilt Journal of Transnational Law 835, 840. In fact the expression dates back at least to the 1970s. See e.g. W.T. Mallison and S.V. Mallison, 'The Juridical Status of Irregular Combatants under the International Humanitarian Law of Armed Conflict' (1977) 9 Case Western Reserve Journal of International Law 39, 56.

48 ICTY Review Committee (n 47), [49, 50].

49 Compare paragraph 50 of the ICTY report with p. 546 in William Fenrick's article: W.J. Fenrick, 'Attacking the Enemy Civilian as a Punishable Offense Symposium: Justice in Cataclysm Criminal Trials in the Wake of Mass Violence' (1997) 7 Duke Journal of Comparative & International Law 539.

50 W.J. Fenrick, 'Targeting and Proportionality during the NATO Bombing Campaign against Yugoslavia' (2001) 12 European Journal of International Law 489, 489 (starred fn).

51 One of the few authors to spot the connection between Fenrick's text and the report is Andreas Laursen; see A. Laursen, 'NATO, the War over Kosovo, and the ICTY Investigation' (2002) 17 American University International Law Review 765, 775–6.

appearance in the ICTY report is, once again, due to the involvement of a lawyer trained in the common law.

Despite the standard's frequent invocation and application by various states and courts, its substantive characteristics are not entirely clear. In an attempt to offer more concrete guidance, the International Committee of the Red Cross has collected from national military manuals examples of situations in which reasonable military commanders would be expected not to attack. Such situations include

> bombing a refugee camp where refugees are knitting socks for soldiers, bombing an isolated fuel tanker in the middle of a densely populated city, bombarding a village because of the presence of a single sniper and the complete destruction of a town in order to eliminate a small pocket of opposing forces.[52]

Examples of situations where a reasonable military commander would give an order to attack include:

> an air strike on an ammunition dump where there is a farmer ploughing a field beside it; an attack on a village occupied by opposing forces at an important crossroads even where such an attack will lead to civilian casualties and damage to civilian property; the targeting of a munitions factory where the collateral damage is limited to the deaths of the civilian factory workers; or the targeting of an oil depot vital for the enemy's logistical operations that might damage a few surrounding houses.[53]

Overall, the standard of the reasonable military commander enjoys widespread support[54] – just like its domestic counterpart. At least at first sight, the standard also appears to share similar functions and characteristics with domestic law's reasonable person. The reasonable military commander standard helps making more concrete a general concept such as the proportionate use of force in armed conflict, and does so in a manner that resembles how the reasonable person test helps to determine, say, whether a person's use of force in self-defence was justified. The reasonable military commander also demarcates the limits of a person's exercise of discretion by bringing in a more objective standard to calibrate that person's subjective perspective – in much the same way as the domestic reasonable person contributes for example to identifying the boundary between negligent and diligent conduct. Furthermore, the standard of the reasonable military commander shares the reasonable person's relatability by anthropomorphising an abstract principle.

[52] L. Gisel, *The Principle of Proportionality in the Rules Governing the Conduct of Hostilities under International Humanitarian Law* (International Committee of the Red Cross 2018) 53 (references omitted).

[53] Ibid., 53–4 (references omitted).

[54] Henderson and Reece (n 47), 845; H. Olásolo, *Unlawful Attacks in Combat Situations: From the ICTY's Case Law to the Rome Statute* (Brill Nijhoff 2008) 229–30; P. Benvenuti, 'The ICTY Prosecutor and the Review of the NATO Bombing Campaign against the Federal Republic of Yugoslavia' (2001) 12 European Journal of International Law 503, 517.

Not only are the functions and characteristics of the reasonable military commander similar to those of the reasonable person, but both figures have faced similar criticisms concerning the standard's vagueness,[55] its unpredictable nature,[56] its fictional character,[57] or its susceptibility to project subjective preferences.[58] All this suggests that the reasonable military commander on the battlefield really is not much more than the domestic reasonable person in military uniform.

Yet, as the reasonable person character wanders onto the battlefield, it is confronted with an existential question: does the reasonable person preserve its identity, as a character rooted in a common sense accessible to all, or does it morph into a different character, that of a soldier, who operates within a different normative cosmos, one where it is permissible to kill innocent farmers ploughing their fields next to an ammunition dump. Asked to assess Lothar Rendulic's decision to burn down Hammerfest in order to hinder a potential Soviet advance, the reasonable person figure we have encountered up to this point may be inclined to conclude that such a course of action would not be reasonable, even assuming that Rendulic's belief was correct. By contrast, a reasonable person figure whose perspective is construed in accordance with military categories may be prepared to accept Rendulic's assessment. The question concerning the reasonable military commander's identity is thus of concrete and practical relevance. But this question also engages matters that go to the very heart of the concept of the reasonable person. We shall explore these matters in the next section.

5.2 Human Rights-niks

The previous section concluded by asking whether the reasonable military commander on the battlefield is the same as the reasonable person in uniform – in other words whether the essential features of this figure remain unaffected by its presence in a theatre of war. Or is the reasonable person on

55 N. Trew, 'Dead Letter Law Arising from Strategic Choices: The Difficulty of Achieving Accountability for the Jus in Bello Rules on Proportionality and Precautions in Attack' (University of Exeter 2017) 34–5; L.A. Whittemore, 'Proportionality Decision Making in Targeting: Heuristics, Cognitive Biases, and the Law' (2015) 7 Harvard National Security Journal 577, 583.

56 I. Henderson, *The Contemporary Law of Targeting: Military Objectives, Proportionality and Precautions in Attack under Additional Protocol I* (Brill Nijhoff 2009) 223; E. Benvenisti, 'The Legal Battle to Define the Law on Transnational Asymmetric Warfare' (2010) 20 Duke Journal of Comparative & International Law 339, 354.

57 W.H. Parks, 'Command Responsibility For War Crimes' (1973) 62 Military Law Review 1, 90.

58 C. von der Groeben, 'Criminal Responsibility of German Soldiers in Afghanistan: The Case of Colonel Klein' (2010) 11 German Law Journal 469, 480. See also R.D. Sloane, 'Puzzles of Proportion and the "Reasonable Military Commander": Reflections on the Law, Ethics, and Geopolitics of Proportionality' (2015) 6 Harvard National Security Journal 299, 302, 318; R. Geiß and M. Siegrist, 'Has the Armed Conflict in Afghanistan Affected the Rules on the Conduct of Hostilities?' (2011) 93 International Review of the Red Cross 11, 33–4.

the battlefield a different kind of person, someone who possesses military training and subscribes to the logic of waging war? This question matters, since the standard of behaviour expected of an ordinary reasonable person may differ from the standard of behaviour expected of an ordinary military person.[59] In the polemical words of a military officer, the former could be 'in the business of saving lives', while the latter is 'in the business of killing'.[60] It also matters because the answer to this question determines the range of people whose views are relevant to evaluating the specific military standard. If a reasonable person on the battlefield is construed as an ordinary reasonable person in uniform, then it is possible to claim that ordinary persons can meaningfully judge whether the decision of a given commander has met a given standard of behaviour. By contrast, if a reasonable person on the battlefield is assumed to possess specialised knowledge and particular military competences, the relevance of the views of ordinary persons who lack such knowledge and competences is precluded.

In the Hostage Case, the US Nuremberg Tribunal appeared to favour the latter option. When evaluating whether Lothar Rendulic failed to comply with the rules that protect prisoners of war in South-Eastern Europe, the Tribunal held that the standard of assessment with respect to the conduct of military personnel was based on persons 'trained in military science',[61] as opposed to a standard based on an ordinary reasonable person. Many commentators and courts share this view.[62] Ian Henderson and Kate Reece, for example, argue that the standard applicable to commanders on the battlefield is explicitly not that of 'a "reasonable person"', who supposedly has a more civilian worldview, but rather a '"reasonable military commander" standard'.[63]

The view of the reasonable person, with which Henderson and Reece contrast the perspective of the reasonable military commander, is often equated with the stance attributed to a human rights lawyer. The authors of the ICTY's 2000 report concerning NATO's bombing campaign against the Federal Republic of Yugoslavia begin by observing that it is 'unlikely that a

[59] While it might be presumed that civilians are less likely to commit war crimes, Noel Trew points out that the opposite can also be the case: Trew (n 55), 124–5.

[60] This account by an anonymous military lawyer is related by D. Luban, 'Military Necessity and the Cultures of Military Law' (2013) 26 Leiden Journal of International Law 315, 315. The lawyer in question described the difference between the perspective of civilians and that of military officers. Luban himself distinguishes the two camps by reference to their starting point: one 'begins with armed conflict', assigning 'military necessity ... axiomatic status', while the other 'begins with humanitarianism', assigning 'human dignity ... primary status' (ibid., 316). See also Benvenisti (n 56), 348.

[61] *Hostage Case* (n 16), 1245–6.

[62] Notably, Rendulic himself observed that he found it particularly irritating that he was asked to justify his conduct during wartime to people who 'by their own admission' had not 'the slightest idea of war': Rendulic (n 28), 444.

[63] Henderson and Reece (n 47), 841. For similar interpretations of the report, see J. Holland, 'Military Objective and Collateral Damage: Their Relationship and Dynamics' (2004) 7 Yearbook of International Humanitarian Law 35, 48–49; Groeben (n 58), 480.

human rights lawyer and an experienced combat commander would assign the same relative values to military advantage and to injury to noncombatants'; then they state that 'the determination of relative values must be that of the "reasonable military commander"'.[64] Sigrid Redse Johansen, too, maintains that, when assessing a commander's conduct, 'the comparison is to be done with a *commander*, not a "human rights lawyer"'.[65]

In a speech given at the US Naval War College in Newport on 24 June 2010, Yoram Dinstein (1936–2024) rejects the idea that the views of civilians, be they human rights lawyers or not, matter on the battlefield in particularly forceful terms. Dinstein's intention is to defend the militaries of 'civilized nations'[66] against alleged criticism from human rights lawyers. At heart, however, Dinstein's speech is an impassioned argument for construing the reasonable person on the battlefield in military terms. Dinstein worries about the growing 'menace' of 'human rights zealots and do-goodniks' ... "human rights-niks" for short'.[67] These people, he says, present a danger to civilised nations that is 'equally acute'[68] as that posed by the 'barbarians'[69] whom these civilised nations fight. The human rights-niks 'would prefer a non-violent solution to every conflict'[70] and are motivated by pacificist motives that resonate 'with the lay (and basically uninformed) public at large'.[71] They would like to introduce a 'system of warfare characterized by zero collateral damage to civilians'.[72] Dinstein fears that too much attention is paid to these kinds of views when assessing a military commander's conduct. As a result, he says, 'in Afghanistan, airstrikes essential to mission accomplishment – and legally unimpeachable – have been scrapped, so as to avoid altogether lawful collateral damage to civilians'.[73] As a consequence of construing the reasonable military commander in too civilian colours, the 'command echelons' on the side of civilised nations 'bend over backward in the application' of the norms that govern armed conflicts.[74] According to Dinstein, this is problematic because it weakens civilised nations in the fight against 'modern barbarians',[75] who conduct hostilities 'in an utterly lawless fashion' and 'slaughter civilians on a large scale'.[76] Consequently, a 'hostile takeover' of the laws of armed conflict by human rights-niks must be resisted,[77] in the interest of preventing complete 'lawlessness'[78] on the battlefield. Reiterating his argument in favour

[64] ICTY Review Committee (n 47), [50]. Again, compare the exact same wording in Fenrick's article which pre-dates the report, Fenrick (n 49), 546.

[65] Johansen (n 35), 86.

[66] Y. Dinstein, 'Concluding Remarks: LOAC and Attempts to Abuse or Subvert It', in R.A. Pedrozo and D.P. Wollschlaeger (eds), *International Law and the Changing Character of War*, vol. 87 (Naval War College 2011) 485.

[67] Ibid., 488. [68] Ibid. [69] Ibid., 484. [70] Ibid., 488.

[71] Ibid. See also Sloane (n 58), 319. [72] Dinstein (n 66), 488. [73] Ibid., 486. [74] Ibid.

[75] Ibid., 484. For a sceptical view of such a portrayal of the enemy, see Gregor Noll, 'Analogy at War: Proportionality, Equality and the Law of Targeting' (2012) 43 Netherlands Yearbook of International Law 205, 223, 225.

[76] Dinstein (n 66), 485. [77] Ibid., 488. [78] Ibid., 489.

of seeing the battlefield as the exclusive domain of the reasonable person construed as a military commander, Dinstein concludes by encouraging the military lawyers gathered at the Naval War College to 'keep poachers' – presumably human rights-niks and uninformed reasonable people – 'off the grass'.[79] Paraphrasing a passage from a text by Michael A. Newton, one could summarise Dinstein's speech by saying that 'the reasonable person on the battlefield belongs to the armed forces of the world'.[80]

As the defensive tone of Dinstein's speech foreshadows, his view is not undisputed. Many deem the reasonable person on the battlefield to be a functional equivalent of domestic law's reasonable person in the sense that the former is the 'reasonable person in the most general sense – the person on the Clapham Omnibus, subject to the normal vagaries of everyday life, not the military commander subject to the completely abnormal vagaries of armed conflict'.[81] The international law and ethics professor William O'Brien (1923–2003), for example, deems the reasonable colonel to be 'the law of war counterpart to the common law "reasonable man"'.[82] The international lawyer Thomas Franck (1931–2009) described the reasonable military commander invoked by the authors of the ICTY report as 'an international version of the common law's reasonable man'.[83] Robert D. Sloane connected the report's standard to 'that old favorite of the law, the reasonable person';[84] and, for Laurie R. Blank, the reasonable military commander fulfils functions that are 'analogous' to those of 'the "reasonable person" in domestic law'.[85] Not all these authors use the term 'reasonable person' in contradistinction to the term 'reasonable military commander', as Henderson and Reece do, for instance. Others, however, leave no doubt that they are referring to a civilian standard. Thus William H. Boothby argues that a reasonable military commander must not do what 'all fair-minded people, including the well-known

79 Ibid., 493.

80 M.A. Newton, 'Modern Military Necessity: The Role and Relevance of Military Lawyers' (2007) 12 Roger Williams University Law Review 877, 900.

81 R. McLaughlin, 'The Law of Armed Conflict and International Human Rights Law: Some Paradigmatic Differences and Operational Implications' (2010) 13 Yearbook of International Humanitarian Law 213, 237. Rob McLaughlin contrasts this understanding of the reasonable person's identity with a narrower construal, in which this figure embodies the reasonable military commander to whom the 'common law "reasonable person"...is irrelevant' (ibid., 232).

82 W.V. O'Brien, 'The Law of War, Command Responsibility and Vietnam' (1972) 60 Georgetown Law Journal 605, 629. See also W.V. O'Brien, *The Yearbook of World Polity* (Praeger 1957) 55. Both times O'Brien attributes the term 'reasonable colonel' to Ernst Feilchenfeld (1898–1956). Attempts to verify this attribution were unsuccessful. Paul Ramsey used the same expression (and also attributes it to Feilchenfeld); see P. Ramsey, *Love and Society: Essays in the Ethics of Paul Ramsey* (James Johnson and David Smith eds, American Academy of Religion 1974) 192.

83 T.M. Franck, 'On Proportionality of Countermeasures in International Law' (2008) 102 American Journal of International Law 715, 737, 765.

84 Sloane (n 58), 317–18.

85 L.R. Blank, 'A New Twist on an Old Story: Lawfare and the Mixing of Proportionalities' (2011) 43 Case Western Reserve Journal of International Law 707, 717.

"man on the Clapham omnibus", would regard . . . as being so excessive as to require prosecution of the person making the decision'.[86] In the context of trying Stanislav Galić for besieging the city of Sarajevo, the ICTY also appeared to suggest that the identity of the reasonable person on the battlefield is to be construed broadly:

> In determining whether an attack was proportionate it is necessary to examine whether a reasonably well-informed person in the circumstances of the actual perpetrator, making reasonable use of the information available to him or her, could have expected excessive civilian casualties to result from the attack.[87]

David Luban, too, while offering a very balanced assessment of the debate, rejects restrictive constructions of the identity of the reasonable military commander. To say that 'military professionals ought to own the laws of war' (or, for that matter, that they ought to own the reasonable person on the battlefield) is 'like saying that Wall Street ought to own securities regulation'.[88] 'Militaries', he says, 'are not the only people in the battle space or the only ones war effects [*sic*].'[89] Thanks in part to the close scrutiny of armed conflicts by the media and by private users of social networks, Luban argues, 'the laws of war are now common property'.[90]

Incidentally, it was again at a colloquium held at the US Naval War College in Newport – the same place where, in 2010, Dinstein shared his concern about human rights-niks appropriating the reasonable person – that Michael Bothe advanced one of the most sustained arguments in favour of a civilian identity for the reasonable military commander. Bothe says that the decision of the authors of the ICTY Report to describe the reasonable military commander as a military figure is 'problematic'[91] and 'not really a satisfactory solution'[92] unless one defines the 'reasonable military commander . . . in more civilian terms'.[93] Bothe's plea for a more civilian identity of the reasonable person on the battlefield is rooted in his own belief that,

> In democratic systems, the values pursued by the military and those by society at large cannot be far apart. The value system on the basis of which the military is operating has to conform to that of the civil society, not *vice versa*. What is necessary in this respect is the dialogue between civil society and the military, which then has to be reflected in military decision-making.[94]

86 W.H. Boothby, *The Law of Targeting* (Oxford University Press 2012) 190.

87 *Prosecutor v Stanislav Galić* (Judgment and Opinion) Case No IT-98-29-T, TC 1 (n 46), [58].

88 Luban (n 60), 338. 89 Ibid.

90 Ibid. To some extent, Dinstein seems to accept this conclusion at least as a matter of fact, Dinstein (n 66), 484.

91 M. Bothe, 'Targeting', in A.E. Wall (ed.), *Legal and Ethical Lessons of NATO's Kosovo Campaign*, vol. 78 (Naval War College 2002) 184.

92 Michael Bothe, 'The Protection of the Civilian Population and NATO Bombing on Yugoslavia: Comments on a Report to the Prosecutor of the ICTY' (2001) 12 European Journal of International Law 531, 535.

93 Ibid. 94 Ibid.

The colloquium proceedings,[95] which reproduce the discussions that followed Bothe's presentation, reveal that his proposal was met with immediate criticism. While Dinstein, who was present in the audience, remained silent, Harvey Dalton (1940–2014), a captain of the US Navy and a Judge Advocate General, declared that he was 'a bit worried' by Bothe's view. 'A military commander knows how to employ the Tomahawk land attack missile . . . better. I'm going to defer to his judgment in terms of weaponizing and employing' such a tool.[96] Leslie C. Green (1920–2011) agreed. He, too, was 'worried about this "reasonable civilian" – this idea of the ordinary civilian and the ordinary soldier'.[97] He asked:

> What was the thought of a reasonable man? A reasonable man is the man on a downtown bus; that is not the reasonable soldier. One of the reasons that I don't like civilian judges trying military offenses is that they don't know the circumstances that were prevailing at the time that led to the soldier's actions. The question of what is reasonable in times of conflict depends on what is reasonable in the eyes of the man who is involved in that conflict. That would only be accepted by those who have similar background knowledge, not by one who has been securely moved up in some Inn of Court.[98]

Bothe responded to these comments by pointing to the particular developments that took place in West Germany after the Second World War. One of the lessons the Federal Republic drew from its history was that it is important

> to integrate the military into a civilian system of values, not to have the military as a state within the State. Arguing that military matters are something which the military knows and the civilian doesn't is utterly a step in the wrong direction.[99]

This exchange concerning the identity of the reasonable person on the battlefield might seem highly specific to the discussion of the law of armed conflict. But, at an elementary level, the issues raised here engage at least with two existential questions that face the reasonable person in any capacity. The first is the permanent problem of how far it is possible for a person who belongs to one community to pass judgement on a person who belongs to another. The same issue arose in discussing the reasonable person's gender in Chapter 3 and in problematising its ethnicity and culture in Chapter 4. Here it would be useful to recall that British colonial courts enlisted local assessors to help English judges understand the local context: interestingly, one respondent to Bothe's presentation at the Naval War College proposed a similar solution. Natalino Ronzitti suggested that the dialogue between civilians and military

[95] A.E. Wall, *Legal and Ethical Lessons of NATO's Kosovo Campaign*, vol 78 (Naval War College 2002).
[96] A.E. Wall (ed.), 'Discussion: Reasonable Military Commanders and Reasonable Civilians', *Legal and Ethical Lessons of NATO's Kosovo Campaign*, vol 78 (Naval War College 2002) 211.
[97] Ibid. [98] Ibid., 212. [99] Ibid.

personnel could be facilitated by inviting military staff to participate in the legal evaluation of military matters in civilian courts.[100] Others suggested that civilian courts could use 'expert witnesses to assess what reasonable conduct' on the part of a military commander 'might look like'[101] or, conversely, that military staff could consult civilian advisors, who are 'likely to possess more empathy than the powerful commander'.[102] If adopted, such proposals could help to integrate and unify the double life that the reasonable person currently leads on the battlefield.

The second existential issue facing the reasonable military commander on the battlefield has been touched upon only implicitly up to this point. It relates to one of the credos of the Scottish sentimentalists – a credo shared by Alderson and Opie – namely the belief in the unity and equality of all humans. The assumed and stipulated equality of humans is a cornerstone of Hume's and Smith's theories about the possibility of deriving truth and norms from an empathetic engagement with others.[103] Hume spoke of a 'string, to which all mankind have an accord and symphony',[104] Alderson of a 'common humanity'.[105] Transporting the reasonable person figure to the battlefield has the potential to seriously shake this foundation, on which the figure itself is erected.

The problem arises most poignantly around the value that the reasonable person on the battlefield is expected to assign to civilian lives in the warring parties. Some argue that a reasonable person embedded in a given state's armed force should give priority to protecting the civilian lives of that state. Thus Sloane observes:

> No state military force that is or has ever been treats enemy civilians and its own civilians equally . . . it is implausible as law . . . [it] would render disproportionate the vast majority of strikes that cause collateral damage.[106]

'States', he says, 'like people, may – and perhaps should – assign greater weight to the welfare of those with whom they have a morally, socially, or politically salient relationship.'[107] Others vehemently disagree. Gregor Noll argues that in the law of armed conflict 'civilians appear as *unqualified* civilians. The proportionality rule relates not to "enemy civilians", but to civilians *at large*,

[100] Ibid. [101] Trew (n 55), 122–3, 125–6. See also Olásolo (n 54), 229–30.
[102] R.S. Adams, 'Power and Proportionality: The Role of Empathy and Ethics on Valuing Excessive Harm' (2019) 80 Air Force Law Review 149, 178.
[103] See Chapter 2.2. See also M.L. Frazer, *The Enlightenment of Sympathy: Justice and the Moral Sentiments in the Eighteenth Century and Today* (Oxford University Press 2010) 142.
[104] D. Hume, *An Enquiry Concerning the Principles of Morals: A Critical Edition* (Tom L Beauchamp ed, Clarendon Press 2006) 75.
[105] C. Alderson, *Selections from the Charges and Other Detached Papers of Baron Alderson* (J.W. Parker & Son 1858) 146. See also Chapter 2.3.
[106] Sloane (n 58), 330. [107] Ibid., 328–9.

regardless of nationality or political allegiance.'[108] To speak of proportionality in the context of the law of armed conflict, in his view, presupposes that there exists a relationship between a given military commander and 'enemy civilians', who might die as a result of the former's decision. They form part of the same *demos*, in fact everyone belongs to the same *demos*.[109] Consequently, a distinction between one's own civilians and 'enemy civilians' is not possible; already 'the first civilian casualty' injures this common *demos*.[110] A reasonable person on the battlefield would be expected to act as an agent of all humanity when it comes to making proportionality decisions. Thus understood, a reasonable military commander in Lothar Rendulic's position could not reasonably have subordinated the interests of the civilian population in occupied Norway to the military interests of the Wehrmacht.

Tempting as that may be, it is not the legal biographer's task to determine which image of the reasonable person is to be preferred, apart from noting that to expect that a reasonable person would distinguish between civilians and enemy civilians, or would treat them differently, is asking a lot from an empathy-based standard. The same applies to the question posed at the beginning of this section concerning the identity of the reasonable person on the battlefield. It is evident that some favour a military image, such that the reasonable person's common sense is accessible only to military staff, while others prefer to construe this figure as a reasonable person in uniform, but rooted in civilian values that are accessible to members of civil society at large. The first alternative represents an understanding of the standard that is the exclusive preserve of a select group of people – such as *paterfamilias* in ancient Rome, or the English as colonial administrators of justice. The second alternative would be in keeping with the egalitarian manifestations of the reasonable person that we have encountered thus far. The point of Egypt's *geru maa* or of the (ideal) man on the Clapham omnibus was precisely their ordinary and accessible character, which was meant to allow everyone to identify the right course of action in any situation by imagining what these characters would do; and this was their appeal, too. Both of these manifestations of the reasonable person exist, and both form part of the reasonable person's biography. Given that the utility of this figure relies on its connection with common sense,[111] one should merely note that the smaller the class of people whose views are permitted to inform the content of that common sense, the

[108] Noll (n 75), 225–6. See also D. Traven, *Law and Sentiment in International Politics: Ethics, Emotions, and the Evolution of the Laws of War* (Cambridge University Press 2021) 274. Eyal Benvenisti appears to reserve judgement on this point; see Benvenisti (n 56), 356.

[109] Noll (n 75), 227–8. [110] Ibid., 228.

[111] For a discussion of common sense in the context of war, see e.g. Johansen (n 35), 403–4; E. Lieblich and E. Benvenisti, 'The Obligation to Exercise Discretion in Warfare: Why Autonomous Weapon Systems Are Unlawful', in N. Bhuta et al. (eds), *Autonomous Weapons Systems: Law, Ethics, Policy* (Cambridge University Press 2016) 253–4.

more reduced is the standard's ability to offer relatable and predictable guidance in concrete situations.

This section addressed two existential and unresolved questions facing the reasonable person on the battlefield. First, is this construct a civilian or a military figure? And, second, is it embedded in human society as a whole or in a particular context that allows it to distinguish between civilians and enemy civilians? The foundational nature of these questions, combined with the fact that answers to them are the subject of fierce debates, impairs the utility of the reasonable person figure on the battlefield. And even if these questions could be resolved, there is still a third existential problem that confronts the subject of this biography: empathy makes killing difficult – or, to put it slightly more polemically, reasonable persons do not kill. We will address this problem in the next section.

5.3 Little Child

Towards the end of the first wave of the destruction of Northern Norway by the Wehrmacht in late November 1944, the officer overseeing the evacuation of the civilian population on the ground, Kurt Herrmann, prepared a report for General Rendulic concerning the measures taken and the results achieved. Towards the end of that report, Herrmann informed his superior that there are certain forms of conduct that make the evacuation of civilians more difficult. These include 'the separation of the men from their families to be deported', 'guarding' these men 'like prisoners', and 'the burning down of houses in the presence of the inhabitants even where an immediate destruction was not necessary'.[112] Herrmann also noted that 'the shelling of the locality Kjoellefjord by units of the navy' while the evacuated population looked on from ships anchored off the town[113] 'hindered the readiness of the population to follow the officially prescribed way'.[114]

Herrmann's reflections come under the heading 'Experiences' – a standard section in these reports that was meant to improve the implementation of military missions in the future. One would think it should be obvious to a reasonable military commander that the needless destruction of homes before the eyes of their inhabitants is not going to make an already difficult mission any easier. Yet the officer's conclusions are less intriguing if it is true that, as numerous studies indicate, persons in positions of power find it difficult to empathise. Thus, what is obvious to many may not be obvious to a military commander focused on turning Northern Norway into an uninhabitable

[112] K. Herrmann, 'Report from Evacuation Staff to 20th Mountain Army Concerning Evacuation of Northern Norway (25 November 1944)'. Reproduced as document NOKW-090 in *Hostage Case* (n 16), 1118–23.

[113] A. Sørenes, 'Tvangsevakuert Som Ti-Åring' *NRK* (Oslo, 26 October 2014).

[114] Herrmann (n 112). Reproduced as document NOKW-090 in *Hostage Case* (n 16), 1118–23.

wasteland. The fact that power impairs its holder's ability to empathise – to understand the views and feelings of others – confronts an empathy-based standard like that of the reasonable person with a considerable challenge. The challenge is complicated by the fact that a lack of empathy actually enhances a military commander's efficiency and ability to conduct missions, especially lethal ones. Against this background, one could argue that the reasonable person's appearance on the battlefield is the result of a misunderstanding, that the character in our story has gone astray, finding itself displaced, thrown in a landscape it was never meant to inhabit. Alternatively, one could argue that there are few places where an empathy-based standard is more urgently needed than the battlefield and that everything we have said about the reasonable person so far comes to the fore in the extreme situation that the battlefield represents. We will consider this option towards the end of the present section, but before doing that we will address the relationship between power and empathy.

Numerous studies have shown that the possession of power significantly influences how a person relates to others. Findings from experiments tell us that power creates a 'psychological distance' between the powerful person and others[115] and 'leads to reduced processing of others' actions and emotions'.[116] Powerful persons struggle to take the perspectives of others into account and, when they attempt it, they reach not very accurate conclusions.[117] Summarising the results of numerous experiments and studies, Adam Galinsky and others have observed that power is 'associated with a reduced tendency to comprehend how other individuals see the world, think about the world, and feel about the world'.[118] Possessing power makes people 'less likely to spontaneously adopt another person's visual perspective, less likely to take into account that another person did not possess their privileged knowledge, and less accurate in detecting the emotional states of other people'.[119]

This relationship between power and perspective taking has numerous consequences. They include a tendency to think in stereotypes,[120] to neglect the interests of less powerful individuals,[121] to objectify others,[122] and to treat people as a means to an end.[123] Gruenfeldt and others observed, for example, that participants in an experiment who were primed to feel powerful reported that they tend to reach out to others only when they need something from

[115] A.D. Galinsky et al., 'Power and Perspectives Not Taken' (2006) 17 Psychological Science 1068, 1069.

[116] J. Hogeveen, M. Inzlicht and S.S. Obhi, 'Power Changes How the Brain Responds to Others' (2014) 143 Journal of Experimental Psychology 755, 759; Adams (n 102), 168, 169.

[117] Galinsky et al. (n 115), 1068. [118] Ibid., 1072.

[119] Ibid. The authors note that the lack of perspective taking is not necessarily the result of a conscious decision; it is rather the case that power 'makes perspective-taking less likely'.

[120] Ibid., 1069, 1072. [121] Hogeveen, Inzlicht and Obhi (n 116), 760.

[122] D.H. Gruenfeld et al., 'Power and the Objectification of Social Targets' (2008) 95 Journal of Personality and Social Psychology 111, 124; Galinsky and others (n 115), 1072.

[123] I.H. Robertson, 'How Power Affects the Brain' (2013) 26 The Psychologist 186, 187.

them and were less likely to like a person who was not useful to them.[124] When asked to write the letter 'E' on their forehead, power-primed participants tended to write the letter as if they were looking at it (resulting in an illegible mirrored 'E'), whereas participants not power-primed wrote the 'E' in a manner that other persons looking at them could read it.[125] Most significantly for our purposes, the possession of power has been linked to a lack of empathy.[126] '[A]s empathy wanes' in a powerful person, notes Keltner,

> so does our capacity for moral sentiments that depend on empathy – namely, concern for others' suffering (compassion), reverence for what others give (gratitude), and inspiration experienced in appreciating others' goodness (elevation).[127]

But, as Scott Adams observes, one must treat the conclusion that power necessarily results in lack of empathy with a degree of caution, since the ability of experiments to simulate the behaviour of people may be limited.[128] Galinsky and others, too, point out that some studies contradict the findings presented above.[129]Still, it appears to be universally accepted, as a general phenomenon, that power tends to produce loss of empathy. Already David Hume had noted that 'oppressive social institutions may successfully shield the feelings of certain others from our view, or may cultivate our own characters so that we are insensible to their feelings'.[130] With respect to slavery, for instance, Hume spoke of the 'little humanity, commonly observed in persons, accustomed, from their infancy, to exercise so great authority over their fellow creatures, and to trample upon human nature'.[131] In other words, great authority can lead to a lack of humanity and of empathy.

This conclusion is problematic for the concept of the reasonable person on the battlefield, since 'great authority' is certainly one of the distinguishing features of military commanders. Indeed, if power is defined as 'an individual's relative capacity to modify others' states by providing or withholding resources or administering punishments',[132] there are few individuals more powerful than military commanders, who have the capacity to modify the states of others existentially, from alive to dead. The power of commanders, coupled with their tendency to lack empathy, is problematic because the standard of the reasonable military commander – which is meant to guide

[124] Gruenfeld et al. (n 122), 127; Robertson (n 123), 187. [125] Galinsky et al. (n 115), 1070.
[126] Robertson (n 123), 187; Galinsky et al. (n 115), 1072. See also Adams (n 102), 152.
[127] D. Keltner, *The Power Paradox: How We Gain and Lose Influence* (Penguin 2016) 101.
[128] Adams (n 102), 172.
[129] A.D. Galinsky, D.D. Rucker and J.C. Magee, 'Power and Perspective-Taking: A Critical Examination' (2016) 67 Journal of Experimental Social Psychology 91, 92.
[130] Frazer (n 103), 53–4.
[131] David. Hume, *Essays: Moral, Political, and Literary* (Lewis 1889) 383.
[132] D. Keltner, D.H. Gruenfeld and C. Anderson, 'Power, Approach, and Inhibition' (2003) 110 Psychological Review 265, 265. The exact definition of the concept of power is disputed. For a similar though slightly different definition, see Galinsky, Rucker and Magee (n 129), 91.

real-life commanders' decision-making processes – presupposes an ability both to engage in perspective taking and to empathise. In concrete terms, there is a risk that the distinct character of the relationship between a soldier and a civilian distorts the accuracy of the soldier's interpretation of the civilian's surroundings. One response to this problem could be to attempt to improve a military commander's ability to empathise. Some studies indicate that this can be done, for example by appealing to the commander's sense of responsibility and accountability.[133] Other studies appear to suggest that the capacity for empathy, once lost, cannot be recovered.[134] Discussing the utility of empathy training presupposes that armies would be interested in enhancing the capacity of their commanders to empathise.

In fact, however, the opposite seems to be the case. This is due to the fact that empathy undermines a person's ability to harm another. Indeed, studies suggest that the closer a soldier gets to the person they are fighting and the stronger their identification with the opponent, the more difficult it is for them to kill that person. An episode from the 1831 Polish–Russian War related by the French colonel Ardant du Picq (1821–70) illustrates the phenomenon:

> two Russian and two Polish regiments of cavalry charged each other. They went with the same dash to meet one another. When close enough to recognize faces, these cavalrymen slackened their gait and both turned their backs. The Russians and Poles, at this terrible moment, recognized each other as brothers, and rather than spill fraternal blood, they extricated themselves from a combat as if it were a crime.[135]

All Quiet on the Western Front, a 1928 bestselling novel by Erich Maria Remarque (1898–1970) based on the author's own experiences in the German army during the First World War, describes this transformation of the enemy from an abstract idea into a concrete human being in some detail. In the relevant passage, Paul Bäumer, the protagonist, lies in a shell hole in the no-man's land between the front lines, next to a French soldier whom Bäumer killed with his bayonet ('the first man I have killed with my hands'[136]). After an extensive period of agony, Bäumer turns to the dead soldier and says:

> Comrade, I did not want to kill you. If you jumped in here again, I would not do it, if you would be sensible too. But you were only an idea to me before, an abstraction that lived in my mind and called forth its appropriate response. It was that abstraction I stabbed. But now, for the first time, I see you are a man like me. I thought of your hand-grenades, of your bayonet, of your rifle; now

133 Galinsky et al. (n 115), 1073. A similar argument had been advanced earlier by S.L.A. Marshall, *Men Against Fire: The Problem of Battle Command in Future War* (Peter Smith 1978) 160–1.

134 Adams (n 102), 170.

135 C.J.J. Ardant du Picq, *Battle Studies: Ancient and Modern Battle* (Macmillan 1921) 45–6.

136 E.M. Remarque, *All Quiet on the Western Front* (A.W. Wheen trans., G.P. Putnam's Sons 1929) 242.

> I see your wife and your face and our fellowship. Forgive me, comrade. We always see it too late.[137]

When Samuel Lyman Atwood Marshall (1900–77), Chief US combat historian of the Second World War, studied the actions of US troops across numerous battles in the Pacific region and in Europe, he found patterns of behaviour that echo those described by du Picq and Remarque. In his book *Men Against Fire*,[138] Marshall presents findings that suggest that 'out of an average one hundred men along the line of fire during the period of an encounter, only fifteen men on the average would take any part with the weapons'.[139] Even in the most aggressive units, 'the figure rarely rose above 25 per cent'.[140] The soldiers who did not fire did not desert the scene or hide, 'they simply would not fire their weapons at the enemy'.[141] Analyses of soldiers' behaviour in the First World War,[142] in the American Civil War,[143] and even in wars fought in ancient Greece and Rome[144] reach similar conclusions.

The studies carried out across these different theatres of war suggest that it is the distance between them that conditions the likelihood of one soldier's killing the other. Jesse Glenn Gray (1913–77), a philosopher with war experience, noted how 'destroying is easier when done at a little remove. With every foot of distance there is a corresponding decrease in reality. Imagination flags and fails altogether when distances become too great.'[145] In a similar vein, Ardant du Picq concludes: 'To fight from a distance is instinctive in man. From the first day he has worked to this end, and he continues to do so.'[146]

At one end of the spectrum are long-range weapons that allow a soldier to 'slay hundreds and never see their blood flow'.[147] At the other end is hand-to-hand combat of the kind described by Remarque, where a soldier's weapon 'becomes a natural extension of his body'[148] that must physically penetrate the adversary. To illustrate this difference, Dave Grossman ponders whether the pilots who bombed Hamburg in July 1943, causing 'horrible deaths, burning and suffocating'[149] to more than 30,000 people, would have carried out their mission if instead they had to 'turn a flamethrower on each one of these … women and children, or worse yet slit each of their throats'.[150] Killing is easier,

137 Ibid., 244. 138 Marshall (n 133). 139 Ibid., 57. 140 Ibid., 56.

141 D. Grossman, *On Killing: The Psychological Cost of Learning to Kill in War and Society* (Little, Brown 1996) 3–4. For an account of one such situation, which takes place in the context of the fight for Makin Island, see Marshall (n 133), 55–6.

142 Grossman (n 141), 27. 143 Adams (n 102), 176. 144 Ardant du Picq (n 135), 110.

145 Jesse Glenn Gray, *The Warriors: Reflections on Men in Battle* (University of Nebraska Press 1999) 178. See also Adams (n 102), 176.

146 Ardant du Picq (n 135), 112.

147 R. Strozzi-Heckler, *In Search of the Warrior Spirit: Teaching Awareness Disciplines to the Green Berets* (North Atlantic Books 2003) 127. See also Grossman (n 141), 97.

148 Grossman (n 141), 121. 149 Ibid., 100–1. 150 Ibid.

it seems, when a distance between the soldier and the person that soldier fights limits the extent to which the former empathises with the latter.[151]

Apart from physical distance, the threshold for killing can be lowered further by dehumanizing the persons one fights on the basis of their cultural, ethnic or class background.[152] With respect to the act of killing itself, the German psychologist and philosopher Erich Fromm (1900–80) notes that there is 'good clinical evidence for the assumption that destructive aggression occurs, at least to a large degree, in conjunction with momentary or chronic emotional withdrawal'.[153] This circumstance is also reflected in the language used to describe the act of killing. Persons killed do not die; they are 'engaged', 'knocked over', 'wasted', 'greased', 'taken out' or 'picked up'.[154] Killed soldiers 'fall' or 'remain' in the field or at sea,[155] enemies are pejoratively called 'Krauts', 'Japs', or 'Rebs',[156] and weapons of mass destruction such as the nuclear bombs dropped by US forces on Hiroshima and Nagasaki receive nicknames like 'Little Boy' or 'Fat Man'.[157]

Just how considerable the distance brought about by these linguistic conventions is becomes apparent when we compare the benign terms given to atomic bombs with a poet's description on the ground. In a poem entitled 'Little Child', Sankichi Tōge (1917–53) describes a scene in Hiroshima after the United States had dropped Little Boy upon the city:

little child, dear child
where can you be?
like a stone stumbled on accidentally
that clear morning, parting
from your eyes, open so wide
you have no mother
suddenly
behind your pupils, which sharply reflect the sky
a dark red cloud rises
and up above is turned inside out and spreads
the disaster of that light with no sound
in front of your endless questions
who will tell you of that day?
little child, dear child
where could you have gone?
leaving you with the neighbors, she went off to work detail
thinking of you
supported only by that devotion

[151] E. Fromm, *The Anatomy of Human Destructiveness* (Holt, Rinehart & Winston 1973) 123.
[152] Grossman (n 141), 160, 161; Fromm (n 151), 121. [153] Fromm (n 151), 123.
[154] For more examples, see Grossman (n 141), 92; R. Holmes, *Acts of War: The Behavior of Men in Battle* (Simon and Schuster 1989) 364.
[155] Ardant du Picq (n 135), 99. [156] Grossman (n 141), 92; Holmes (n 154), 364.
[157] Grossman (n 141), 92; Holmes (n 154), 364.

your mother raced to you through burning streets
not strong enough to be bothered
by even the maggots beginning to fester on the putrefying soles of her feet
in the darkness of a temporary aid station
silently died. . .[158]

Confronted with these existential horrors of war captured in Tōge's poem, and lacking the distancing tools discussed earlier – social, cultural, physical, linguistic or other – human beings do what comes naturally to them: 'Some load, some pass weapons, some tend the wounded, some shout orders, a few run, a few wander off in the smoke or find a convenient low spot to sink into, and a few, a very few, shoot.'[159] Similarly, Marshall concluded:

> the average and normally healthy individual – the man who can endure the mental and physical stresses of combat – still has such an inner and usually unrealized resistance towards killing a fellow man that he will not of his own volition take life if it is possible to turn away from that responsibility.[160]

Consequently, if the armies of the world want their soldiers to shoot, they must actively train these 'average and healthy individuals', 'ordinary men, who do not like combat at all',[161] specifically to kill. For Colonel Ardant du Picq, the entire purpose of an army is to 'make men fight in spite of themselves'.[162] Otherwise 'the civilized man, in war, which is opposed to civilization, returns' to his peaceful instincts.[163]

This is precisely what modern armies decided to do. One of the first to act in this spirit appears to have been the German army. Grieving the dead French soldier he had killed, Remarque's First World War protagonist, the German soldier Bäumer, had cried out: 'Why do they never tell us that you are poor devils like us, that your mothers are just as anxious as ours, and that we have the same fear of death, and the same dying and the same agony . . . ?'[164] The answer is that the German 1915 *War Book* already noted that 'sentimentality'[165] and 'humanitarian considerations'[166] undermine a soldier's fighting spirit and must be kept in check. Rendulic's own order to implement a scorched earth policy 'ruthlessly' and without pity for the civilian population equally reflects an awareness of the potential of empathy to undermine the successful implementation of a mission. The US Army, too, confronted with Marshall's findings, took action after the Second World War.[167] Measures

158 S. Tōge, 'Little Child', in his *Poems of the Atomic Bomb* (K. Thornber trans., University of Chicago 2012) 38–9.

159 Grossman (n 141), 20. 160 Marshall (n 133), 79. 161 G. Dyer, *War* (Crown 1985) 118.

162 Ardant du Picq (n 135), 111, 110. 163 Ibid., 112. 164 Remarque (n 136), 244.

165 Great General Staff of the German Army, *The War Book of the German General Staff* (J.H. Morgan trans., McBride, Nast & Co. 1915) 71–2.

166 Ibid.

167 For a general overview of the manner in which Marshall's studies influenced the US Army and of the most important criticisms of his theories, see F.D.G. Williams, *SLAM: The Influence of*

such as 'rehearsing and mimicking'[168] the act of killing, or replacing abstract target circles with human-shaped targets[169] during shooting practice, are considered to be among the reasons why the firing rates of soldiers increased from '15 to 20 percent in World War II to 90 to 95 percent in Vietnam'.[170]

With this, we now return to the question of the reasonable person on the battlefield. Rather than focusing on countering the de-empathising effect of power on military commanders (discussed above), armies specifically desire and nurture soldiers' distance and non-empathetic engagement with those they are fighting. This can be problematic for many reasons. But it also raises a challenge to the utility of an empathy-based standard such as that of the reasonable person. If it is the case, as the discussion in this chapter aimed to show, that the reasonable person does not kill and that a military commander's power impairs that commander's ability to empathise, one could argue that the application of the reasonable person standard on the battlefield is misguided.

Instead, one could operate with less empathy-charged concepts, for example reasonableness per se, or with general notions of proportionality, and banish the reasonable person from the battlefield. The outcomes of such a course of action need not be disastrous. Some have argued, for instance, that reducing empathy in the field furthers the swift conclusion of hostilities.[171] Conversely, one could say that the reasonable person's being naturally opposed to killing makes this figure uniquely suited for deployment on the battlefield and that the world would be a better place if battlefields were exclusively populated by reasonable persons who are capable of feeling empathy.[172] An extreme example of harnessing the violence-controlling effects of empathy is the proposal of Roger Fisher (1922–2012), a US professor of law, to implant the US nuclear launch codes in the chest of a US volunteer. In case the US president and commander-in-chief would want to launch a nuclear weapon, that president would then have to kill the volunteer first. 'He has to look at someone and realize what death is – what an innocent death is. Blood on the White House carpet. It's reality brought home.'[173]

Again, it is not my task to resolve the questions posed by the biography of the reasonable person – at least not at this stage. However, it is important to

S.L.A. Marshall on the United States Army (S. Canedy ed., Office of the Command Historian, United States Army Training and Doctrine Command 1999) chs 4–5.

168 Grossman (n 141), 132. 169 Ibid., 253. 170 Ibid., 132.

171 Great General Staff of the German Army (n 165), 71–2. See also Adams (n 102), 175–6.

172 A. Saab, 'Emotions and International Law' (2021) 10 ESIL Reflections 5. See also E.J. Buis, 'International Law's Invisible Frames Symposium: Inter-Temporality, Legal Fictions and Wartime Emotions in the Investigation of International Humanitarian Law Violations' (*Opinio Juris*, 25 January 2022), http://opiniojuris.org/2022/01/25/international-laws-invisible-frames-symposium-inter-temporality-legal-fictions-and-wartime-emotions-in-the-investigation-of-international-humanitarian-law-violations.

173 R. Fisher, 'Preventing Nuclear War' (1981) 37 Bulletin of the Atomic Scientists 11, 16.

acknowledge that the appearance of this figure on the battlefield, first in connection with the Nuremberg trials, after the Second World War, and then in the form of the reasonable military commander, in the context of the ICTY's 2000 NATO report, raises existential questions related both to the figure itself and to the character of those whose conduct the standard is meant to guide. We will revisit some of these questions in connection with the reasonable person's encounter with other artificial creations in the next chapter. There, however, they are not confined to the battlefield but permeate all areas of life.

6

The Reasonable Person in the Future

As we have seen in the previous chapter, one noteworthy feature of the ICTY's 2000 report concerning the legality of NATO's use of force against Yugoslavia is the explicit discussion of the standard of the reasonable military commander. Another noteworthy feature is the absence of any discussion, explicit or otherwise, of one aspect that set NATO's Yugoslavia campaign apart from previous conflicts: that operation, on the eve of the millennium, was the first war that heavily relied on the use of unmanned aerial vehicles, colloquially known as drones. From the outset, NATO's declared aim was to minimise the risk of its soldiers dying in combat.[1] The replacement of human aircraft pilots with remote-controlled, unmanned drones was one way of meeting this objective. The Czech author Karel Čapek (1890–1938) predicted that this would happen – and that it would happen in the Balkans. His 1920 play *R.U.R.*, set in the year 2000, describes a dystopian future in which tasks hitherto reserved to humans would be gradually transferred to machines, or rather, to be precise, to entities that Čapek decided to call 'robots'.[2] The term now universally used to describe programmable machines with various degrees of autonomy derives from the Czech noun *robota*, which means 'hard labour'.[3] Curiously, Čapek's play discusses the consequences of replacing human soldiers with robots, specifically with reference to a war in the Balkans.[4] Concerning that war, one of the play's protagonists can be heard reading out a newspaper article that reports: 'Robot soldiers spare nobody in the occupied territory. They have assassinated over seven hundred thousand citizens.'[5] The play's central question, however, is not about robot soldiers, in

[1] W.K. Clark, *Waging Modern War: Bosnia, Kosovo, and the Future of Combat* (Public Affairs 2001) 183. See also G. Chamayou, *A Theory of the Drone* (Janet Lloyd trans., New Press 2015) 127–8.

[2] In 1933, Karel Čapek reported that the term was invented and suggested to him by his brother Josef (1887–1945); see K. Čapek, 'O Slove Robot', *Lidové noviny* (Prague, 24 December 1933), 12.

[3] Ibid.

[4] K. Čapek, *R.U.R.: Rossum's Universal Robots* (Paul Selver and Nigel Playfair trans., Doubleday, Page 1923) 44.

[5] Ibid., 45.

the Balkans or anywhere else, but about a robot's ultimate identity. Are they human, are they objects, are they something else altogether? The question comes up in the play's first act, in a dialogue between Harry Domin and Helena Glory. Domin, 'a handsome man of 35',[6] is the general manager of the robot factory, Rossum's Universal Robots. Glory, 'a vital, sympathetic, handsome girl of 21',[7] is the daughter of Domin's employer, the factory owner, and has come to visit the remote island where the plant is situated. Domin explains to Glory that the founder of Rossum's invented robots with the aim of producing cheap and simple labourers:

DOMIN: He rejected everything that did not contribute directly to the progress of work. Everything that makes man more expensive. In fact he rejected man and made the Robot. My dear Miss Glory, the Robots are not people. Mechanically they are more perfect than we are; they have an enormously developed intelligence, but they have no soul.
GLORY: How do you know they have no soul?
DOMIN: Have you ever seen what a Robot looks like inside?
GLORY: No.
DOMIN: Very neat, very simple. Really a beautiful piece of work. Not much in it, but everything in flawless order. The product of an engineer is technically at a higher pitch of perfection than a product of Nature.
GLORY: But man is supposed to be the product of God.
DOMIN: All the worse. God hasn't the slightest notion of modern engineering. . .
GLORY: I saw the first Robots at home. The Town Council bought them for – I mean engaged them for work.
DOMIN: No, bought them, Miss Glory. Robots are bought and sold.
GLORY: These were employed as street-sweepers. I saw them sweeping. They were so strange and quiet.
DOMIN: Rossum's Universal Robot factory doesn't produce a uniform brand of Robots. We have Robots of *finer* and *coarser* grades. The best will live about twenty years.
GLORY: Then they die?
DOMIN: Yes, they get used up.

Shortly after this exchange, it becomes apparent that Glory is not just the daughter of Domin's employer, but also the president of the Humanity League, an organisation that advocates treating robots 'like human beings'.[8] Glory believes robots can have a soul, can feel, can love, can revolt. Domin rejects this idea. Robots are things (they are 'bought', not 'engaged'), even though he himself at times describes them in language used of humans (they 'live' about twenty years). Throughout the entire play, the protagonists debate the question of a robot's identity. Gradually, however, it becomes clear that this is, just as much, a question about a human's identity. The question 'what is that?' becomes 'who am I?'. The protagonists' confrontation with a

[6] Ibid., 7. [7] Ibid. [8] Ibid., 28.

perceived other – the robots – turns their attention to themselves, sharpening their own sense of identity. Embracing this phenomenon, the present chapter explores the reasonable person's encounter with entities that possess artificial intelligence (AI). Naturally, all the previous chapters explored the reasonable person's encounter with an other. But the encounter with AI is particularly acute, since it has been argued that the advent of AI will lead to the demise of the reasonable person. As we approach the end of this biography, it is thus apposite to ask to what extent the concept can deal with the emergence of AI-empowered digital agents. We begin by considering the applicability of the reasonable person concept to cases where AI entities act as human avatars (Section 6.1), before exploring the prospect of treating AI as legal actors in their own right (Section 6.2). The chapter concludes with a discussion of proposals to personalise the reasonable person concept with the help of big data (Section 6.3).

6.1 Avatars

An accurate understanding of the way in which entities that possess AI challenge the reasonable person presupposes an accurate understanding of what exactly AI-empowered entities are and which tasks they can perform.[9] At the most foundational level, AI is composed of lines of computer code – written sets of instructions that control how a given computer program executes specific tasks. In most cases, AI is just that – a few lines of code. In other cases, however, AI takes a more embodied form, for example when it is used to empower self-driving cars or vacuum-cleaning robots. *R.U.R.*'s robots, too, were controlled by preconfigured mechanical operations, but appeared in human form. Since embodied AI poses the most acute challenge to the concept of the reasonable person, we shall focus on this type of AI here and in the next section.

When it comes to the tasks that it can perform, AI runs along a spectrum of competence and autonomy. Some AIs[10] are classical tools, in the sense that they enhance the capacity of humans to carry out certain tasks: calculators, for example, or programs that can solve Sudoku puzzles fall in this category. At the other end of the spectrum, one finds AIs that are given a certain objective to achieve and then use sophisticated machine-learning techniques to identify the best means of achieving that objective. This type of AI is autonomous in the sense that it 'teaches itself by running experiments or

[9] For an overview of the different legal statuses of various types of robots and AI-empowered machines, see N.M. Richards and W.D. Smart, 'How Should the Law Think about Robots?' and C.E.A. Karnow, 'The Application of Traditional Tort Theory to Embodied Machine Intelligence', both in R. Calo, A.M. Froomkin and I. Kerr (eds), *Robot Law* (Edward Elgar 2016).

[10] In this chapter I am using 'AI' not only for artificial intelligence but also as a shorthand for an AI-empowered object or entity; thus 'AIs' (in the plural) will cover AI programs, AI devices, AI robots, and so on.

making other sorts of real or virtual attempts at a solution, corrects for error, and approximates a result that it then implements'.[11] Sometimes it may be possible for human operators to predict the means a machine would choose and how these means would produce a particular result. At other times the means or the eventual output (or both) may be unpredictable from the perspective of a human operator. For example, certain AI-empowered programs can be used to identify suitable medical treatments without human users being able to understand on what basis the AI issued its recommendation.[12] It is these AIs – the ones that are both autonomous and unpredictable – that engage the concept of the reasonable person most directly. For the purposes of this chapter, we shall consider to what extent the concept of the reasonable person can accommodate embodied forms of AI that are autonomous and unpredictable or is threatened by them.

The spheres of AI and of the reasonable person begin to overlap most notably when an AI performs a task that impairs another person's interests. In the world of *R.U.R.*, this could happen, for example, if one of the robots causes harmful substances to be baked into the bread they are making (tort), or if the clothes they weave turn out to be faulty (contract). In the contemporary world, conventional examples of undesired machine behaviour include accidents caused by autonomous vehicles, as when Uber's self-driving car collided with and killed Elaine Herzberg (1968–2018) as she was crossing a road,[13] or software biases that discriminate between people on the basis of their ethnicity, as when Google's Photos app associated African Americans with 'gorillas'.[14] One way of addressing these situations is to treat them as cases of faulty products regardless of whether one deals with robots, mechanical machines, or software programs and regardless of the degree of autonomy that these entities possess.[15] *R.U.R.*'s robots would then be, not actors in their own right, but rather artefacts. Similarly, the algorithms regulating the behaviour of a self-driving car or categorizing digital images would be considered not independent entities but mere extensions or products of their human creators. Treating such situations in this manner would mean holding the creators of these products strictly liable for the behaviour of their creations. Thus *R.U.R.* would be liable for the mistakes of its robots no matter whether it intended to cause its robots to make faulty clothes or to bake contaminated

[11] Karnow (n 9), 52.

[12] For an overview of the legal issues raised by 'black-box' applications in the medical sector, see N.W. Price, 'Black-Box Medicine' (2015) 28 Harvard Journal of Law & Technology 419.

[13] S. Levin and J.C. Wong, 'Self-Driving Uber Kills Arizona Woman in First Fatal Crash Involving Pedestrian', *The Guardian* (London, 19 March 2018).

[14] A. Barr, 'Google Mistakenly Tags Black People as "Gorillas," Showing Limits of Algorithms', *Wall Street Journal* (New York, 1 July 2015). https://www.wsj.com/articles/BL-DGB-42522. In this regard, it is also telling that the algorithm that generated Figure 6.1 portrayed the reasonable person as white.

[15] A.D. Selbst, 'Negligence and AI's Human Users' (2020) 100 Boston University Law Review 1315, 1320.

bread. Similarly, the manufacturer of the AI system that controls the car that killed Elaine Herzberg would be liable for her death regardless of whether the manufacturer was negligent. If one adopts this strict liability approach, which reflects the law in many jurisdictions,[16] the emergence of AI does not pose a particular challenge to the concept of the reasonable person. Treating AI-empowered entities in the same way products are treated means that the concept is simply not engaged.

But some argue that treating AIs as if they were products is unsatisfactory for reasons that resemble those invoked in support of the development of modern negligence law at the turn of the eighteenth century: a strict liability system makes innovation expensive, because it places the responsibility exclusively on those who invent and operate new machines.[17] In consequence, even technological innovations that could increase overall welfare risk not being pursued.[18] Instead, it is argued, the legal assessment of AIs should be based on a negligence standard that takes into account that such entities act autonomously, and often in a manner that humans cannot predict.[19] In view of this, there are at least two possible ways of using the reasonable person standard: one could subject AIs to the same reasonable person standard that is currently applied to human conduct; or one could develop a negligence standard specifically tailored towards AI conduct. I will address the first option in this section and the second option in the next.

At first sight, it may seem counterintuitive to suggest that the reasonable person standard, a standard made by humans for humans, could be applied to an artefact like an autonomous car. However, as we have seen, one of the very first cases in which the concept of the reasonable person featured was not actually concerned with the conduct of a human entity, but with the conduct of an artificial person: the Birmingham Waterworks. In fact the standard is frequently applied to companies,[20] and not just to companies: the conduct of organisations and of public authorities, too, has been evaluated by using the

[16] B. Casey, 'Robot Ipsa Loquitur' (2019) 108 Georgetown Law Journal 225, 240; R. Abbott, *The Reasonable Robot: Artificial Intelligence and the Law* (Cambridge University Press 2020) 50. For a defence of a strict liability model, see A. Lior, 'The AI Accident Network: Artificial Intelligence Liability Meets Network Theory' (2021) 95 Tulane Law Review 1103.

[17] R. Abbott, 'The Reasonable Computer: Disrupting the Paradigm of Tort Liability' (2018) 86 George Washington Law Review 1, 12–13; K. Chagal-Feferkorn, 'The Reasonable Algorithm' (2018) 2018 Journal of Law, Technology & Policy 111, 121; Casey (n 16), 267; Abbott (n 16), 51.

[18] Abbott (n 16), 51; B.W. Jackson, 'Artificial Intelligence and the Fog of Innovation: A Deep-Dive on Governance and the Liability of Autonomous Systems' (2018) 35 Santa Clara High Technology Law Journal 35, 49–50.

[19] Abbott (n 17), 12–13; Chagal-Feferkorn (n 17), 121; Casey (n 16), 267; Abbott (n 16), 51.

[20] Contrary to the opinion of Justice Langstaff in *Arriva London Ltd.*, it is not at all remarkable, against that background, to apply the standard of 'the man on the Clapham omnibus' to a company; cf. *Arriva London Ltd v Mr K Eleftheriou* UKEAT/0272/12/LA (Employment Appeal Tribunal) [16] (Justice Langstaff).

standard.[21] In these cases, however, companies, organisations and authorities feature merely as an avatar of the people who are acting on their behalf. In *Blyth*, the crux of the matter was really the conduct of the 'proprietors' of the waterworks and of the 'company's servants', and whether they could have foreseen that the water pipe would burst.[22] The International Military Tribunal at Nuremberg, concerned as it was with the criminal conduct of organisations, analysed their collective conduct through the lens of individual human members.[23] In *Wednesbury*, the English case that introduced the standard of the reasonable person to public authorities, the question was whether a public authority had acted reasonably when it prohibited a cinema from admitting children under the age of 15 on Sundays. Here, too, the court was concerned with the conduct of a non-human entity, but in effect it referred to the conduct of a 'person entrusted with a discretion', someone who 'must, so to speak, direct himself properly in law'.[24] Formally the court probed a public authority's conduct, but *de facto* it considered the conduct of a human administrator who acted on behalf of that authority. Thus, when considering whether the reasonable person standard can accommodate the negligent behaviour of AI, it is important to be clear about whose conduct is really at issue.[25] Is AI an avatar of human actors, or does one attribute agency to AI itself? In the former case, there is nothing extraordinary about applying the reasonable person standard to AI. If a self-driving car abruptly changes lanes on the motorway, the question 'did the car behave as a reasonable person would have?' would then really mean, 'did the humans who used or programmed the car behave as a reasonable person would have?'. Strictly speaking, it would be the human actor's negligence and not the car's behaviour that is at issue.[26]

More challenging are situations where an AI is itself treated as an actor.[27] This could happen when a self-driving car has been granted a degree of autonomy for the purposes of dealing with various types of situations that it could encounter on the road. Confronted with a child who runs unexpectedly into the car's path, the car might decide autonomously whether to avoid the collision by swaying into the opposite lane, by sweeping onto the pavement or

21 *Associated Provincial Picture Houses Ltd v Wednesbury Corp* [1947] EWCA Civ 1; [1948] 1 KB 223 (Court of Appeal); John Gardner, 'The Many Faces of the Reasonable Person' [2015] Law Quarterly Review 563, 564.

22 *Blyth v The Company of Proprietors of the Birmingham Waterworks* (1856) 11 Exch 781 (Court of Exchequer) 784.

23 See the introductory section in Chapter 5.

24 *Associated Provincial Picture Houses Ltd v Wednesbury Corp* [1947] EWCA Civ 1; [1948] 1 KB 223 (n 21), 229 (Greene MR).

25 Richards and Smart (n 9), 19.

26 J.M. Balkin, 'The Three Laws of Robotics in the Age of Big Data' (2017) 78 Ohio State Law Journal 1217, 1224. See also Selbst (n 15), 1320.

27 For a detailed argument in favour of scrutinizing the 'action (or decision) of the algorithm itself . . . rather than the decisions of the humans involved', see Chagal-Feferkorn (n 17), 115, 121–30.

by triggering its emergency break mechanism.[28] The car might be programmed to make this type of decision by itself, and at such a speed that no kind of human intervention is possible. Assessing this type of situation on the basis of a negligence standard would mean that the AI takes 'the place of a person in the traditional negligence paradigm'.[29] According to Abbott, letting the AI take the place of the person in the traditional negligence paradigm could 'accelerate automation' and 'improve safety'[30] by eliminating the risks associated with human errors. This may or may not be the case. But for our purposes the key question is whether it is meaningful to apply to artefacts a perspective-taking concept such as the reasonable person standard as opposed to a general, non-personified negligence standard. The issue rests on the question whether one believes that it is possible to empathise with an AI or to adopt its perspective. Asking for a situation to be assessed by stepping into the shoes of another, in accordance with the credo of the Scottish sentimentalists, makes sense only if it is possible to step into the shoes of that other, or rather if there is such an other to begin with – one into whose shoes one could step.

In *R.U.R.*, protagonists like Helena Glory believed that artificially intelligent entities like robots could be such an other. Clearly empathising with the robot Radius, Helena pleads for his 'life' to be spared towards the end of the play.[31] Similarly, Mr Alquist, head of Rossum's Building Department, thinks that taking a robot apart amounts to 'murder'.[32] Others, such as Harry Domin or Mr Fabry, Rossum's technical engineer, explicitly reject the idea that one could take a robot's perspective and maintain that robots are simply objects. Notwithstanding the views of Domin and Fabry, there is clear evidence that humans do empathise with robots. Joanna Malinowska has shown, for instance, that people who see 'robots being abused (being kicked or bitten) . . . have reacted similarly to how they react when seeing other people being abused in analogues ways'.[33] Referring to neuroscientific research, Malinowska explains that the 'brain activity of "observers" associated with empathising was noticed regardless of whether they were looking at humans or robots'.[34] Kate Darling, too, explains that human interaction with robots

[28] For a general discussion of these kinds of 'trolley problems' in relation to the regulation of autonomous cars, see e.g. S.S. Wu, 'Autonomous Vehicles, Trolley Problems, and the Law' (2020) 22 Ethics and Information Technology 1, 3–5.

[29] Abbott (n 16), 62.

[30] Ibid., 58, 63. Abbott suggests that the manufacturers or suppliers of negligent machines would still be responsible for satisfying judgments against the machines by compensating injured parties (ibid., 51).

[31] Čapek (n 4), 49–50. [32] Ibid., 84.

[33] J.K. Malinowska, 'What Does It Mean to Empathise with a Robot?' (2021) 31 Minds and Machines 361, 369. See also Richards and Smart (n 9), 18 and U. Pagallo, *The Laws of Robots: Crimes, Contracts, and Torts* (Springer 2013) 122–4.

[34] Malinowska (n 33), 369.

can – depending on their appearance[35] – trigger 'emotional projection'[36] and 'follow social behavior patterns'.[37] To illustrate the point, Darling refers to an article in which Joel Garreau discusses military robots.[38] One particular test robot resembled an insect with six legs. Whenever the robot triggered a mine, one of the legs was lost, causing the robot to limp on. Garreau reports that the colonel in charge of the experiment soon discontinued the tests:

> The colonel just could not stand the pathos of watching the burned, scarred and crippled machine drag itself forward on its last leg. This test, he charged, was inhumane.[39]

However, if one assumes that there is no 'little person'[40] endowed with feelings or with good or bad intentions[41] sitting inside the AI program that steers a robot or a self-driving car, but rather lines of code, the perspective that humans are in fact taking when they empathise with AI must be an imagined one.[42] As Malinowski explains, 'we have no idea what it is to be a robot and we only project our fantasies, beliefs, experiences and expectations onto these entities'.[43] The military colonel is not empathising with a pain or an emotion that the military test robot actually feels, but rather with a projection that is based on the colonel's analogising the situation of the robot to that of an animal, for instance. Would this mean that the reasonable person standard cannot meaningfully be used for assessing the conduct of AI-empowered robots? Not necessarily. As we have seen in Chapter 2, imagination is central to the operation of the concept of the reasonable person, and many would say that taking another's perspective and feeling what others feel always leads to a more or less accurate prediction, one based on what we imagine the other feels (rather than a reflection of what the other actually does feel). Moreover, taking the perspective of the reasonable person itself – an imaginary character, after all – requires imagining what the reasonable person might think or feel regardless of the possibility that the imagined entity would not actually feel or think anything. But this is not extraordinary. As the German philosopher and theologian Edith Stein (1891–1942) has pointed out, '[e]ven a creature of

[35] Referring to David Hume's arguments presented earlier, Mark Coeckelbergh has shown that, just like inter-human empathy, a human's empathy with an object is also conditioned by our familiarity with that object; see M. Coeckelbergh, 'Artificial Companions: Empathy and Vulnerability Mirroring in Human-Robot Relations' (2010) 4 Studies in Ethics, Law, and Technology 7.

[36] K. Darling, 'Extending Legal Protection to Social Robots: The Effects of Anthropomorphism, Empathy, and Violent Behavior towards Robotic Objects', in R. Calo, A.M. Froomkin and I. Kerr (eds), *Robot Law* (Edward Elgar 2016) 218.

[37] Ibid., 214.

[38] Ibid., 218. The article in question is J. Garreau, 'Bots on the Ground', *Washington Post Sunday* (Washington, DC, 6 May 2007).

[39] Garreau (n 38). [40] Balkin (n 26), 1223. See also Chagal-Feferkorn (n 17), 132.

[41] Balkin (n 26), 1223; C. Misselhorn, 'Empathy with Inanimate Objects and the Uncanny Valley' (2009) 19 Minds and Machines 345, 352.

[42] Misselhorn (n 41), 352; Malinowska (n 33), 368–9. [43] Malinowska (n 33), 370–1.

the free imagination can be an intelligible person'.[44] Similarly, Nussbaum showed that empathising with characters from novels, poems or movies allows us to shed light on concrete normative questions despite the characters' fictional nature.[45] However, when we empathise with any of these imaginary persons, we do so by referring to our own knowledge and experience of what it means to be that particular character:

> Together with other human beings, we belong to a single species and although we do not really know exactly what it is like to be a person X, we know what it is like to be a human, and therefore, although our conclusions about the affective state of X may not be factual, they are justified to some extent.[46]

As we move away from a reference point that is familiar to us, our ability to empathise and to engage in perspective taking decreases. Illustrating this point, Edith Stein explains that we might understand a sensation felt by a dog in its paw – we do not have paws, but by comparing the paw to our own hand we can understand what it means to have a 'sensitive limb of a living body'.[47] But, unlike with a dog's paw, we lack an understanding of what it means to be 'a non-biological being like a robot'[48] or an AI. Thus, while it is not remarkable to take the perspective of an imagined entity on the basis of a set of shared characteristics, it is quite extraordinary to take the perspective of an artefact that categorically differs from us.[49]

In some cases it may be possible to get around this problem by replacing an AI actor with a fictional human. The setup described here is then reversed, and it is this human fictional actor that becomes the AI's avatar. Abbott suggests, for example, that one could meaningfully ask: did the car run a red light, and would 'a reasonable person . . . have done the same'?[50] Running a red light is an action humans frequently engage in, and one in which they normally do not have any legal discretion. However, in situations where the abilities of the object with which one seeks to empathise clearly differ from one's own, empathising and perspective taking by replacing the AI with a fictitious human becomes not only more difficult but also implausible.[51] As we have seen, the reasonable person standard, informed by the thoughts of the Scottish

44 E. Stein, *Zum Problem der Einfühlung* (Buchdruckerei des Waisenhauses 1917) 125 (my translation).

45 See e.g. M.C. Nussbaum, 'Poets as Judges: Judicial Rhetoric and the Literary Imagination' (1995) 62 The University of Chicago Law Review 1477; also Coeckelbergh (n 35), 7.

46 Malinowska (n 33), 370–1.

47 Stein (n 44), 66 (my translation). For a discussion of the application of the reasonable person standard to animals more generally, see K. Barnett and J. Gans, *Guilty Pigs: The Weird and Wonderful History of Animal Law* (La Trobe University Press 2022) 99–100.

48 Malinowska (n 33), 370–1. See also Y. Suzuki et al., 'Measuring Empathy for Human and Robot Hand Pain Using Electroencephalography' (2015) 5 Scientific Reports 1, 5.

49 J. Turner, *Robot Rules: Regulating Artificial Intelligence* (Springer 2018) 89–90.

50 Abbott (n 16), 63.

51 K. Colonna, 'Autonomous Cars and Tort Liability Note' (2012) 4 Case Western Reserve Journal of Law, Technology and the Internet 81, 103 (n 145).

sentimentalists, is a standard tailored to a 'weak and imperfect creature as man',[52] as opposed to a 'perfect being'[53] like the 'great Superintendant of the universe'.[54] Thus, '[i]f we met an invulnerable god or machine that was entirely alien to us, we could not put ourselves in its shoes by any stretch of our imagination and feeling'.[55] As a result, applying the reasonable person standard to an AI-empowered entity's conduct, which differs, in whole or in part, from the conduct of a human being, risks producing inaccurate conclusions. If a self-driving car's algorithm failed to bring the car to a halt before it collided with a pedestrian, it makes little sense to ask what a reasonable person would have done, provided that no human could have reacted as the car did. Moreover, it is difficult to see how the concept of the reasonable person could apply to situations in which an AI enjoys a significant degree of discretion and engages in complex analytical processes, which perhaps differ considerably from the processes humans engage in.[56] If, for example, the car that collided with the pedestrian had the option of swaying into the opposite lane or of crashing into a traffic light instead, it would not be possible to subject its decision-making process to a reasonable person analysis without attributing to AI a deeply human capacity of weighing competing interests.[57] A reasonable person could have come to the same conclusion as the AI – namely that colliding with the pedestrian is the best, though suboptimal, outcome in the given situation. However, it would be misleading to describe in similar terms the AI's decision-making process, based as this was on preprogrammed parameters. Despite occasional suggestions to the contrary, the reasonable person is not an automaton.[58] It is a device that assesses behaviour through an intersubjective feedback process, which considers and subjectively weighs the interests of the humans concerned on the basis of a human community's common sense.[59] This is not to say that AI decision-making processes could not be scrutinised for their reasonableness. It could be that a 'reasonableness assessment is indifferent to the type and nature' of the actors whose conduct it assesses.[60] The reasonable person standard, however, is not. It is a standard

[52] A. Smith, *The Theory of Moral Sentiments* (D.D. Raphael and A.L. Macfie eds, Clarendon 1976) 77.

[53] Ibid. [54] Ibid., 292. [55] Coeckelbergh (n 35), 7, 4. [56] Chagal-Feferkorn (n 17), 146.

[57] E. Lieblich and E. Benvenisti, 'The Obligation to Exercise Discretion in Warfare: Why Autonomous Weapon Systems Are Unlawful', in Nehal Bhuta et al. (eds), *Autonomous Weapons Systems: Law, Ethics, Policy* (Cambridge University Press 2016) 9–10; R. Calo, 'Robotics and the Lessons of Cyberlaw' (2015) 103 California Law Review 513, 542.

[58] W. Pengilley, *Advertising and the Trade Practices Act* (CCH Australia 1981) 10–12, also cited by S. Kapnoullas and B. Clarke, 'The Legal Regulation of Comparative Advertising: Old Game, New Rules' (1995) 11 Queensland University of Technology Law Journal 7, 13–14.

[59] K. Chagal-Feferkorn, 'How Can I Tell if My Algorithm Was Reasonable?' (2021) 27 Michigan Technology Law Review 213, 252–3; M.A. Lemley and B. Casey, 'Remedies for Robots' (2019) 86 University of Chicago Law Review 1311, 1371.

[60] Chagal-Feferkorn (n 59), 250.

intimately connected to the humaneness of the persons to whom and by whom it is applied.

It follows from all this that the emergence of AI-empowered entities such as autonomous cars does not necessarily need to lead to the demise of the reasonable person. If one treats AI entities like products, the reasonable person concept is not engaged; and, where AI-empowered entities act as avatars for human actors, the reasonable person standard can be applied in an ordinary manner. But the challenge posed by digital entities is more acute when it comes to AI-empowered entities that act in their own right. While humans can and do empathise with AI, there is a risk that a human's attempt to take the perspective of an AI leads to inaccurate conclusions. Moreover, there is also a risk that analysing a digital decision-making process according to an empathy-based standard means humanising a process that is in fact a purely rational deduction. Naturally, rational processes of deduction can and should be scrutinised, but not through a standard that is founded on the conviction that finding the truth or distinguishing between right and wrong requires resonance between real human beings who have a sense common to all. Thus, applying the reasonable person standard to AIs based on the strength of the conviction that they are 'just like people' undermines the very rationale of the reasonable person concept.[61] Against this background, the next section discusses suggestions to introduce a standard tailored specifically to AI-empowered entities, with the aim of determining whether such a standard would merely supplement a reasonable person standard or risks displacing it.

6.2 Artificial Intelligence

As we have seen, the possibility of applying the concept of the reasonable person to AI is limited to situations where AI is treated as a product, where an AI acts as an avatar of human decision-makers, or where the conduct of an AI can plausibly be assessed through the lens of a human avatar. Against that background, the present section explores the argument that AI conduct should be assessed not with reference to the perspective of a reasonable person but with reference to a reasonable AI instead – and, specifically, the implications of this argument for the concept of the reasonable person itself. Writing in 1985 about the regulation of robots (which are equated with AI for the purposes of this chapter), an early proponent of such an approach mused:

> Robots, by analogy to humans, must conform to a 'reasonable computer' standard. Sentient computers and their software should be held to the standard of competence of all other data processing systems of the same technological generation. Thus, if all 'sixth generation' computers ought to be smart enough to

61 Richards and Smart have described this tendency of equating AIs with people as the android fallacy; see Richards and Smart (n 9), 4.

> detect bogus input in some circumstances, then, given that circumstance, a court will presume that a 'sixth generation' computer knew or should have known the input data were bogus.[62]

Thus the reference point for an AI's conduct is not a reasonable person but a reasonable artificial peer – another robot, another AI, another computer. Two contemporary commentators have recently advanced similar arguments. Ryan Abbott proposes that in areas where the safety of AI-empowered computers exceeds that of humans, such computers should 'be held to the reasonable computer standard'.[63] 'For instance', Abbott explains,

> if a self-driving Audi collided with a child running in front of the vehicle, the negligence test could take into account the stopping times of self-driving Volvo cars. There are a variety of ways to determine the reasonable computer standard, for example, considering the industry customary, average, or safest technology.[64]

Arguing along the same lines, Karni Chagal-Feferkorn considers that a novel concept – that of 'the reasonable algorithm' – 'could be applied to algorithms just as the concept of the "reasonable person" ... applies to humans'.[65] According to Chagal-Feferkorn, this would mean evaluating the behaviour of a 'non-human decision-maker' with reference to other non-human decision-makers.[66] In a medical setting, for example, the reasonableness of a 'robo-doctor' would be compared 'with the actions of other robo-doctors'.[67] Both Abbott and Chagal-Feferkorn suggest that the standard of competence expected of a reasonable AI would be higher than that currently expected of a reasonable person.[68] The substantive content of the standard could be informed by established industry standards[69] and would have a dynamic character, which allows the standard to become stricter as the technology it relates to improves.[70] While Abbott is confident that the application of a reasonable AI standard is relatively straightforward,[71] Chagal-Feferkorn is more cautious and acknowledges that the operationalisation of a reasonable algorithm standard would 'require much thought and adjustments'.[72] Others, too, have noted that there is 'very little guidance, up to now, on what a "reasonable algorithm" might look like'.[73] It is unlikely that the questions concerning the exact function of a reasonable algorithm or reasonable

[62] R.A. Freitas, 'End Note: Can the Wheels of Justice Turn for Our Friends in the Mechanical Kingdom?' (1985) 13 Student Lawyer 54, 55–6.

[63] Abbott (n 17), 41. See also M.S.Gal, 'Algorithmic Challenges to Autonomous Choice' (2018) 25 Michigan Technology Law Review 59, 100.

[64] Abbott (n 17), 41. [65] Chagal-Feferkorn (n 17), 146. [66] Ibid., 138. [67] Ibid.

[68] Abbott (n 17), 42; Chagal-Feferkorn (n 17), 122, 129, 145. See also Gal (n 63), 100.

[69] Abbott (n 17), 41.

[70] Ibid., 42; Chagal-Feferkorn (n 17), 129; Chagal-Feferkorn (n 59), 228–9.

[71] Abbott (n 17), 37. [72] Chagal-Feferkorn (n 17), 145.

[73] M. Infantino and W. Wang, 'Algorithmic Torts: A Prospective Comparative Overview' (2019) 28 Transnational Law and Contemporary Problems 309, 347.

computer standard will be answered very soon. For our purposes, however, it suffices to note the ways in which the proposed standard relates to the concept of the reasonable person.

At first sight, the introduction of a reasonable AI standard would merely lead to the advent of yet another novel legal creature alongside the established concept of the reasonable person. As we have seen in Chapter 1, the reasonable person is hardly the first of its kind, and it is unlikely to be the last. As the common law's reasonable person ventured beyond its original field of tort law, numerous other legal creations have joined the concept's journey through time and space. Among the 'siblings'[74] of the reasonable person we can find reasonable policemen, reasonable doctors, reasonable soldiers. All these figures are designed to account both for the specific skills of certain groups of professionals and for the expectation that specific persons meet a certain level of skill when exercising their profession. In that sense, these figures could be seen to respond to a challenge similar to the one identified by Abbott and Chagal-Feferkorn regarding the regulation of a highly competent AI. So, again, one could think that the concept of reasonable AI is just the latest member of that illustrious family of legal creations. There are, however, categorical differences between the family of reasonable persons we encountered so far and the concept of reasonable AI.

The first difference concerns the importance of empathy: by comparison with both the reasonable person itself and its siblings, the reasonable AI standard is not based on empathetic perspective taking. As explained earlier, the proponents of the new standard envision that the behaviour of a reasonable AI behaviour is assessed on the basis of established industry standards or with reference to the behaviour of other algorithms.[75] Thus the assessment would be based on empirical studies of the behaviour of similar artefacts. Empathetic perspective taking does not come in. This does not necessarily undermine the utility of the standard in assisting with the evaluation of AI conduct. It does mean, however, that the reasonable AI standard is categorically different from the reasonable person standard, which is informed by the conviction that rational deduction alone is insufficient for identifying desirable conduct in a given situation and that empathising with fellow human beings clarifies our understanding of what is right and wrong. Thus the reasonable AI standard is not just another incarnation of the reasonable person standard; it is a completely different standard.

A second difference concerns the time at which the conduct of the reasonable AI is being assessed. While the reasonable person standard can be used to guide the behaviour of legal subjects prospectively, for example when a

[74] C. Dent, 'The Reasonable Man, His Nineteenth-Century Siblings, and Their Legacy' (2017) 44 Journal of Law and Society 406.

[75] Chagal-Feferkorn (n 17), 129. Chagal-Feferkorn notes that a 'comparison of reasonableness with algorithms' peers is not yet available'. Chagal-Feferkorn (n 59), 253.

reasonable military commander contemplates how to behave in a coming battle,[76] it is most commonly applied retrospectively, when courts assess the conduct of legal subjects. The situation is reversed in the case of the reasonable AI standard. Although it is conceivable for the standard to be used to assess the conduct of AIs retrospectively, it is a standard that predominantly informs decisions before such an entity has executed a given operation. This is so because AIs act exclusively in accordance with, and on the basis of, instructions they received.[77] Thus, if a reasonable AI is meant to act in accordance with a reasonable AI standard, the parameters of that standard need to be coded into that entity before the latter acts. The specificity of these instructions may vary from AI to AI and from situation to situation. A self-driving car may be instructed to stop at a red light without exception. Or a self-driving car might be instructed to select the best out of a limited number of alternatives when facing the choice between collision with a pedestrian, collision with a bridge and collision with on-coming traffic. But the fact that the AI has a higher degree of discretion in the latter scenario does not undermine the fact that it makes use of that discretion exclusively in accordance with a precoded, or at least pre-approved decision-making process. By contrast, few human drivers will, before they get into their car in the morning, reflect upon how they would behave in a situation of tragic choice. And even if they decided in advance to select, say, the option that causes the least harm to anyone, in the heat of the moment few humans would preserve enough control of their faculties to be able to implement that choice. The reasonable AI, by contrast, will have been instructed in advance how to behave, and will be able to follow these instructions in an emergency situation with ease, since a car does not get stressed, fearful, sweaty or frozen. Considering that the reasonable person standard, too, can be used prospectively, one may well ask whether this temporal aspect does not really set the two types of standard apart.

It matters that the reasonable AI acts only in accordance with instructions received in advance, because this makes it impossible for the law to reserve judgment on certain questions until after a decision or an act occurred. Instead of determining in advance how to balance the rights to life of different stakeholders in a collision scenario, it is often enough to consider whether, in hindsight, a given driver made a justifiable decision. Reserving judgement in this manner avoids a ranking of interests that would be difficult, if not impossible, to do *ex ante*. It also keeps open the class of acts that a reasonable person would engage in. The reasonable AI standard, however, demands an answer to such questions in advance. It does not have to be a fixed answer (e.g. 'always prioritise the protection of youngest life'), but it must be sufficiently

[76] Eyal Benvenisti, 'The Legal Battle to Define the Law on Transnational Asymmetric Warfare Symposium: War Bound by Law: Non-State Actors and the Law of Armed Conflict in the Twenty-First Century' (2010) 20 Duke Journal of Comparative & International Law 339, 354.

[77] Lemley and Casey (n 59), 1371.

detailed to allow the car to make a decision in the situation (e.g. 'do what protects most lives'). One could argue that this novel 'technological window of opportunity'[78] that AI provides is a chance to look at law's legal tragic choice scenarios with more 'clarity and forethought',[79] for it allows for an 'exact weighing' of the 'relative importance'[80] of legal interests. Conversely, one may be of the view that not providing answers in advance for certain tragic choices between competing legal norms would be, on the whole, a better way of protecting and honouring the legal interests affected.[81] In any case, the unavoidable need for *ex ante* instructions distinguishes the reasonable AI standard clearly from the reasonable person standard.

That the reasonable AI acts only in accordance with instructions received in advance also matters, because this means that there must be an actor that supplies these instructions to the AI. This brings us to a third difference between the reasonable AI and the reasonable person. At heart, the reasonable person is an egalitarian, a character that anyone can know and relate to. The position of the reasonable AI is different. Since an assessment of an AI's behaviour requires expert knowledge of industry norms and of the behaviour of comparable AIs, it is difficult for ordinary members of society to predict and understand the substantive standard that a reasonable AI is supposed to meet.[82] Instead, the content of the reasonable AI standard is determined by professional programmers. In fact even professional programmers can struggle with predicting, or relating to, an AI's behaviour, because commercial interests mean that the exact modifications of AIs are often a well-kept secret.[83] By comparison with the reasonable person standard, the reasonable AI standard is thus not a commonly accessible concept but the preserve of a select group of experts.

The difference between the reasonable AI standard and its human counterpart becomes further apparent if one considers the process by which the substantive content of the two standards evolves. In the case of the reasonable person, the person's characteristics emerge from a patchwork of courtrooms where juries are regularly told: 'The law does not say what a reasonably careful

78 M. Cunneen et al., 'Artificial Driving Intelligence and Moral Agency: Examining the Decision Ontology of Unavoidable Road Traffic Accidents through the Prism of the Trolley Dilemma' (2019) 33 Applied Artificial Intelligence 267, 282.

79 O. Ben-Shahar and A. Porat, *Personlized Law: Different Rules for Different People* (Oxford University Press 2021) 36.

80 Ibid.

81 For a theory for dealing with such irresolvable norm conflicts, see V. Jeutner, *Irresolvable Norm Conflicts in International Law: The Concept of a Legal Dilemma* (Oxford University Press 2017).

82 S. Holm, C. Stanton and B. Bartlett, 'A New Argument for No-Fault Compensation in Health Care: The Introduction of Artificial Intelligence Systems' (2021) 29 Health Care Analysis 171, 183; Turner (n 49), 90; M. Sword, 'To Err Is both Human and Non-Human Comments' (2019) 88 UMKC Law Review [i], 225.

83 Selbst (n 15), 1322, 1364; Lior (n 16), 1119; G.I. Zekos, *Economics and Law of Artificial Intelligence: Finance, Economic Impacts, Risk Management and Governance* (Springer 2021) 384.

person using ordinary care would or would not do under such circumstances. That is for you to decide.'[84] As a result, the substantive content of the concept of the reasonable person emerges slowly from countless ad hoc determinations made by juries and judges.[85] Over time, certain manifestations of the standard become accepted, others fade out.

Crucially, though, there are numerous different manifestations of the reasonable person. What seems reasonable to one jury or judge in a particular place and at a particular time may not seem reasonable to another jury or judge. Ideally, the different manifestations of the reasonable person resemble one another to some extent, but they certainly represent a wide spectrum of justifiable behaviour. With respect to the reasonable AI standard, the situation is quite different. Not only is the group of human actors who program an AI – and thereby determine how it behaves – small, but the range of behaviours that the AI engages in is limited to what this small group has anticipated. While the substantive content of the standard of the reasonable person is not pre-configured and open to retrospective modification, the substantive content of the standard of the reasonable AI is a codified and fixed standard. In this sense, the narrowing of the group of people capable of understanding and assessing the behaviour of a reasonable AI also leads to a narrowing of the range of actions that a reasonable AI would engage in. The fact that algorithms can be scaled up easily – that is, that one algorithm authored by a small group of persons can be used to control millions of programs – amplifies this effect. Towards the end of *R.U.R.*, one of the protagonists captures parts of this phenomenon when, confronted with an army of robots, he observes: 'We made the Robots' faces too much alike. A hundred thousand faces all alike, all facing this way. A hundred thousand expressionless bubbles. It's like a nightmare.'[86] The reference to Rossum's robots is particularly fitting because just like the formula that created the robots, the instructions given to an AI at once constitute and regulate the actors whose behaviour they govern. In other words, the codes governing the behaviour of AI do not simply guide the behaviour of an AI as a legal actor; they create legal actors. This has far-reaching implications. For example, unlike human persons, AIs behave exactly as they are told. This means that norm-deviating behaviour (e.g. civil disobedience) is not just impermissible,

[84] South Dakota Pattern Jury Instructions, as quoted by P.J. Kelley and L.A. Wendt, 'What Judges Tell Juries about Negligence: A Review of Pattern Jury Instructions' (2002) 77 Chicago-Kent Law Review 587, 672. Cf. e.g. the California Civil Jury Instructions (630), the Model Utah Jury Instructions-Civil (674), and the Wyoming Civil Pattern Jury Instructions (682), all quoted in this article (pp. 630, 674 and 682). For model jury instructions invoking the reasonable person in England and Wales, see M. Picton et al. (eds), *The Crown Court Compendium: Part I (Jury and Trial Management and Summing Up)* (Judicial College 2021), ch 7–4(18–21).

[85] See also M. Del Mar, *Artefacts of Legal Inquiry: The Value of Imagination in Adjudication* (Hart 2020) 360.

[86] Čapek (n 4), 64.

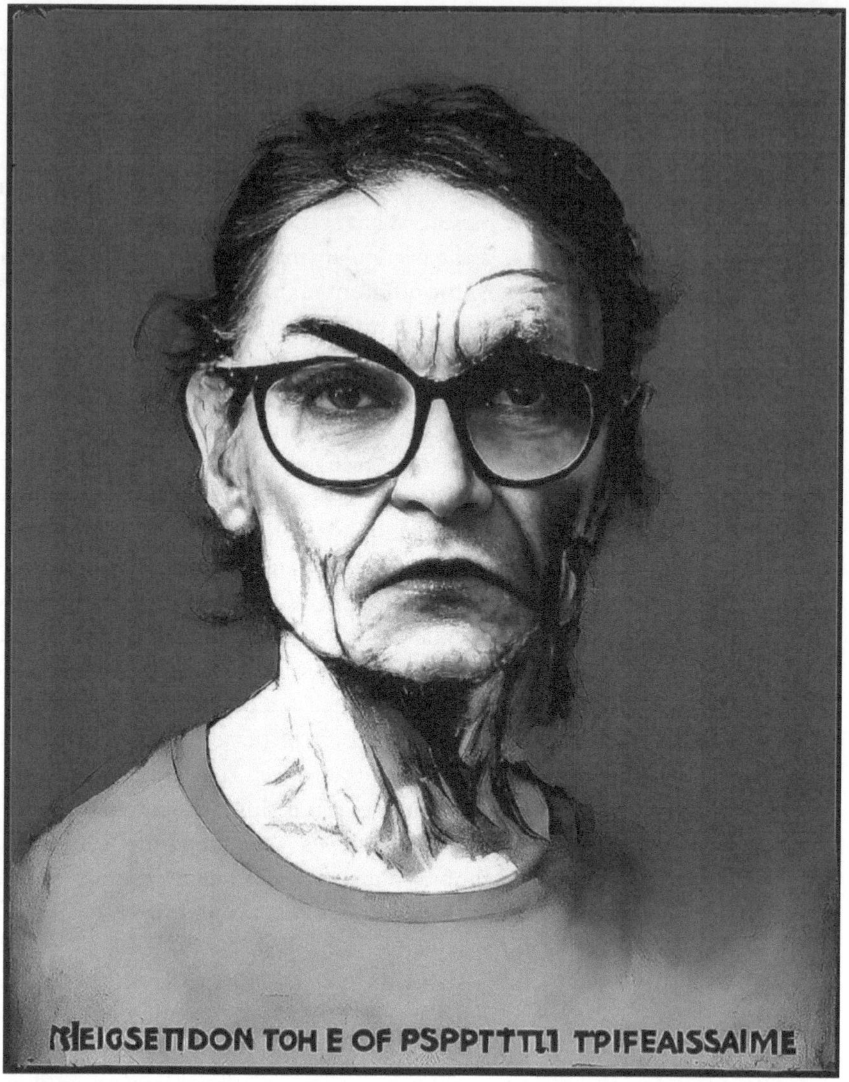

Figure 6.1 Image created by an artificially intelligent software program in response to this input: 'Create a portrait of the reasonable person'.
Credits: Valentin Jeutner / Deep Dream Generator

it is outright impossible. Thus, those who create the code that facilitates the transplantation of the reasonable person into the digital realm (Figure 6.1) possess the power to create an artificial legal archetype that corresponds in all respects to their specific preferences.

From the perspective of the reasonable person, the most threatening aspect of the proposed introduction of a reasonable AI standard is the risk that this novel archetype of the reasonable AI displaces its empathetic human predecessor. While noting that 'it will still make sense to apply the reasonable person standard'[87] to tasks that are difficult to delegate to AIs, Abbott argues explicitly, for instance, that 'the reasonable person standard should be replaced with the reasonable robot standard'[88] for all the tasks that AI can perform better than humans. Abbott supports his view with a reference to a driver who was involved in a collision:

> To take a simple case, imagine an individual driving on dry pavement at forty miles per hour colliding with a child running into the road 150 feet ahead of the driver's vehicle. To determine whether the driver is liable under the reasonable computer standard, a plaintiff could present a jury with evidence that when a child runs in front of the same make and model of car being operated by automated software under the same conditions, the vehicle stops in about 100 feet. Because the reasonable computer would not have collided with the child, the human driver would be liable.[89]

Thus Abbott envisions that future humans will be judged not with reference to a reasonable person standard informed by the behaviour of other humans, but with reference to a standard based on the most advanced AI.[90] Among many other things, this could mean that it would become altogether unreasonable to perform certain acts that AI can perform better. Abbott explains that, as 'self-driving cars become safer than traditional vehicles, a jury might find that it is unreasonable to drive yourself'.[91] Whereas Abbott deems such a development to be positive, since it promises to replace human drivers with less accident-prone AI-controlled entities, Anat Lior is concerned that the advent of the reasonable AI standard could mean 'that humans will not be allowed to do anything on their own because a "reasonable computer" could have done it in a safer way, thus stifling human actions and behaviors we cherish and encourage as a society'.[92]

Apart from these more direct ways in which the introduction of a reasonable AI standard could displace the reasonable person standard, the behaviour of reasonable AI could also affect human behaviour. In relation to the reasonable person standard, each person works out how to behave in specific circumstances. When, in the collision scenario mentioned at the beginning of this chapter, a child runs in front of the car, it is for the driver to decide how to avoid the collision by swaying into the opposite lane, by taking the pavement or, if it is not too late, by engaging the car's breaks. It is for the driver to account for the consequences and, almost more importantly, it is for a jury and judges to reflect critically upon the driver's decision. The assessment of these kinds of decisions on the basis of a reasonable AI standard not only replaces this traditional process of collective human reflection with an empirical analysis of AI conduct but also deprives the humans involved in the

87 Abbott (n 16), 70. 88 Ibid., 69, 70; Abbott (n 17), 37. 89 Abbott (n 17), 37–8.
90 Abbott (n 16), 51. 91 Abbott (n 17), 39.
92 Lior (n 16), 1119. See also Zekos (n 83), 384–5.

process of the chance to practice the skill of empathetic perspective-taking, on which the standard of the reasonable person relies. There is thus a risk that, as the reasonable AI standard is introduced, humans will gradually become worse at applying the reasonable person standard.

Moreover, the possibility of treating AI entities as legal actors in their own right, which the reasonable AI standard envisions, incentivises human beings to delegate decisions to these entities instead of making their own decisions in critical situations. The US military, for instance, has announced that it will develop algorithms meant to assist with military decision-making in situations where 'trusted [human] decision-makers disagree'.[93] Such situations exist when there is 'no right answer', 'uncertainty', 'time pressure' and 'conflicting values'.[94] The new decision-making system, styled the In the Moment program,[95] is supposed to provide a 'rigorous, quantifiable, and scalable approach to evaluating and building algorithmic systems for difficult decision-making where objective ground truth is unavailable'.[96] If a future military commander can rely on the outputs of the In the Moment program when facing such difficult decisions, there is little or no reason for that commander to engage in an independent analysis of the given situation, since it is significantly more convenient to attribute responsibility to an AI. And, even if decisions made by AIs would initially be limited to highly specific contexts (e.g. military operations or car collision scenarios), there is a risk that those decisions would over time influence decision-making in other fields as well. If human actors realise, for instance, that AI programs are instructed to follow a utilitarian logic that always optimises the interests of the most people, they will be less hesitant to apply that same logic to their own conduct instead of following a deontological approach that optimises norm compliance regardless of its consequences. Thus, gradually, the standardised behaviour of reasonable AIs could influence the behaviour of human actors and, ultimately, the legislative or judicial conceptualisation of law's analogue reasonable person. As a result, the power of those determining the behaviour of reasonable AIs in the military or automobile sector may eventually extend beyond the digital realm and may come to shape notions of reasonableness in the analogue world. As the ideal of an egalitarian concept of the reasonable person, a concept composed of a multiplicity of perspectives, gives way to the notion of a reasonable AI informed by the views of a select group of experts, there is a risk that a society that abolishes the need to learn how to work out difficult legal puzzles

[93] Defense Advanced Research Projects Agency, 'Developing Algorithms That Make Decisions Aligned with Human Experts' (3 March 2022). https://www.darpa.mil/news-events/2022-03-03.

[94] Ibid.

[95] Defense Advanced Research Projects Agency, 'In the Moment (ITM)' (2 March 2022). https://sam.gov/opp/3e904257ba51463d953014fcc6212f98/view.

[96] Defense Advanced Research Projects Agency (n 93).

degenerates into a synchronised collective of uniform actors who are no more than shadows of their former (reasonable) selves.

At present, the view that a reasonable AI standard should be introduced to assess the conduct of AIs and that this new standard should eventually displace even the reasonable person standard for human beings is upheld by a minority of commentators. In any event, the displacement of the reasonable person by the reasonable AI would be a slow process. In the meantime, AI could trigger the extinction of the reasonable person standard not by confronting it with digital actors but by facilitating the concept's encounter with the actual human beings to whom it is meant to relate. It is this encounter of the reasonable person with actual human beings that we are going to address in the next section.

6.3 You

When, at the beginning of the nineteenth century, the Belgian astronomer Adolphe Quetelet, whom we encountered in Chapter 3, set out to catalogue the behaviour of all human beings, in search for the qualities of the average human, he conceded that this undertaking could seem absurd. He himself deemed it absurd – not because the idea was in principle misguided, but because there was a 'want of a sufficient number of accurate observations'[97] of human behaviour. In the future, he hoped, 'a registration of all human actions',[98] combined with 'long and laborious'[99] studies and 'immense researches'[100] carried out with 'infinite care',[101] would allow for a precise identification of the features of society's *homme moyen*. That future is now here. Modern digital technologies and databases mean that behavioural patterns of vast numbers of humans can be identified in ways that are neither long nor laborious. As Sheila Jasanoff observes, '[a]lmost everything that people do in hightech societies leaves informational traces'.[102] And these traces are not limited to Quetelet's humble indicators concerning people's age, diet or height. Smart phones, cars, washing-machines, watches, computers collect large amounts of data about their users: what they search for on the Internet, how often they do laundry and at what temperature, how much they move and where they go. The ability to collect and collate large quantities of data allows for the possibility of creating quite accurate behavioural profiles, both of groups and of individuals. GoogleMaps, for example, collects and collates data received from the smart phones of car drivers in order to predict the behaviour of road users.[103] This allows it to identify traffic jams and to suggest alternative routes to its users.

[97] A. Quetelet, *A Treatise on Man and the Development of His Faculties* (R. Knox trans., William and Robert Chambers 1842) 74.
[98] Ibid., 6. [99] Ibid., vi. [100] Ibid., 9. [101] Ibid.
[102] S. Jasanoff, *The Ethics of Invention: Technology and the Human Future* (Norton 2016) 3.
[103] J. Lau, 'Google Maps 101: How AI Helps Predict Traffic and Determine Routes' (Google, The Keyword, 3 September 2020) https://blog.google/products/maps/google-maps-101-how-ai-helps-predict-traffic-and-determine-routes.

One may think that these modern phenomena are of little consequence to the concept of the reasonable person, since we saw in Chapters 2 and 3 that, in spite of Quetelet's approach to identifying the *homme moyen*, the concept is, quite clearly, meant to be not an empirically verifiable standard but a standard controlled by judges. Indeed, in *Blyth*, Baron Alderson did not survey how the proprietors of waterworks in cities other than Birmingham maintain their pipes during winter in order to establish the waterworks' comparative diligence. Even if he wanted to, and even if the data had been available, it would have been a most time-consuming task. Nowadays this kind of information would be considerably easier to procure. Although such information could not be relied upon directly when assessing, for instance, whether a person or an entity was negligent, it could contribute to the operation of the reasonable person standard in indirect ways. This is because the substantive content of the concept of the reasonable person needs to be informed by empirical data. While not necessarily mirroring reality, it needs to be anchored to it. The characteristics of the reasonable person must bear some resemblance to those of the real human beings whose conduct one wishes to assess. Baron Alderson himself recognised the importance of empirical data and, as we have seen,[104] relied on statistical studies carried out by the first Earl of Lovelace when determining whether a reasonable member of society would engage in civil unrest or not.

By comparison with the more or less systematic studies of the first Earl of Lovelace, modern technologies allow for the collection and collation of significantly larger amounts of data and for the significantly more accurate identification of behavioural patterns. There is, for example, a growing body of empirical data to suggest that it is 'statistically impossible that health care professionals do not make mistakes in the course of their careers'.[105] In fact accidents in the healthcare sector are not rare 'but common, systematic, ubiquitous'.[106] This type of data can have an effect on the legal assessment of whether an individual doctor's conduct conformed to what is expected of a reasonable person or not. Alan Merry explains:

> Data demonstrating that the vast majority of anaesthetists have given the wrong drug at some stage of their career show that giving the wrong drug may be the sort of error any reasonable anaesthetist could make on occasion. On the other hand, if an anaesthetist had chosen not to put labels on his or her syringes when preparing several for use in a case, this violation of a widely understood and accepted rule antecedent to the error in question, might be construed as something a reasonable anaesthetist would never do.[107]

[104] See the discussion in Section 2.3.

[105] L. Wahlberg, 'Skäligt Straffansvar För Misstag Inom Medicinsk Vård Och Behandling' (2019) Nordisk socialrättslig tidskrift 115, 128 (my translation). For an in-depth study of the accident rates in hospitals, see also Institute of Medicine, *To Err Is Human: Building a Safer Health System* (National Academies Press 2000).

[106] W.B. Runciman, A.F. Merry and F. Tito, 'Error, Blame, and the Law in Health Care: An Antipodean Perspective' (2003) 138 Annals of Internal Medicine 974, 974.

[107] A.F. Merry, 'How Does the Law Recognize and Deal with Medical Errors?' (2009) 102 Journal of the Royal Society of Medicine 265, 269–70.

Similarly, statistical data could be used when applying the reasonable person standard in connection with traffic offences. Already sensors of modern cars collect a vast amount of information, not just about themselves but about their human drivers and passengers.[108] The data that the car itself collects can be supplemented with information gathered by the driver's personal devices, such as phones or smart watches. The data collected this way allow for the compilation of 'reliable statistics regarding average conduct on myriad driving behaviors, such as speed, braking, turning, tire pressure, use of directional or headlights, and even movement'.[109] These data can be supplemented with information about '[e]nvironmental conditions, such as precipitation, wind, visibility, and temperature',[110] in order to create high-resolution images of people's driving behaviour. In a concrete case, these statistics can be used to determine whether someone who failed to break in time to avoid colliding with a pedestrian on a rainy day at a busy junction behaved how most other drivers would have behaved or whether their conduct was below average. The finding that a driver's conduct resembled the conduct of most other drivers under similar circumstances could affect the way in which the reasonable person standard is used in two main ways.

First, the data about general driving patterns could be used to inform the substantive content of the standard and ensure that the standard does not expect of drivers behaviour that no driver actually engages in. Second, this information could make it clear that it is not just a driver in a concrete case, but drivers in general who fail to meet a standard that the law deems to be desirable.[111] Hence, in order to bring about a change in conduct, judges could decide to depart intentionally from the behaviour of actual human drivers by imposing a stricter normative standard. The way in which statistical data collected by modern technologies are used to 'develop evidence-based reasonable person judgments'[112] is a delicate exercise. If the standard of the reasonable person becomes too normative and the discrepancy between it and the actual human beings to which it relates becomes too large, it is not only the case that the standard loses its ability to guide the actions of persons; the authority of law as a whole risks being undermined. As noted previously, Gustav Radbruch observed, for instance, that a legal system that relies on an 'inaccurate conception' of the individuals to whom it relates will 'collapse'.[113] The advent of digital technologies and large databases has made the need to

[108] B. Sheppard, 'The Reasonableness Machine' (2021) 62 Boston College Law Review 2259, 2289–90.

[109] Ibid., 2290. [110] Ibid.

[111] On the importance of customs for identifying the substantive content of the standard of the reasonable person, see C.B. Jaeger, 'The Empirical Reasonable Person' (2020) 72 Alabama Law Review 887, 934.

[112] R. Dresser, 'The Reasonable Person Standard for Research Disclosure: A Reasonable Addition to the Common Rule' [2019] The Journal of Law, Medicine & Ethics 194, 199.

[113] G. Radbruch, 'Law's Image of the Human' (2020) 40 Oxford Journal of Legal Studies 667, 674. See also L. Zwiffelhoffer, *Die Figur des Durchschnittsmenschen im Verwaltungsrecht* (Mohr Siebeck 2020) 256.

pay careful attention to the degree of resemblance between the reasonable person and actual human beings particularly acute. This is because, for the first time, the countless sensors that track the customs, habits and behaviour of real-life humans slowly but surely make the characteristics of these individuals visible on a very large scale. The normative figure of the reasonable person is for the first time confronted with its empirical counterpart.

In principle, this should not cause many problems for the standard, simply because the standard is normative. However, the availability of verifiable statistics about how people in fact behave means that the reasonable person could face competition from its empirical counterpart. Historically, given the lack of empirical data, it was sufficient for US Supreme Court Justice Oliver Wendell Holmes (1841–1935) to point out that the reasonable person standard must be a normative one, on account of the lack of an empirical alternative or, as he put it, in light of the 'impossibility of nicely measuring a man's powers and limitations'.[114] Such an argument no longer holds. A choice is now possible between a normative reasonable person standard and a standard based on empirically verifiable average behaviour; and the latter could turn the reasonable person analysis into a 'bright-line test' of whether a person's conduct in a particular case violated 'a numerical minimum or maximum'.[115] Consequently, a judicial assessment of individual conduct could be streamlined by stating, for instance, that, '[i]f a majority of people perform X and defendant did not perform X, then liability attaches'.[116]

The contrast between the reasonable person standard and this latter, statistics-based approach makes it very clear just how normative the reasonable person standard is and how different it is from what actual people do. Hence the standard's normativity must be more explicitly justified. If a court imposes on drivers a standard that is evidently not met by anyone, such a standard cannot be justified by appeals to vague notions of what reasonable people might do. Instead, courts might have to explain why a particularly high standard is desirable – and do so on the basis of the standard's ability to protect certain legitimate interests. In many cases this might not be a problem, since there are good reasons for expecting humans to meet a standard that exceeds average behaviour. But the available data do confront both judges and the reasonable person with an extra layer of scrutiny; and this layer can limit the discretion of judges, who were previously protected by the simple fact that it was impossible to verify how people behave on a larger scale. The reasonable person used to be able to occupy a comfortable twilight zone between the outright normative and the outright empirical. It was possible to maintain that the concept relied on

[114] O.W. Holmes, *The Common Law* (Macmillan 1882) 108. Notably, the lack of data about individual characteristics was just one of the reasons Holmes provided for adopting a normative standard. The more important reason, he says, is that the general welfare of society requires 'a sacrifice of individual peculiarities going beyond a certain point'.

[115] Sheppard (n 108), 2289. [116] Ibid.

people's actual behaviour without having to prove that it actually did so.[117] The advent of digital technologies does not dispel this twilight zone but sharpens its edges, making it very clear whether, in a given case, the standard falls within or without that zone and, if the latter, on which side. The availability of empirical data puts a new kind of pressure on the concept of the reasonable person, not only by revealing how the standard can implement subjective preferences and biases but also by showing how it fails to account for specific attributes of concrete persons in concrete legal proceedings. In short, the reasonable person's confrontation with its empirical counterpart shows that the former is often no more than an approximation of actual human beings. For some, such as Radbruch, this circumstance is unavoidable, since law must by definition be general and cannot be tailored to 'the actual, real human being who walks the surface of the earth, to their peculiarities and moods, to their dottiness, to the entire herbarium of strange plants that we call mankind'.[118]

But, for others, the fact that the reasonable person is a mere approximation of actual human beings is not an inevitability, but rather a defect – and one that can now be remedied, thanks to the availability of big data and the omnipresence of sensors that track our behaviour. Omri Ben-Shahar and Ariel Porat outline the most comprehensive version of this argument in their book *Personalized Law: Different Rules for Different People.*[119] There they propose that the standard of the reasonable person be replaced 'by a multitude of personalized rules, each person with their own "reasonable you" standard'.[120] The following account captures Ben-Shahar and Porat's vision of how human conduct would be assessed in a legal system where the reasonable person has given way to the reasonable you:

> What is reasonable for an individual defendant would be determined, not by reference to the average traits of some reference group, but instead by the skills and riskiness of this defendant. A young person with good eyesight and quick reflexes, who does not take drowsing medications, would be allowed to drive faster and over longer hours in the same road conditions as someone without these traits. The speed limit tailored to this young person could change by the hour of the day, as subjective factors affecting the predicted degree of alertness change – including how fatigued they become and whether they are having a conversation while driving. A one-size-fits-all speed limit sign posted alongside

[117] Zwiffelhoffer (n 113), 253. [118] Radbruch (n 113), 7.

[119] Ben-Shahar and Porat (n 79). For similar arguments presented by others, see e.g. A.J. Casey and A. Niblett, 'Self-Driving Laws' (2016) 66 University of Toronto Law Journal 429; Benjamin Alarie, 'The Path of the Law: Towards Legal Singularity' (2016) 66 University of Toronto Law Journal 443; P. Hacker, 'Personalizing EU Private Law: From Disclosures to Nudges and Mandates' (2017) 25 European Review of Private Law 651; C. Busch, 'Implementing Personalized Law: Personalized Disclosures in Consumer Law and Data Privacy Law' (2019) 86 The University of Chicago Law Review 309; J. McGinnis and S. Wasick, 'Law's Algorithm' (2015) 66 Florida Law Review 991.

[120] Ben-Shahar and Porat (n 79), 1.

> the road would be replaced by a flashing speed limit screen in the driver's car, displaying an algorithmically derived command.[121]

The 'skills and riskiness' of a given defendant would be calculated from big data sourced from government databases[122] and from data held by commercial actors.[123] Data deemed relevant for the purposes of building profiles of individual behaviour would include not only information about people's physical characteristics,[124] for example height, allergies and health records, but also about people's '*[m]ental, cognitive, and emotional characteristics*'.[125] In the context of traffic offences, this could include, for example, information about their 'impulsiveness, reaction speed, spatial awareness, and risk aversion'.[126] Information about personal preferences, derived for instance from people's 'sex, income, wealth, family size, religious affiliation, or marital history',[127] could also be relied on when evaluating a person's conduct.

The aim of the 'reasonable you' standard is to respect a person's 'dignity' by treating that person 'as an individual, not a population'.[128] According to Ben-Shahar and Porat, the general norms that a reasonable person embodies can be too strict for some and too lenient for others. For example, a general rule 'like the 55 miles per hour highway speed limit', which

> is based on the average risks and skills among all drivers, reflecting the traits of the "reasonable person" and ignoring any individual differences . . . imposes a restriction that is too harsh and potentially unfair for those excellent drivers who could safely drive faster. It visits on them the failing of mediocre and bad drivers.[129]

Their hope is that a 'reasonable you' standard would mean that '[s]ome people in some areas might have to meet more exacting duties because they pose higher specific risks. Simultaneously, countless other people will enjoy less burdensome duties and greater access.'[130] As a result,

> Better drivers would be free to drive faster, more skilled doctors would be held to higher standards of care, vulnerable employees would receive stronger protections, age restrictions for the young and the elderly would vary according to individual competence, and each borrower would be entitled to a personalized loan disclosure tailored to their specific concerns and delivered in a format fitting their mental capacity.[131]

[121] Ibid., 62. See also 19–20.

[122] The authors note that government records contain detailed information about 'income, resources, physical and other disabilities, types of expenses, living arrangements, and much more': Ben-Shahar and Porat (n 79), 210.

[123] Ibid. [124] Ibid., 203–204. [125] Ibid. (emphasis in original). [126] Ibid.

[127] Ibid., 205. [128] Ibid., 7. [129] Ibid., 147. [130] Ibid., 12.

[131] Ibid., 1. Presumably the 'reasonable you' standard would also be able to address the legal challenge posed by 'cyborgs', persons whose abilities have been enhanced by technological means such as implanted antennas or cameras and who for that reason may need to be assessed on their own rather than collectively or in group; see M.R.M. Protasio, 'The Reasonable Man in the 21st Century' (Tilburg University 2018) 46; L.H. Scholz, 'Two Cheers

The proposed standard of 'the reasonable you' raises a plethora of questions and has attracted a significant amount of criticism concerning the insufficiently precise description of how this standard would operate in practice,[132] its commitment to welfare optimization at the expense of other legal values,[133] the uncertain technological capabilities that the system presupposes,[134] possible effects on individual autonomy, the fact that personalised law could be abused,[135] or the worry that this standard could be just as difficult to apply as the reasonable person standard.[136] The most fundamental objection to the proposal is the concern that the very concept of law might not survive the introduction of a 'reasonable you' standard.[137] For our purposes, we need not get involved in that debate. Suffice it to note that, even if a 'reasonable you' standard could somehow become compatible with the notion of law, the concept of the reasonable person would certainly not survive its introduction.

The emergence of 'the reasonable you' standard would lead to the reasonable person's demise, since the former displaces both of the foundational elements of the reasonable person: empathy and perspective taking. With respect to the element of empathy, it would not be a shared, common sense, a 'fellow feeling' that were to inform a person's (or a judge's) assessment of the situation, but rather a set of empirical data. As Ben-Shahar and Porat write, this would be a 'data-driven' standard, as opposed to a standard based on human intuition.[138] Moreover, since everyone would have 'their own personal

for Cyborgs' (*The University of Chicago Law Review Online*, 9 March 2022), https://lawreviewblog.uchicago.edu/2022/03/09/bp-scholz.

132 S.G. Mayson, 'But What Is Personalized Law?' (*The University of Chicago Law Review Online*, 9 March 2022). https://lawreviewblog.uchicago.edu/2022/03/09/bp-mayson.

133 H. Eidenmüller, 'Why Personalized Law?' (*The University of Chicago Law Review Online*, 9 March 2022), https://lawreviewblog.uchicago.edu/2022/03/09/bp-eidenmuller. For less sceptical responses to the authors' proposal, see J.H. Kordi, 'Personalized Enfranchisement' (*The University of Chicago Law Review Online*, 9 March 2022), https://lawreviewblog.uchicago.edu/2022/03/09/bp-kordi; C. Goanta, 'The Ancient Alien: Good Faith as the Facilitator of Personalized Law' (*The University of Chicago Law Review Online*, 9 March 2022), https://lawreviewblog.uchicago.edu/2022/03/09/bp-goanta; C. Coglianese, 'Moving Toward Personalized Law' (*The University of Chicago Law Review Online*, 9 March 2022), https://lawreviewblog.uchicago.edu/2022/03/09/bp-coglianese; L.H. Scholz (n 131); G. Klass, 'Tailoring Ex Machina: Perspectives on Personalized Law' (*The University of Chicago Law Review Online*, 9 March 2022), https://lawreviewblog.uchicago.edu/2022/03/09/bp-klass.

134 P.N. Salib, 'Complex Algorithmic Law' (*The University of Chicago Law Review Online*, 9 March 2022), https://lawreviewblog.uchicago.edu/2022/03/09/bp-salib.

135 A. Davidson, 'Personalized Law, Political Power, and the Dangerous Few' (*The University of Chicago Law Review Online*, 9 March 2022), https://lawreviewblog.uchicago.edu/2022/03/09/bp-davidson.

136 J.I. Mayer, 'Implementing Personalized Negligence Law' (*The University of Chicago Law Review Online*, 9 March 2022), https://lawreviewblog.uchicago.edu/2022/03/09/bp-mayer; Hans Christoph Grigoleit, 'Personalized Law: Distinctions and Procedural Observations' (*The University of Chicago Law Review Online*, 9 March 2022), https://lawreviewblog.uchicago.edu/2022/03/09/bp-grigoleit.

137 T. Endicott and K. Yeung, 'The Death of Law? Computationally Personalized Norms and the Rule of Law' (2022) 72 University of Toronto Law Journal 373. See also Radbruch (n 113) 7.

138 Ben-Shahar and Porat (n 79), 37.

legal system',[139] the second foundational element of the concept of a reasonable person – the practice of taking another's perspective – would also become irrelevant. When one reflects upon one's own action, considering how others may behave 'would not help'[140] and would be irrelevant. Under the heading 'Know Thyself' – the English version of the Enlightenment's credo *sapere aude* – the authors make it plain that individuals would no longer have to 'guess' or 'extrapolate' what other members of society deem to be reasonable.[141] They would merely have to relate to their 'personalized care standards' instead.[142] This personalised standard of care, the authors argue, would be relatively easy to acquire and also 'grounded and accurate',[143] since people know whether 'they are clumsy, slow-reacting, narrow-visioned, distractable, or shaky'[144] and can adjust their behaviour accordingly. Compared to a legal system that uses the reasonable person, a system of personalised law would 'require no learning' insofar as individuals 'harness information' that they 'already have about themselves'.[145]

Whether or not one shares the vision of Ben-Shahar and Porat, its implementation would sound the death knell for the reasonable person. Born amid the technological revolution at the turn of the eighteenth century, the reasonable person would perish in the wake of the technological revolution of the twenty-first century. Even if one doubts that personalised law would ever or could ever become a reality, we have seen that the appearance both of artificially intelligent actors and of the empirical human being in the wake of the ongoing digital revolution puts considerable pressure on the concept of the reasonable person – a pressure that edges the concept away from its normative roots towards an empirical base, away from empathy and towards rationality, away from an egalitarian standard rooted in a common, shared sense and towards a standard controlled by a smaller group of experts. Some might welcome this development, in the hope that technology and empirical data can overcome some of the problems inherent in a reasonable person standard – for instance its incorporation of biases, its vagueness, or its generality, which causes it to pay too little attention to a person's unique characteristics. Against this background, the book's final chapter offers an emphatic plea for retaining and cherishing the reasonable person standard as a perspective-taking device despite its all-too-human flaws.

[139] Ibid., 201. [140] Mayer (n 137).

[141] Ben-Shahar and Porat (n 79), 214. The flipside is that this argument makes it difficult for others to assess an individual's specific act, because the only person who can tell whether that individual behaved in a blameworthy manner or not is the actor in possession of data related to the individual in question.

[142] Ibid. [143] Ibid. [144] Ibid. [145] Ibid.

Conclusion

Throughout this legal biography, we have encountered the reasonable person at different times, in different places and in many shapes and forms. We traced the concept's ancestors to ancient Egypt, Greece and Rome (Chapter 1). We explored how industrialisation and Scottish sentimentalism facilitated the concept's emergence in Birmingham (Chapter 2) and we pondered over the significance of the concept's association with the man on the Clapham omnibus (Chapter 3). We followed the reasonable person into the courtrooms of colonial Africa (Chapter 4) and onto the battlefield (Chapter 5). We even considered the reasonable person of the future, by studying its encounter with AI and big data (Chapter 6). The reasonable person we met at these different times and in these different settings was not always the same. Egypt's *geru maa* was the epitome of an egalitarian standard of law and fairness. Its Roman and, to a lesser extent, its Greek counterpart were claimed by the elites. The reasonable person of Chapter 2 was an empathy-infused character with humanitarian convictions. But we saw that, once it was construed in the shape of the man on the Clapham omnibus, the standard was soon tied to the customs of middle-class men and excluded women and the lower classes (and many more besides). At times, the reasonable person in colonial courts was an Englishman. At times it took the shape of a member of the local community. In Chapter 5 the reasonable person appeared variously as a civilian in uniform or as someone thinking in distinctly military categories. At last, we encountered digital variants of the reasonable person, and even arguments to the effect that such a person does, or at least should, resemble us. In light of this illustrious group of reasonable persons, one might wonder whether there is anything that unites them. Or is the reasonable person simply a legal shapeshifter, at best controlled by context and, at worst, by the subjective preferences of judges?

In this concluding chapter I want to address this question by arguing that the reasonable person possesses an essence that can be traced across time and across the different jurisdictions we encountered. This essence is the concept's fundamental acceptance that ours is always just one perspective among many and that the best way to understand and accurately assess what others think, do and feel is by empathising with them. But, as we have seen, the standard is not always understood in this manner, in fact it is frequently applied in violation of this principle. For this reason, the concluding chapter will offer a restatement of the function and rationale of the common law's most illustrious character. The aim is to contribute to the realisation of the concept's potential and to make it easier to identify instances of misuse. The chapter unfolds in three parts, which correspond to the three steps of making judgments through empathetic perspective taking: the intention to take the reasonable person's perspective (Section C.1); the assumption of the reasonable person's perspective (Section C.2); and the making of a judgment by reference to the reasonable person's perspective (Section C.3). As each of these steps is considered, it will become obvious that the most fundamental points of criticism are levelled not at the concept itself but at how it is used by some. The concept itself, this final chapter argues, has significant potential to facilitate the making of tolerant and humane judgements in a diverse, globalised and dynamic society, provided that one remembers that the reasonable person is always someone else.

C.1 An Other

In the Introduction I observed that the reasonable person's most important characteristic is that the reasonable person is not you. This feature is important because it captures the heart of the concept: the conviction that a judgement of what is right and wrong requires a consideration of the views and feelings of others. As we have seen, the *geru maa* of ancient Egypt represented a worldview that expected everyone, kings and slaves alike, to listen and relate to the perspective of other community members. The *spoudaios* in the ancient Greek world was meant to remove decision-makers from 'egocentric selfishness'.[1] Similarly, the Roman writer Lucius Junius Moderatus Columella (4–70) describes Rome's *bonus paterfamilias* as a person who takes 'especial pains to consult on every point' and to gauge 'the opinions and teachings' of others.[2] We have seen that the common law's reasonable person emerged in a social and intellectual climate shaped by Scottish sentimentalists like David Hume and Adam Smith. They maintained that the Enlightenment was not just an age of reason but also an age of feeling,[3] and that the cognitive, analytical faculty must be complemented by a 'moral sense'[4] that allows any individual to relate

[1] V.J. Bourke, 'The Ethical Role of the Impartial Observer' (1978) 6 The Journal of Religious Ethics 279, 284.

[2] Lucius Junius Moderatus Columella, *De re rustica*, 1.1.3.

[3] S. Moyn, 'Empathy in History, Empathizing with Humanity' (2006) 45 History and Theory 397, 399.

[4] Or 'moral taste', as David Hume calls it. See D. Hume, *A Treatise of Human Nature* (L.A. Selby-Bigge ed., Clarendon 1896) 581.

to the shared feelings of other members of the community.[5] Crucially, this 'moral sense' is calibrated through the perspective of an external observer. The third Earl of Shaftesbury referred to this actor as 'the common honest Man',[6] David Hume presented it as a 'model character'[7] and, most famously, Adam Smith assigned this external point of view to an 'impartial spectator'. The common law's versions of this external observer figure of Scottish sentimentalists are Baron Alderson's reasonable man, Lord Bowen's 'man on the Clapham omnibus',[8] and, eventually, the reasonable person. Just like the impartial spectator, each of these characters invokes an external point of view with the aim of facilitating the understanding of ourselves and others through the eyes of an observer.

Accordingly, the first step in applying the reasonable person standard is for a judge to position herself in relation to an external observer. Doing this means that the judge must split into a spectator and an agent – the two persons discussed in Chapter 2 around Adam Smith. This division of perspectives alienates the judge both from herself and from the situation at hand. One could compare this process of alienation to the *Verfremdungseffekt* ('alienation, estrangement, distancing effect') related to the stage – a concept introduced by the German playwright Berthold Brecht (1898–1956).[9] In theatre, the *Verfremdungseffekt* enables the audience to take a critical distance from what it observes; and it does so by irritating the audience – for example by interrupting a performance with critical comments, by switching genres or by addressing the audience directly. The split of the judge into two persons – spectator and agent – has a similar effect. Here the tool used to bring about the *Verfremdung*, the estrangement, is *Verdopplung* – a 'duplication' of actors and perspectives. The judge suddenly has to relate to a spectator, namely the reasonable person. This reasonable person is a figure sufficiently familiar to the judge to invite identification, yet it is also sufficiently different to cause a degree of cognitive dissonance, of estrangement. It is this sensation of alienation and estrangement that reminds the judge that the other – the spectator, the reasonable person – is not the judge herself but someone else.

This recognition of the other entails acknowledging the relevance and legitimate existence of a different perspective. Thus, as we saw in Chapter 1, Rensi son of Meru, who was the High Steward tasked with adjudicating the

5 M.L. Frazer, *The Enlightenment of Sympathy: Justice and the Moral Sentiments in the Eighteenth Century and Today* (Oxford University Press 2010) 4.

6 A. A. Cooper, *Characteristicks of Men, Manners, Opinions, Times*, vol 1 (Philip Ayres ed, Clarendon Press 1999) 72.

7 D. Hume, *Essays: Moral, Political, and Literary* (Lewis 1889) 158.

8 *Tichborne v Lushington* (Court of Common Pleas, 1872).

9 B. Brecht, 'Über experimentelles Theater', in B. Brecht, *Ausgewählte Werke in sechs Bänden*, vol 6 (Suhrkamp 1997) 418–21. For a discussion of the connection between Brecht's *Verfremdungseffekt* and Viktor Shklovsky's (1893–1984) *priyom ostraneniya*, see D. Robinson, *Estrangement and the Somatics of Literature: Tolstoy, Shklovsky, Brecht* (Johns Hopkins University Press 2008) 167–9.

conflict between a peasant named Khunanup and the official who stole his donkeys and goods, did not reach a decision right away. It is only after having listened to Khunanup and being reminded by him of what the *geru maa* would do that Rensi decided the case. In Herodotus' story King Xerxes, too, explicitly enquires about the perspectives of others when pondering over his next move during the conflict with Greek cities. He consults the members of his war council – including Artemisia, queen of Halicarnassus; he does not listen to her and ends up making the wrong decision. But this is beside the point; the important fact here is that both Rensi and Xerxes acknowledge that there are perspectives other than their own that are worthy of consideration. That Rensi would be tempted to consider the views of Khunanup, who appeared before him no less than nine times, or that Xerxes would consult the members of his war council, who provided crucial support to his campaign, seems hardly worthy of note. Yet the distinct function of the concept of the reasonable person is to invite a person who evaluates a specific situation – a judge – to relate to an external perspective regardless of the physical presence of other human beings. A solitary person, for instance someone stranded on an island who deliberates whether it is permissible to start a fire or to kill an animal, can still meaningfully acknowledge another's perspective by asking herself what a reasonable person would do in her place.

The recognition of another's perspective also entails acknowledging one's own perspective. In other words, supplementing one's own perspective with that of an imaginary other not only leads to a more accurate recognition of another person's perspective; it also reveals the coordinates of our own position,[10] and consequently helps us to understand that our view is just one out of many.[11] Relating to another's perspective means accepting that other views and other interpretations of circumstances exist, and that they need to be considered if one wishes to acquire a comprehensive understanding of a given situation. As the Scottish sentimentalists would take it, to position oneself in relation to another means recognising the defeasibility of the reasons that inform one's own understanding of the world. In this sense, the rationale of the reasonable person is based on the view that the truth, legal or otherwise, may derive in part from objective principles and through rational deductions, but it is always also co-owned and co-constituted. Everyone owns a share of the truth; and everyone's share is just a part of the larger whole.

This process of positioning oneself in relation to another not only creates and makes apparent a distance between oneself and another; it also brings about a separation of the judge from the judge's perspective. It creates a distance between the judge and the judge's perspective. This process of estrangement makes it clear that the judge has a perspective but is not that

[10] E. Stein, *Zum Problem der Einfühlung* (Buchdruckerei des Waisenhauses 1917) 70–1.

[11] Edith Stein goes even further, stipulating that the recognition of our own individuality presupposes that we view ourselves through the eyes of another; see ibid., 73.

perspective. The process of perspective taking transforms a judge's view from an essential characteristic into an attribute. Instead of 'being' conservative, a judge recognising the defeasibility of the reasons that inform her position will 'hold' conservative views. This separation between person and perspective, this detachment of the person of the judge from the view the judge holds allows for a discussion of different perspectives without threatening the person, character or identity of the judge. Person, character and identity will no doubt be relevant when it comes to explaining the judge's specific perspective; but they are not inextricably linked to the judge's position. In this sense, the subjectification and relativisation of a judge's views in fact objectifies them; it turns them into objects of rigorous reflection. Ideally, this circumstance makes it easier to explore why it is that one holds the particular belief one does. Thus understood, the debates concerning the perspectives and characteristics of the reasonable person are then not about objective truths or accurate processes of reasoning; rather, they are debates about more or less plausible interpretations of a given situation.

In the theatre it is directors and actors who confront members of the audience with a *Verfremdungseffekt* that, ideally, triggers a cognitive dissonance and leads to a duplication of perspectives. When we judge others, by contrast, we must initiate this process of estrangement ourselves. If we do not consciously decide to take another's perspective, nobody will do it for us.[12] There is no doubt that many of the judges we encountered failed to understand that invoking the reasonable person implies accepting that one's own truth is not the only one there is. In *Daniels v Clegg*, Chief Justice Christiancy – along with many other judges we encountered in Chapter 3 who seemingly equated the law's perspective with their own – appears to apply the reasonable person standard in violation of the concept's rationale. Similarly, Chief Justice Tredgold's observation, in *Jackson*, that the concept of the reasonable person must refer to only one norm, which 'cannot . . . be varied in any way',[13] a view shared by many of the other judges encountered in Chapter 4, directly contradicts the concept's rationale. Against this background, it is understandable that some have concluded that the 'reasonable man test is based on an assumption, that there can be one ideal, one truth, one and only one appropriate behaviour in any given situation',[14] or that the 'reasonable person

[12] In the same way, Maksymilian Del Mar has argued with respect to the figure of the officious bystander that its ability to assist with meaningful judgment making presupposes that it 'actually functions as an artefact' and that 'persons actually imagine it': M. Del Mar, *Artefacts of Legal Inquiry: The Value of Imagination in Adjudication* (Hart 2020) 332.

[13] *Attorney-General for Nyasaland v Jackson* [1957] R & NLR 443 (Federal Supreme Court of Rhodesia and Nyasaland) 448–9 (Tredgold CJ). In *Mbombela*, De Villiers JA expressed exactly the same view: *R v Mbombela* 1933 AD 269 (Appellate Division (South Africa)) 272 (De Villiers JA).

[14] R. Martin, 'A Feminist View of the Reasonable Man: An Alternative Approach to Liability in Negligence for Personal Injury' (1994) 23 Anglo-American Law Review 334, 342.

standard encourages conformism and the suppression of different voices'.[15] While certain episodes of judicial practice related to the reasonable person standard undoubtedly support such a conclusion, the concept's genesis and rationale are diametrically opposed to a worldview that presumes the existence of one and only one standard for every member of the human species. Indeed, the concept powerfully counters 'the myth' of law's 'perspectivelessness'[16] – the idea that law can be made, adjudicated, applied and understood in an objective manner, without regard for the person who is making, adjudicating, applying or understanding it. This means that, even in situations where the reasonable person concept is used as a proxy for a judge's own perspective, an awareness of the concept's genesis can facilitate a fundamental critique of the use of the concept on its own terms. An internal critique of the concept is aided, in particular, by an accurate understanding of the second step in applying the reasonable person concept.

C.2 A Listener

Having initiated a process of perspective taking, a judge needs to take the second step, namely to actually assume the perspective of the reasonable person. For the purposes of clarifying what exactly this entails, it is helpful to begin by situating the reasonable person's perspective amid at least three perspectives.

The reasonable person must relate to the perspectives of at least three stakeholders: the person assessing a given situation (the 'judge'), the person whose conduct is at issue (e.g. a defendant) and society at large. The ability of the perspective of the reasonable person to shed light on a given situation presupposes that it does not drift too close to any of these three perspectives. If it maintains this distance, the concept is particularly suitable to facilitating the making of adequate judgements in a diverse, globalised, dynamic society. On the other hand, if it does not, the concept will find its rationale of facilitating empathetic perspective taking undermined. If the reasonable person's perspective resembles the perspective of the judge too closely, the standard will become a proxy for the judge's own views,[17] and this leads to the collapse of Smith's distinction between agent and spectator. This is what happened in cases such as *Jackson*[18] or *Mawema*,[19] discussed in Chapter 4,

[15] L. Bender, 'A Lawyer's Primer on Feminist Theory and Tort' (1988) 38 Journal of Legal Education 3, 23.

[16] K.W. Crenshaw, 'Toward a Race-Conscious Pedagogy in Legal Education' (1988) 11 National Black Law Journal 12.

[17] For the same reason, Berthold Brecht's *Verfremdungseffekt* was explicitly not meant to trigger an all-encompassing identification of the audience with the feelings and experiences of the actors: Brecht (n 9), 415.

[18] *Attorney-General for Nyasaland v Jackson* [1957] R & NLR 443 (n 13).

[19] *Mawema v R* [1961] R & NLR 655 (High Court of Southern Rhodesia).

where colonial courts equated the reasonable person's view and characteristics with their own views and characteristics. If the standard resembles too closely the perspective of the person whose conduct is at issue, it will become itself subjective and will lose its normative force. An extreme example of such a development is the proposed 'reasonable you' standard encountered in Chapter 6. Finally, if the standard gets too attached to the perspective of a particular societal context, it risks replacing the rule of law with the rule of the majority, and thereby puts minority interests at risk. Cases concerning the practice of religious minorities, briefly touched upon towards the end of Chapter 3, and the discussion of the proposed fusion of the reasonable person standard with standards derived from empirically verifiable majority behaviour in Chapter 6, illustrate this problem.

With respect to the reasonable person's perspective, a judge must assume it through imagination and empathy. Both elements are crucial. The horizon in which a judge has the ability to imagine the perspective of another is determined to a large extent by the judge's knowledge and experience of other people. Judges must be firmly rooted in the world,[20] in the sense of possessing an accurate understanding of the social context in which they act. With respect to empathy, too, the extent to which a judge senses what others feel will be a matter of experience, but also presupposes, fundamentally, that the judge is prepared to use her own moral sense, in an attempt to touch that Humean string to which all mankind is connected. When doing so, judges must resist the understandable temptation to form a concrete image of the reasonable person. The dedication of songs and poems to the reasonable person character, and judicial (usually gratuitous, often humorous) speculations about its features – where it lives, what religion it follows, what mode of public transport it uses – enhance the concept's tangibility and its communicative power. The downside to such fetishizing practices is that they overemphasise particular features of the external observer.[21] To picture heroes of songs and poems or travellers on busses and other public transport when you try to adopt the reasonable person's perspective is fundamentally to misunderstand how the standard is supposed to function. It is not the figure itself of the reasonable person, but its perspective that is of importance. The process of assuming the reasonable person's perspective requires the judge to walk backwards towards the position occupied by the reasonable person. The objective is not to see the reasonable person but to see what it sees, to hear what it hears, to feel what it feels.

In this regard, it is telling that the key characteristics of ancient Egypt's *geru maa* were to be silent and to listen. Silence is important because it creates a

[20] C. Kemp Allen, 'The Judge as Man of the World' (1930) 46 Law Quarterly Review 151, 151. See also *Watt v Longsdon* [1930] 1 KB 130 (Court of Appeal) 139 (Scrutton LJ).

[21] L. Zwiffelhoffer, *Die Figur des Durchschnittssmenschen im Verwaltungsrecht* (Mohr Siebeck 2020) 259.

space for the feelings and thoughts of others. Likewise, when assuming the perspective of a reasonable person, an ideal judge exercises restraint and modesty and recedes into the background. Listening is the act of taking in the thoughts, feelings, perspectives that fill the silence. To listen in the legal sense requires not just an accurate understanding of the applicable norms (the teachings of the elders in ancient Egypt; precedent and statute law in modern common law jurisdictions) but also presence and attentiveness to the circumstances at hand. It also means refraining, at least initially,[22] from filtering and categorising what is heard in accordance with one's own convictions. In this respect, when judges emulate the perspective of the reasonable person, they should strive to adopt the attitude of a silent listener.

The contours of this process of combining imagination and empathy are further clarified by considering two fundamental concerns about the concept of the reasonable person as an empathetic perspective-taking device. The first concern relates to the problem of biases – that is, the risk that a judge's impression of what the reasonable person sees will necessarily be coloured by the identity and preferences of the judge herself. The most severe problem in this area occurs when judges who purport to engage in empathetic perspective taking do so in an egocentric manner. This means that the question 'What would a reasonable person do in situation x?' becomes 'What would I do in situation x?' Both questions use empathy but, while the author of the first question empathises with, and takes the perspective of, another, the author of the second question empathises with themselves and takes their own perspective.[23] It is rare to find explicit examples of egocentric perspective taking in the judicial context. However, in decisions such as *Palamba*[24] or *Mawema*,[25] the judges come close to producing such examples when they dismiss outright perspectives that conflict with their own. One can contrast cases of this type with the decisions in *Fabiano*[26] or *Nyandoro*,[27] where the judges were able to take the defendants' views into account, despite the fact that they did not share

[22] Ultimately the insights gained through empathetic perspective taking need to be filtered (see Section C.3); for otherwise the perspective of the author of an act of empathy would become identical with the perspective taken by the author of a given act. See, in this regard, Hannah Arendt's treatment of Kant's discussion of impartial perspective taking: H. Arendt, 'Lectures on Kant's Political Philosophy' in Ronald Beiner (ed.), *Lectures on Kant's Political Philosophy* (University of Chicago Press 1982) 42–4. But, as Martha Nussbaum observes, 'the sense of what was really experienced is a crucial step, without which any spectatorial assessment will likely be off the mark': M.C. Nussbaum, 'Poets as Judges: Judicial Rhetoric and the Literary Imagination' (1995) 62 The University of Chicago Law Review 1477, 1488.

[23] D. Traven, *Law and Sentiment in International Politics: Ethics, Emotions, and the Evolution of the Laws of War* (Cambridge University Press 2021) 41.

[24] *R v Palamba s/o Fundikila, Kamumbi s/o Sikulu* (1947) 14 EACA 96 (Court of Appeal for Eastern Africa).

[25] *Mawema v R* [1961] R & NLR 655 (n 19).

[26] *R v Fabiano Kinene s/o Mukye, Seperiano Kiwanuka s/o Kintu, Albert Iseja s/o Kintu* (1941) 8 EACA 96 (Court of Appeal for Eastern Africa).

[27] *R v Nyandoro* [1958] R & NLR 932 (High Court of Southern Rhodesia).

those defendants' assumptions on the existence of witchcraft or on colonial history.

Egocentric empathetic perspective taking results in complete failure on the part of a judge to adopt the reasonable person's perspective. Such cases aside, biases can materialise in more subtle ways, too. David Hume and Adam Smith were acutely aware that it is relatively easy to empathise accurately with people whom one knows and likes.[28] For the purposes of empathetic perspective taking, this means that, in appealing to the reasonable person figure as an external observer, a judge risks assessing the behaviour of a person known or similar to the judge in more favourable terms than the behaviour of a person not known or not similar to the judge.[29] Indeed, examples of instances where the reasonable person appeared to reflect the characteristics of those who apply the concept can be found in each episode of the concept's biography. The reasonable person's Greek and Roman ancestors, discussed in Chapter 1, belonged to the ruling class; the reasonable person of Chapters 2 and 3 was a predominantly male figure; many of the reasonable person's manifestations in the colonial courts presented in Chapter 4 resembled an Englishman; and, in Chapter 5, we learned that the extent to which reasonable military commanders can favour their own nationals is one of the key questions in the law of armed conflict. In Chapter 6 it became clear how the use of algorithms and AI can amplify the subjective preferences and biases of human beings.

Accordingly, and in light of recent studies that established the exclusionary potential of empathetic perspective taking,[30] it is understandable that many have criticised the standard of the reasonable person on the grounds that it discriminates against women,[31] people of colour,[32] persons with cognitive

[28] Frazer (n 5), 45, 100.

[29] J. Prinz, 'Against Empathy' (2011) 49 The Southern Journal of Philosophy 214, 227; J. Conaghan, 'Tort Law and the Feminist Critique of Reason', in A. Bottomley (ed.), *Feminist Perspectives on The Foundational Subjects of Law* (Cavendish Publishing 1996) 53; Kemp Allen (n 20), 152.

[30] See, for instance, M. Cikara et al., 'Their Pain Gives Us Pleasure: How Intergroup Dynamics Shape Empathic Failures and Counter-Empathic Responses' (2014) 55 Journal of Experimental Social Psychology 110, 120; K. Stueber, 'Empathy', in E.N. Zalta (ed.), *The Stanford Encyclopedia of Philosophy* (2019, Stanford University 2019), https://plato.stanford.edu/archives/fall2019/entries/empathy; Prinz (n 29); P. Bloom, *Against Empathy: The Case for Rational Compassion* (Random House 2017) 9; T. Fuchs, 'Empathy, Group Identity, and the Mechanisms of Exclusion: An Investigation into the Limits of Empathy' (2019) 38 Topoi 239; N.S. Kteily and E. Bruneau, 'Darker Demons of Our Nature: The Need to (Re)Focus Attention on Blatant Forms of Dehumanization' (2017) 26 Current Directions in Psychological Science 487.

[31] N.R. Cahn, 'Looseness of Legal Language: The Reasonable Woman Standard in Theory and in Practice' (1992) 77 Cornell Law Review 1398; C. Forell and D. Matthews, *A Law of Her Own: The Reasonable Woman as a Measure of Man* (NYU Press 2001); A. Phillips, 'When Culture Means Gender: Issues of Cultural Defence in the English Courts' (2003) 66 The Modern Law Review 510.

[32] P. Lenta, 'The Tikoloshe and the Reasonable Man: Transgressing South African Legal Fictions' (2004) 16 Law and Literature 353; Crenshaw (n 16); R.B. Seidman, 'Mens Rea and the

disabilities,[33] members of society considered to belong to the lower classes[34] – in short, against anyone who does not fall in the category of white middle-class male individuals, who traditionally serve as judges in common law courts. Thus it has been argued that the standard should be replaced by a 'gender-free'[35] and 'truly universal standard'[36] applicable to all, or by one related to the behaviour of a '"neighbor" or "social acquaintance" or "responsible person with conscious care and concern for another's safety"'.[37] But the reasonable person can possess all these attributes – or rather, when construed in accordance with its rationale, the reasonable person is meant to be understood in precisely these terms.[38] In light of the frequent disregard for the concept's rationale in the cases encountered in this biography, this might be cold comfort to all those whose interests are ignored as a result of judges' reliance on the reasonable person standard.

However, bias in the administration of justice is a general issue and pertains to the concept of the reasonable person only insofar as this concept is an established element of a legal system susceptible to human biases. John Gardner noted: 'If the reasonable person often ends up giving effect to a male standard of justification that is not because he sets a male standard of justification. It is because he sets no particular standard of justification.'[39] And thus, much like the algorithms encountered in Chapter 6, the reasonable person channels the biases of those who invoke the standard.[40] This figure 'can accommodate prejudice, bias, superstition, and gullibility to the extent that he is landed, as he so easily is, with the prejudice, bias, superstition, and gullibility of those who use him'.[41] All these would exist with or without the reasonable

Reasonable African: The Pre-Scientific World-View and Mistake of Fact' (1966) 15 The International and Comparative Law Quarterly 1135.

[33] J. Chriscoe and L. Lukasik, 'Re-Examining Reasonableness: Negligence Liability in Adult Defendants with Cognitive Disabilities' (2015) 6 Alabama Civil Rights & Civil Liberties Law Review 1; M. Moran, *Rethinking the Reasonable Person: An Egalitarian Reconstruction of the Objective Standard* (Oxford University Press 2003) 150; K. Harlow, 'Applying the Reasonable Person Standard to Psychosis: How Tort Unfairly Burdens Adults with Mental Illness' (2007) 68 Ohio State Law Journal 1733.

[34] Moran (n 33), 210.

[35] R.K.L. Collins, 'Language, History and the Legal Process: A Profile of the Reasonable Man' (1976) 8 Rutgers Camden Law Journal 311, 323.

[36] W. Parker, 'The Reasonable Person: A Gendered Concept?' (1993) 23 Victoria University of Wellington Law Review 105, 112.

[37] Bender (n 15), 25. For discussions of additional alternatives to the reasonable person, see also Martin (n 14), 353, 357–358; L.M. Finley, 'A Break in the Silence: Including Women's Issues in a Torts Course' (1989) 1 Yale Journal of Law and Feminism 41, 63.

[38] Thus, one must distinguish the critique of the reasonable person concept as such from the critique of particular manifestations of the concept. For a recent argument that critiques a particular construal of the reasonable person (rather than the concept itself), see A. Hochman Bloom, 'Objective Enough: Race Is Relevant to the Reasonable Person in Criminal Procedure' (2023) 19 Stanford Journal of Civil Rights & Civil Liberties 1.

[39] J. Gardner, 'The Many Faces of the Reasonable Person' [2015] Law Quarterly Review 563, 568.

[40] Zwiffelhoffer (n 21), 251.

[41] Gardner (n 39), 568.

person; but the standard's distinct, tangible and anthropomorphic character makes such pre-existing biases and prejudices particularly visible. This is so not despite, but precisely because of, the fact that the reasonable person invites those who apply it to individuate and particularize[42] otherwise seemingly perspectiveless, abstract standards of behaviour. Male notions of reasonableness dominated (and in many ways still dominate) the administration of justice in many jurisdictions. But few tools make this circumstance as clear as the fact that a legal system's standard of behaviour is represented in the form of a reasonable man (and it is for the same reason that Gardner explicitly and intentionally refers to the reasonable person as a 'he' in the passage just quoted).[43] One might wonder whether the drafters of the 1900 German Civil Code in the late nineteenth century would have paid any particular attention to the interests of housewives, actresses, children and domestic staff if the *paterfamilias* standard had not illustrated the blatant implausibility of measuring their behaviour against that of a patriarch. Likewise, the colonial courts' use of, and explicit engagement with, a standard of the reasonable person depicted as a man on the streets of England makes the widespread absurdity of the colonial administration of justice especially obvious. Again, this makes perhaps little difference in practice, but the use of the standard introduces a certain degree of procedural transparency, no doubt limited, that renders biases clear and allows for a rigorous review of problematic judicial decisions. Thus, when construed in accordance with its rationale, the reasonable person figure is 'not an obstacle to normative judgement, but is, or at least can be, a more careful, more subtle, though also often more difficult, way of exercising it'.[44] Accurately applied, the reasonable person is meant to temper the detrimental effects of human biases by forcing those who apply the standard to confront other perspectives and to challenge their own. Inaccurately applied, the reasonable person standard makes deviations from its rationale apparent and allows for the critique of discriminatory judicial practices.

The second concern related to the concept is that, even if human biases could be kept in check, there are inherent limits to a person's ability to empathise with, and to take the perspective of, another. Proponents of this view accept that empathetic perspective taking might be a welcome technique of judgment making in relatively homogenous settings, but one that it is unable to assist in heterogenous social, ethical, cultural and political contexts. The theories of David Hume and Adam Smith, for example, have been

42 S. Stern, 'From Clapham to Salina: Locating the Reasonable Man' (2023) Law & Literature 1, 2. While Stern maintains that this effect of anthropomorphised standards is concerning, I consider the individuating and particularizing effect to be one of the reasonable person's most valuable and most important characteristics.

43 Despite his criticism of the reasonable person, Stern, too, acknowledges that the figure of the 'man on the Clapham omnibus', for instance, 'helped reveal some of the problems and complications underlying "reasonableness" as a standard' (ibid 22).

44 Del Mar (n 12), 386.

criticised for presupposing 'an implausible degree of uniformity' among human beings.[45] There is certainly a risk that perspective taking and empathy beyond the situations with which a judge is familiar produce inaccurate results. Johann Gottfried Herder (1744–1803), one of the few German representatives of the sentimental Enlightenment, remarked that one 'often needs a magic mirror'[46] to identify common points of reference when trying to assess the behaviour of people from unfamiliar contexts. But this, too, is a challenge that confronts law in general. Any judgment that seeks to claim a degree of objectivity and generality presupposes that legal subjects are, at least in some respects, equal and uniform.[47] In the words of Gustav Radbruch that I quoted in Chapter 6, it is simply not possible to tailor law to 'the actual, real human being who walks the surface of the earth, to their peculiarities and moods, to their dottiness, to the entire herbarium of strange plants that we call mankind'.[48] Nevertheless, the legal process must of course strive towards an accurate assessment of the relevant circumstances, across and beyond contexts with which judges may be familiar. In the cases we encountered in Chapter 4, the assessors of colonial courts were supposed to mediate between different cultural and social contexts. English judges often dismissed the assessors' views; but there are also cases where judges appeared to make a conscious effort genuinely to understand and relate to the persons whose conduct was at issue. The first instance decision in *Jackson* is such an example.

In the non-colonial context, the role of assessors can be performed by juries composed of members who represent all sections of society. Indeed, in cases where the application of the reasonable person standard is delegated to juries, the involvement of a multiplicity of persons greatly enhances the ability of the standard to produce accurate results across cultural, social and ethnic boundaries. And yet, in spite of these safeguards, the application of the reasonable person standard will always remain to some extent subjective. As the next section argues, this is not necessarily problematic.

C.3 A Human

For a judge, as we have seen, the first step in applying the reasonable person concept in conformity with its rationale is to position herself in relation to the reasonable person, understood as an external observer. The second step is to adopt the perspective of the reasonable person, understood as a silent listener. The third step, which will be discussed in this section, entails that the judge

45 Frazer (n 5), 13.

46 J.G. Herder, 'On the Change of Taste (1766)', in M.N. Forster (ed.), *Philosophical Writings* (Cambridge University Press 2002) 255.

47 D.A. Donovan and S.M. Wildman, 'Is the Reasonable Man Obsolete: A Critical Perspective on Self-Defense and Provocation' (1981) 14 Loyola of Los Angeles Law Review 435, 466–7.

48 G. Radbruch, 'Law's Image of the Human' (2020) 40 Oxford Journal of Legal Studies 667, 7. See also Zwiffelhoffer (n 21), 259–60.

passes judgment by reference to the perspective of the reasonable person by reassuming the judge's own position. That the judge passes judgment by reassuming her own position at this final step has at least two implications.

The first implication is that the judgment of the judge is not identical with the reasonable person's perspective adopted at the second stage. Rather than reflecting the reasonable person's perspective itself, at this third stage, the judge calibrates the reasonable person's perspective by reference to any applicable legal norms. Such legal norms may regulate the concept's application in both concrete and more general senses. Concretely, legal norms often regulate and limit the way in which the reasonable person standard can be applied. Customary practices in certain fields (e.g. in the financial or trade sectors) and professional codes of conduct (e.g. in a medical or engineering context) can inform the way in which the reasonable person standard is calibrated when applied to specialists. Apart from such specialised standards, judges must construe the reasonable person in relation to generally applicable legal norms. When military commanders apply the standard of the reasonable person to the situations discussed in Chapter 5 the scope of permissible interpretations of this standard is always limited by the general provisions of the law of international armed conflict. Whatever insights a judge may have gained at the second stage, a reasonable military commander's actions must, by law, conform to the requirement that attacks be both proportionate and necessary to the achievement of a military objective. In *Jackson*, discussed in Chapter 4, Tredgold CJ explained that one of the reasons why he equated the reasonable person with an Englishman was that, in his view, the applicable statute did not allow for any alternative interpretation.[49] This passage of the *Jackson* decision is interesting, because it seems to reveal that Tredgold CJ himself noticed a dissonance between the insights he gained at the second stage and the legal requirements with which he was confronted at the third.

In a more general sense, a judge must also calibrate the reasonable person's perspective by reference to previous judicial pronouncements. In each of the cases discussed in this book, the judges related their interpretation of the reasonable person to the interpretations of others; they did it sometimes with approval, sometimes with disapproval, sometimes by explicitly inviting future courts to revisit questions raised in particular cases. In *Muddarubba*,[50] to mention just one example, Kriewaldt J declared that he would continue to apply the reasonable person standard in the manner he deemed preferable 'until put right by a higher court'.[51] Indeed, the common law's sheer number of judicial assessments across time and space offers a rich and dense corpus of decisions within which each new reasonable person analysis must situate itself.

49 *Attorney-General for Nyasaland v Jackson* [1957] R & NLR 443 (n 13), 448.
50 *R v Aboriginal Muddarubba* [1956] (1) NTJ 317 (Supreme Court of the Northern Territory of Australia).
51 Ibid., 322 (Kriewaldt J).

In this way the reasonable person standard 'allows a legal community to engage in collective inquiry over time', and this enquiry 'slowly and casuistically' generates 'insight as to what values, vulnerabilities and interests might be at stake'[52] in a particular case. For this reason, it is not surprising that the figure of the reasonable person has enjoyed a particularly enduring existence within the family of common law jurisdictions grounded so firmly in the belief in the casuistic administration of justice.

The existence of these legal limitations on the range of permissible interpretations of the perspective of the reasonable person means that the concept is less vulnerable to one of the core criticisms raised by sentimental Enlightenment sceptics. This criticism relates to the fact that empathetic perspective taking can lead to a diversity of potentially contradictory assessments of a given situation,[53] whereas adherents of the rational variant of Enlightenment[54] 'can derive a single set of authoritative standards from a single universal faculty of reason'.[55] The different episodes of the reasonable person's biography confirm that the standard does indeed manifest itself in different ways, depending on time and space. But in legal contexts – unlike in moral philosophy – the operation of the reasonable person concept is conditioned by the legal norms discussed earlier. As a result, the way in which the identity of a judge can shape the outcome of the same judge's reasoning and the extent to which the concept can adapt to the specific context in which it is applied are limited.

The second crucial implication of the fact that the judge passes judgment at the third stage by re-assuming her own position is that the reasonable person never speaks for themselves. Ordinarily, judgments portray the view of the reasonable person in terms that suggest that they represent the outcome of the second step, namely that the judicial pronouncement of the reasonable person's perspective reflects the reasonable person's perspective. But, as we have seen, this is not the case. The reasonable person's perspective – its voice, its views, its thoughts – are always mediated by a human judge, and the process of mediating, calibrating and assessing the perspective of the standard is necessarily informed by the judge's identity. As a result, any judicial account of the reasonable person is but an imperfect representation of its perspective, which can vary from judge to judge, from courtroom to courtroom and from epoch to epoch. In this way the standard is inherently contingent, in the sense that no statement about the reasonable person can ever claim absolute validity. This immunises the concept against hegemonic instrumentalization. Any pronouncement as to what the reasonable person may or may not do must always be seen in its specific context and with due appreciation of the fact that

[52] Del Mar (n 12), 360.
[53] J. Goudkamp and P. Cane, *Atiyah's Accidents, Compensation and the Law* (9th ed., Cambridge University Press 2018) 30.
[54] Frazer (n 5), 142–4. [55] Ibid., 13.

the reasonable person itself never speaks. The reasonable person is co-constituted and co-owned by all participants in the legal process. This means that the standard can be used to identify as justified, defensible, plausible or legal a wide range of behaviour. For this reason, it can come across as an inherently relativistic standard. But its relative nature is limited by its core commitment to respecting and protecting other perspectives. The standard cannot be used for purposes that violate this most fundamental aspect of the concept's rationale.

One may find the reasonable person's flexible characteristics, ever-changing appearance and unsteady nature dissatisfying. One may have hoped that the reasonable person's first biography would offer more concrete information about who this person actually is. But, as I tried to show throughout this book, the reasonable person's ability to assist in the making of judgments in a meaningful manner rests precisely on the character's indeterminate nature. The character's indeterminate nature means that the standard must always be applied afresh to every situation it encounters. Understood in this way, the standard protects legal analysis from petrification and prevents a judge's preconceived notions of how things are or should be from unduly influencing the judgment. Ultimately, the standard's relative indeterminacy is the cost of a concept that bridges the gap between legal norms and their application to concrete situations, between law's normative image of human beings and their actual, empirical counterparts. Indeed, it is the standard's relative indeterminacy that allows for the features of the actual human being whose conduct is at issue to shine through the legal template that the law otherwise imposes upon them. And thus, as we approach the end of this biography, we return to the actual human beings whose conduct the reasonable person standard is meant to help assess.

The human is at the heart of the reasonable person concept at every stage of the empathetic perspective-taking process. At the first stage, the perspective of the other, created by the judge, is the perspective of another human that reminds the judge of her own humanity. At the second stage, the perspective adopted is a fundamentally human one, in the sense that the imagined spectator is fallible and imperfect, as opposed to omnipotent and flawless. At the third stage, the perspective of the reasonable person is mediated and communicated by a human judge, which renders any representation of that standard incomplete, contingent and susceptible to critique. Importantly, the standard focuses on the human not just as a singular individual but as an individual embedded within a human collective composed of countless different perspectives on what is right and wrong, lawful and unlawful. The reasonable person never walks alone. The reasonable person is a social character who is interested in others. As we have seen, the concept is frequently applied in practice in a way that violates this rationale. This is why I set out to tell the story of the reasonable person with the aim of showing that, properly applied, this concept has enormous potential to facilitate a more tolerant, inclusive, and human administration of law and justice. Far from facing imminent demise, the reasonable person is poised to play an even more meaningful role in the future. As we witness how our world becomes once again more polarised, the reasonable person's unquestioning acceptance of different perspectives has the potential to facilitate understanding across social, political, cultural, economic and religious contexts – provided that we remember that the reasonable person is always someone else.

Bibliography

Abbott, R., 'The Reasonable Computer: Disrupting the Paradigm of Tort Liability' (2018) 86 George Washington Law Review 1.

Abbott, R., *The Reasonable Robot: Artificial Intelligence and the Law* (Cambridge University Press 2020).

Adams, R.S., 'Power and Proportionality: The Role of Empathy and Ethics on Valuing Excessive Harm' (2019) 80 Air Force Law Review 149.

Adébísí, F., *Decolonisation and Legal Knowledge: Reflections on Power and Possibility* (Bristol University Press 2023).

Alarie, B., 'The Path of the Law: Towards Legal Singularity' (2016) 66 University of Toronto Law Journal 443.

Alderson, C., 'Life and Literary Remains of Baron Alderson' (1859) 9 The Monthly Christian Spectator 206.

Alderson, C., *Selections from the Charges and Other Detached Papers of Baron Alderson* (John W. Parker and Son 1858).

Allott, A.N., 'The Authority of English Decisions in Colonial Courts' (1957) 1 Journal of African Law 23.

Amann, E., *The Omnibus: A Cultural History of Urban Transportation* (Springer Nature 2023).

Anonymous, *The Omnibus: A Satire* (Trubner 1865).

Ardant du Picq, C.J.J.J., *Battle Studies: Ancient and Modern Battle* (Macmillan 1921).

Arendt, H., 'Lectures on Kant's Political Philosophy', in Ronald Beiner (ed.), *Lectures on Kant's Political Philosophy* (University of Chicago Press 1982).

Arendt, H., '*On Revolution* (17th ed., Penguin Books 1990).

Aristotle, *Nicomachean Ethics* (R.C. Bartlett and S.D. Collins trans., University of Chicago Press, 2011).

Aristotle, *Nikomachische Ethik* (F. Dirlmeier ed., 8th ed., Akademie Verlag 1983).

Asante, S.K.B., 'Over a Hundred Years of a National Legal System in Ghana' (1987) 31 Journal of African Law 70.

Assmann, J., *Ma'at: Gerechtigkeit und Unsterblichkeit im Alten Ägypten* (2nd ed., C.H. Beck 2006).

Austin, R.T., 'Better Off with the Reasonable Man Dead, or The Reasonable Man Did the Darndest Things' (1992) 2 Brigham Young University Law Review 479.

Bagehot, W., 'Average Government' (*The Saturday Review*, 29 March 1856), 428.

Bagehot, W., *The English Constitution* (Chapman & Hall 1867).

Bairoch, P., *Cities and Economic Development: From the Dawn of History to the Present* (University of Chicago Press 1988).

Baker, J., *Introduction to English Legal History* (5th ed., Oxford University Press 2019).

Balkin, J.M., 'The Three Laws of Robotics in the Age of Big Data' (2017) 78 Ohio State Law Journal 1217.

Barak-Corren, N., 'Personalization and the Constitution' (*University of Chicago Law Review Online*, 9 March 2022). https://lawreviewblog.uchicago.edu/2022/03/09/bp-barak-corren.

Barnett, K. and Gans, J., *Guilty Pigs: The Weird and Wonderful History of Animal Law* (La Trobe University Press 2022).

Barr, A., 'Google Mistakenly Tags Black People as "Gorillas," Showing Limits of Algorithms' (*Wall Street Journal*, 1 July 2015). www.wsj.com/articles/BL-DGB-42522.

Barrett, J., 'Counter-Conduct and Its Intra-Modern Limits' (2020) 34 Global Society 260.

Bateson, M. (ed.), *Borough Customs, vol. 2* (Seldon Society 1906).

Beard, M., *Woman as a Force in History* (Macmillan 1946).

Bender, L., 'A Lawyer's Primer on Feminist Theory and Tort' (1988) 38 Journal of Legal Education 3.

Bennet, T., *Straffansvar vid atypiska sinnestillstånd* (Norstedts Juridik 2020).

Ben-Shahar, O. and Porat, A., *Personlized Law: Different Rules for Different People* (Oxford University Press 2021).

Benvenisti, E., 'The Legal Battle to Define the Law on Transnational Asymmetric Warfare' (2010) 20 Duke Journal of Comparative & International Law 339.

Benvenuti, P., 'The ICTY Prosecutor and the Review of the NATO Bombing Campaign against the Federal Republic of Yugoslavia' (2001) 12 European Journal of International Law 503.

Birks, P., *The Roman Law of Obligations* (E. Descheemaeker ed., Oxford University Press 2014).

Blackstone, W., *Commentaries on the Laws of England*, vol. 1 (Clarendon 1765).

Blackstone, W., *Commentaries on the Laws of England*, vol. 1 (3rd ed., Clarendon 1768).

Blank, L.R., 'A New Twist on an Old Story: Lawfare and the Mixing of Proportionalities' (2011) 43 Case Western Reserve Journal of International Law 707.

Bloom, A.H., 'Objective Enough: Race Is Relevant to the Reasonable Person in Criminal Procedure' (2023) 19 Stanford Journal of Civil Rights & Civil Liberties 1.

Bloom, P., *Against Empathy: The Case for Rational Compassion* (Random House 2017).

Bohannan, P., 'Ethnography and Comparison in Legal Anthropology', in L. Nader (ed.), *Ethnography and Comparison in Legal Anthropology* (University of California Press 1969).

Bohannan, P., *Justice and Judgment among the Tiv* (Oxford University Press 1968).

Boothby, W.H., *The Law of Targeting* (Oxford University Press 2012).

Bothe, M., 'The Protection of the Civilian Population and NATO Bombing on Yugoslavia: Comments on a Report to the Prosecutor of the ICTY' (2001) 12 European Journal of International Law 531.

Bothe, M., 'Targeting', in A.E. Wall (ed.), *Legal and Ethical Lessons of NATO's Kosovo Campaign*, vol. 78 (Naval War College 2002).

Bourke, V.J., 'The Ethical Role of the Impartial Observer' (1978) 6 Journal of Religious Ethics 279.

Bourke, V.J., 'Rationalism', in D.D. Runes (ed.), *The Dictionary of Philosophy* (Philosophical Library 1951).

Brecht, B., 'Über experimentelles Theater', in B. Brecht, *Ausgewählte Werke in sechs Bänden*, vol. 6 (Suhrkamp 1997).

Brockhaus, F.A. (ed.), 'Omnibus', *Allgemeine deutsche Real-Encyklopädie für die gebildeten Stände: Conversations-Lexikon* (8th ed., Brockhaus 1835).

Brown, B., 'The "Ordinary Man" in Provocation: Anglo-Saxon Attitudes and "Unreasonable Non-Englishmen"' (1964) 13 International and Comparative Law Quarterly 203.

Brunner-Traut, 'Weiterleben der ägyptischen Lebenslehren in den koptischen Apophthegmata am Beispiel des Schweigens', in E., Hornung and O. Keel (eds), *Studien zu altägyptischen Lebenslehren* (Vandenhoeck & Ruprecht 1979).

Busch, C., 'Implementing Personalized Law: Personalized Disclosures in Consumer Law and Data Privacy Law' (2019) 86 University of Chicago Law Review 309.

Butler, J., *The Works of Bishop Butler* (D.E. White ed., University of Rochester Press 2006).

Cahn, N.R., 'Looseness of Legal Language: The Reasonable Woman Standard in Theory and in Practice' (1992) 77 Cornell Law Review 1398.

Calcutta Review, 'Review of: The Letters of Civis on Indian Affairs from 1842-1849 by Henry Russell', *Calcutta Review (XXV/XIII)* (Sanders, Cones and Co. 1850).

Calo, R., 'Robotics and the Lessons of Cyberlaw' (2015) 103 California Law Review 513.

Campbell, T., *Adam Smith's Science of Morals* (Routledge 2012).

Čapek, K., *R.U.R.: Rossum's Universal Robots* (P. Selver and N. Playfair trans., Doubleday, Page 1923).

Čapek, K., 'O Slove Robot' *Lidové noviny* (Prague, 24 December 1933) 12.

Carlsgaard, L.J., 'Reasonable Person and I' (2016) 27 Hastings Women's Law Journal 165.

Casey, A.J. and Niblett, A., 'Self-Driving Laws' (2016) 66 University of Toronto Law Journal 429.

Casey, B., 'Robot Ipsa Loquitur' (2019) 108 Georgetown Law Journal 225.

Castermans, A.G. et al. (eds), *De maatman in het burgerlijk recht* (Kluwer 2008).

Chagal-Feferkorn, K., 'The Reasonable Algorithm' (2018) 2018 Journal of Law, Technology & Policy 111.

Chagal-Feferkorn, K., 'How Can I Tell if My Algorithm Was Reasonable?' (2021) 27 Michigan Technology Law Review 213.

Chamayou, G., *A Theory of the Drone* (J. Lloyd trans., New Press 2015).

Chivanda, C.G., 'The Mashona Rebellion in Oral Tradition: Mazoe District' (University College of Rhodesia 1966).

Chriscoe, J. and Lukasik, L., 'Re-Examining Reasonableness: Negligence Liability in Adult Defendants with Cognitive Disabilities' (2015) 6 Alabama Civil Rights & Civil Liberties Law Review 1.

Cikara, M. et al., 'Their Pain Gives Us Pleasure: How Intergroup Dynamics Shape Empathic Failures and Counter-Empathic Responses' (2014) 55 Journal of Experimental Social Psychology 110.

Clark, W.K., *Waging Modern War: Bosnia, Kosovo, and the Future of Combat* (Public Affairs 2001).

Clarke, B., 'Proportionality in Armed Conflicts: A Principle in Need of Clarification?' (2012) 3 Journal of International Humanitarian Legal Studies 73.

Clarke, B.R., *The Death of the Reasonable Man* (Faculty of Business, Swinburne Institute of Technology 1990).

Coeckelbergh, M., 'Artificial Companions: Empathy and Vulnerability Mirroring in Human-Robot Relations' (2010) 4 Studies in Ethics, Law, and Technology 1.

Coglianese, C., 'Moving Toward Personalized Law' (*The University of Chicago Law Review Online*, 9 March 2022). https://lawreviewblog.uchicago.edu/2022/03/09/bp-coglianese.

Collins, R.K.L., 'Language, History and the Legal Process: A Profile of the Reasonable Man' (1976) 8 Rutgers Camden Law Journal 311.

Colonna, K., 'Autonomous Cars and Tort Liability Note' (2012) 4 Case Western Reserve Journal of Law, Technology and the Internet 81.

Conaghan, J., 'Tort Law and the Feminist Critique of Reason', in A. Bottomley (ed.), *Feminist Perspectives on the Foundational Subjects of Law* (Cavendish Publishing 1996).

Cooper, A.A., *Characteristicks of Men, Manners, Opinions, Times*, vol. 1 (P. Ayres ed., Clarendon 1999).

Cooper, B., *Family Fictions and Family Facts: Harriet Martineau, Adolphe Quetelet and the Population Question in England 1798-1859* (Routledge 2007).

Corder, H., *Judges at Work: The Role and Attitudes of the South African Appellate Judiciary, 1910-1950* (Juta 1984).

Cosgrave, I.M., '"White Lies": Amelia Opie, Fiction, and the Quakers' (University of Exeter 2014).

Cosgrove, I.J., 'The Illusive Reasonable Person: Can Neuroscience Help the Mentally Disabled' (2015) 91 Notre Dame Law Review 421.

Cottrell, J., 'The Functions of the Law of Torts in Africa' (1987) 31 Journal of African Law 161.

Crane, R.S., 'Suggestions Toward A Genealogy of the "Man of Feeling"' (1934) 1 ELH 205.

Crenshaw, K.W., 'Toward a Race-Conscious Pedagogy in Legal Education' (1988) 11 National Black Law Journal 1.

Crouter, R., *Reinhold Niebuhr: On Politics, Religion, and Christian Faith* (Oxford University Press 2010).

Cunneen, M. et al., 'Artificial Driving Intelligence and Moral Agency: Examining the Decision Ontology of Unavoidable Road Traffic Accidents through the Prism of the Trolley Dilemma' (2019) 33 Applied Artificial Intelligence 267.

Dagault, M., 'Bureau des Voitures Dames Blanches Dites Omnibus' (1892) 31 Bulletin de la Sociéte Archéologique de Nantes 116.

Darling, K., 'Extending Legal Protection to Social Robots: The Effects of Anthropomorphism, Empathy, and Violent Behavior towards Robotic Objects', in R. Calo, A.M. Froomkin and I. Kerr (eds), *Robot Law* (Edward Elgar 2016).

Daube, D., *Roman Law: Linguistic, Social and Philosophical Aspects* (Edinburgh University Press 1969).

Davidson, A., 'Personalized Law, Political Power, and the Dangerous Few' (*The University of Chicago Law Review Online*, 9 March 2022). https://lawreviewblog.uchicago.edu/2022/03/09/bp-davidson.

De Vinne, M.J., 'The Reasonable Person as a Living Fossil Evolution' (2010) 37 Litigation 15.

Defense Advanced Research Projects Agency, 'In the Moment (ITM)' (2 March 2022). https://sam.gov/opp/3e904257ba51463d953014fcc6212f98/view.

Defense Advanced Research Projects Agency, 'Developing Algorithms That Make Decisions Aligned with Human Experts' (3 March 2022). www.darpa.mil/news-events/2022-03-03.

Del Mar, M., 'Common Virtue and the Perspectival Imagination: Adam Smith and Common Law Reasoning' (2018) 9 Jurisprudence 58.

Del Mar, M., *Artefacts of Legal Inquiry: The Value of Imagination in Adjudication* (Hart 2020).

Denning, A., *The Due Process of Law* (Oxford University Press 1980).

Dent, C., 'The Reasonable Man, His Nineteenth-Century Siblings, and Their Legacy' (2017) 44 Journal of Law and Society 406.

Déplanche, N., 'From Young People to Young Citizens: The Emergence of a Revolutionary Youth in France, 1788–1790' (2011) 45 Journal of Social History 225.

Devlin, P. et al., 'Report of the Nyasaland Commission of Inquiry' (Colonial Office 1959).

Dillon, J., *The Heirs of Plato: A Study of the Old Academy (347–274 BC)* (Clarendon 2003).

Dinstein, Y., 'Concluding Remarks: LOAC and Attempts to Abuse or Subvert It', in R.A. Pedrozo and D.P. Wollschlaeger (eds), *International Law and the Changing Character of War*, vol. 87 (Naval War College 2011).

Donovan, D.A. and Wildman, S.M., 'Is the Reasonable Man Obsolete: A Critical Perspective on Self-Defense and Provocation' (1981) 14 Loyola of Los Angeles Law Review 435.

Dorsey, G.A., *Man's Own Show: Civilization* (Harper & Brothers 1931).

Dresser, R., 'The Reasonable Person Standard for Research Disclosure: A Reasonable Addition to the Common Rule' (2019) 47 The Journal of Law, Medicine & Ethics 194.

du Bois, W.E.B., *The Souls of Black Folk* (2nd ed., McClurg 1903).

du Plessis, P.J., *Borkowski's Textbook on Roman Law* (Oxford University Press 2020).

Duhaime, L., 'The Reasonable Man: The Law's Ghost God' (*Duhaime.org: Learn Law*, 26 April 2014). https://web.archive.org/web/20170409075430/http://www.duhaime.org/LegalResources/TortPersonalInjury/LawArticle-1378/The-Reasonable-Man–Laws-Ghost-God.aspx.

Duke, G., *Aristotle's Legal Theory: The Politics of Nomos* (Cambridge University Press 2019).

Dyer, G., *War* (Crown 1985).

Eberle, E.J. and Grossfeld, B., 'Law and Poetry' (2006) 11 Roger Williams University Law Review 353.

Ehrenreich, N., 'Pluralist Myths and Powerless Men: The Ideology of Reasonableness in Sexual Harassment Law' (1990) 99 Yale Law Journal 1177.

Eidenmüller, H., 'Why Personalized Law?' (*The University of Chicago Law Review Online*, 9 March 2022). https://lawreviewblog.uchicago.edu/2022/03/09/bp-eidenmuller.

Emiliano, J.B., 'International Law's Invisible Frames Symposium: Inter-Temporality, Legal Fictions and Wartime Emotions in the Investigation of International

Humanitarian Law Violations' (*Opinio Juris*, 25 January 2022). http://opiniojuris.org/2022/01/25/international-laws-invisible-frames-symposium-inter-temporality-legal-fictions-and-wartime-emotions-in-the-investigation-of-international-humanitarian-law-violations.

Encyclopaedia Britannica (ed.), 'Birmingham', *The Encyclopaedia Britannica* (11th ed., Cambridge University Press 1910) 983.

Endicott, T. and Yeung, K., 'The Death of Law? Computationally Personalized Norms and the Rule of Law' (2022) 72 University of Toronto Law Journal 373.

Erman, A., *The Literature of the Ancient Egyptians* (A.M. Blackman trans., Benjamin Blom 1971).

Fenrick, W.J., 'Attacking the Enemy Civilian as a Punishable Offense Symposium: Justice in Cataclysm Criminal Trials in the Wake of Mass Violence' (1997) 7 Duke Journal of Comparative & International Law 539.

Fenrick, W.J., 'Targeting and Proportionality during the NATO Bombing Campaign against Yugoslavia' (2001) 12 European Journal of International Law 489.

Finley, L.M., 'A Break in the Silence: Including Women's Issues in a Torts Course' (1989) 1 Yale Journal of Law and Feminism 41.

Fiori, R., 'The *vir bonus* in Cicero's *De officiis*: Greek Philosophy and Roman Legal Science', in A.M. Shirvindt (ed.), *Aequum ius* (Statut 2014).

Fisher, R., 'Preventing Nuclear War' (1981) 37 Bulletin of the Atomic Scientists 11.

Flexer, G.G., 'From Fire Plug to Fire Hydrant' (1966) 58 Journal (American Water Works Association) 1417.

Foblets, M.-C. and Renteln, A.D. (eds), *Multicultural Jurisprudence: Comparative Perspectives on the Cultural Defense* (Bloomsbury Publishing 2009).

Fontein, J., *The Silence of Great Zimbabwe: Contested Landscapes and the Power of Heritage* (Routledge 2016).

Forell, C. and Matthews, D., *A Law of Her Own: The Reasonable Woman as a Measure of Man* (NYU Press 2001).

Foucault, M., 'What Is Enlightenment?', in P. Rabinow (ed.), *The Foucault Reader* (Pantheon Books 1984).

Franck, T.M., 'On Proportionality of Countermeasures in International Law' (2008) 102 American Journal of International Law 715.

Frankfort, H., *Ancient Egyptian Religion* (Columbia University Press 1948).

Frazer, M.L., *The Enlightenment of Sympathy: Justice and the Moral Sentiments in the Eighteenth Century and Today* (Oxford University Press 2010).

Freitas, R.A., 'End Note: Can the Wheels of Justice Turn for Our Friends in the Mechanical Kingdom?' (1985) 13 Student Lawyer 54.

Fromm, E., *The Anatomy of Human Destructiveness* (Holt, Rinehart and Winston 1973).

Fuchs, T., 'Empathy, Group Identity, and the Mechanisms of Exclusion: An Investigation into the Limits of Empathy' (2019) 38 Topoi 239.

Fyfe, P., *By Accident or Design: Writing the Victorian Metropolis* (Oxford University Press 2015).

Gal, M.S., 'Algorithmic Challenges to Autonomous Choice' (2018) 25 Michigan Technology Law Review 59.

Galinsky, A.D. et al., 'Power and Perspectives Not Taken' (2006) 17 Psychological Science 1068.

Galinsky, A.D., Rucker, D.D. and Magee, J.C., 'Power and Perspective-Taking: A Critical Examination' (2016) 67 Journal of Experimental Social Psychology 91.

Gardner, J., 'The Mysterious Case of the Reasonable Person' (2001) 51 The University of Toronto Law Journal 273.

Gardner, J., 'The Many Faces of the Reasonable Person' (2015) 131 Law Quarterly Review 563.

Garreau, J., 'Bots on the Ground' *The Washington Post Sunday* (Washington, DC, 6 May 2007).

Garvey, S.P., 'Self-Defense and the Mistaken Racist' (2008) 11 New Criminal Law Review 119.

Geiß, R. and Siegrist, M., 'Has the Armed Conflict in Afghanistan Affected the Rules on the Conduct of Hostilities?' (2011) 93 International Review of the Red Cross 11.

Gisel, L., *The Principle of Proportionality in the Rules Governing the Conduct of Hostilities under International Humanitarian Law* (International Committee of the Red Cross 2018).

Gluckman, M., *The Judicial Process among the Barotse of Northern Rhodesia* (Manchester University Press 1955).

Gluckman, M., 'Concepts in the Comparative Study of Tribal Law', in L. Nader (ed.), *Concepts in the Comparative Study of Tribal Law* (University of California Press 1969).

Goanta, C., 'The Ancient Alien: Good Faith as the Facilitator of Personalized Law' (*The University of Chicago Law Review Online*, 9 March 2022). https://lawreviewblog.uchicago.edu/2022/03/09/bp-goanta.

Good, A., 'Folk Models and the Law' (2015) 47 The Journal of Legal Pluralism and Unofficial Law 423.

Goudkamp, J. and Cane, P., *Atiyah's Accidents, Compensation and the Law* (9th ed., Cambridge University Press 2018).

Graves, C.L., *The Life and Letters of Sir George Grove* (Macmillan 1903).

Gray, J., 'Opinions of Assessors in Criminal Trials in East Africa as to Native Custom' (1958) 2 Journal of African Law 5.

Gray, J.G., *The Warriors: Reflections on Men in Battle* (University of Nebraska Press 1999).

Great General Staff of the German Army, *The War Book of the German General Staff* (J.H. Morgan trans., McBridge, Nast & Company 1915).

Green, L.C., '"Civilized" Law and "Primitive" Peoples' (1975) 13 Osgoode Hall Law Journal 233.

Greer, D.S., 'Requiem for the Reasonable Man' (1967) 18 Northern Ireland Legal Quarterly 437.

Grigoleit, H.C., 'Personalized Law: Distinctions and Procedural Observations' (*The University of Chicago Law Review Online*, 9 March 2022). https://lawreviewblog.uchicago.edu/2022/03/09/bp-grigoleit.

Grossman, D., *On Killing: The Psychological Cost of Learning to Kill in War and Society* (Little, Brown 1996).

Grover, J.W., *Old Clapham* (2nd ed., Bachhoffner 1892).

Gruenfeld, D.H. et al., 'Power and the Objectification of Social Targets' (2008) 95 Journal of Personality and Social Psychology 111.

Hacker, P., 'Personalizing EU Private Law: From Disclosures to Nudges and Mandates' (2017) 25 European Review of Private Law 651.

Harlow, K., 'Applying the Reasonable Person Standard to Psychosis: How Tort Unfairly Burdens Adults with Mental Illness' (2007) 68 Ohio State Law Journal 1733.

Hausmaninger, H., 'Diligentia Quam in Suis: A Standard of Contractual Liability from Ancient Roman to Modern Soviet Law' (1985) 18 Cornell International Law Journal 179. DOI: https://doi.org/10.1093/ref:odnb/303.

Hedley, S., 'Alderson, Sir Edward Hall', *Oxford Dictionary of National Biography* (Oxford University Press 2014).

Heighington, W., 'The Lament of the Reasonable Man' (1926) 4 Canadian Bar Review 644.

Henderson, I., *The Contemporary Law of Targeting: Military Objectives, Proportionality and Precautions in Attack under Additional Protocol I* (Brill Nijhoff 2009).

Henderson, I. and Reece, K., 'Proportionality under International Humanitarian Law: The "Reasonable Military Commander" Standard and Reverberating Effects' (2018) 51 Vanderbilt Journal of Transnational Law 835.

Henry, O., 'The Atavism of John Tom Little Bear' (1903) 9 Everybody's Magazine 57.

Herbert, A.P., 'Fardell v. Potts', in *Alan Patrick Herbert, Uncommon Law* (Methuen 1948).

Herbert, A.P., *Uncommon Law* (Methuen 1948).

Herder, J.G., 'On the Change of Taste (1766)', in M.N. Forster (ed.), *Philosophical Writings* (Cambridge University Press 2002).

Herodotus, *Herodotus*, vol. 4 (A.D. Godley trans., William Heinemann 1930).

Herrmann, K., Report from Evacuation Staff to 20th Mountain Army Concerning Evacuation of Northern Norway (25 November 1944). Reproduced as Document NOKW 090 in *United States v Wilhelm List et al.* (Judgment of 19 February 1948), Trials of War Criminals before the Nuerenberg Military Tribunals under Control Council Law No. 10, vol. 11 (1950) 1118–23.

Hinshaw, J. and Stearns, P.N., *Industrialization in the Modern World: From the Industrial Revolution to the Internet*, vol. 1 (ABC-CLIO 2013).

Historical Section of the Foreign Office, *Nyasaland* (Historical Section of the Foreign Office 1920).

Hoffmann, L., 'Anthropomorphic Justice: The Reasonable Man and His Friends' (2010) 29 The Law Teacher 127.

Hogeveen, J., Inzlicht, M. and Obhi, S.S., 'Power Changes How the Brain Responds to Others' (2014) 143 Journal of Experimental Psychology 755.

Holdsworth, W.S., *A History of English Law*, vol. 3 (Methuen 1909).

Holland, J., 'Military Objective and Collateral Damage: Their Relationship and Dynamics' (2004) 7 Yearbook of International Humanitarian Law 35.

Holm, S., Stanton, C. and Bartlett, B., 'A New Argument for No-Fault Compensation in Health Care: The Introduction of Artificial Intelligence Systems' (2021) 29 Health Care Analysis 171.

Holmes, O.W., *The Common Law* (Macmillan 1882).

Holmes, R., *Acts of War: The Behavior of Men in Battle* (Simon & Schuster 1989).

Honsell, H., Mayer-Maly, T. and Selb, W., *Römisches Recht* (4th ed., Springer 1987).

Hookey, J.F., 'The "Clapham Omnibus" in Papua New Guinea', in B.J. Brown (ed.), *Fashion of Law in New Guinea* (Butterworths 1968).

Human Rights Council, 'Human Rights in Palestine and Other Occupied Arab Territories: Report of the United Nations Fact-Finding Mission on the Gaza Conflict', UN DOC A/HRC/12/48.

Human Rights Watch, 'Making the Case: The Dangers of Killer Robots and the Need for a Preemptive Ban' (2016). www.hrw.org/sites/default/files/report_pdf/arms1216_web.pdf.

Hume, D., *Essays: Moral, Political, and Literary* (Lewis 1889).

Hume, D., *A Treatise of Human Nature* (L.A. Selby-Bigge ed., Clarendon 1896).

Hume, D., *An Enquiry Concerning the Principles of Morals: A Critical Edition* (T.L. Beauchamp ed., Clarendon 2006).

Hunt, L., *Inventing Human Rights: A History* (Norton 2007).

Hyde, T., *Ugliness and Judgment: On Architecture in the Public Eye* (Princeton University Press 2019).

Ibbetson, D., *A Historical Introduction to the Law of Obligations* (Oxford University Press 2001).

ICTY Review Committee, 'Final Report to the Prosecutor by the Committee Established to Review the NATO Bombing Campaign against the Federal Republic of Yugoslavia' (2000). www.icty.org/en/press/final-report-prosecutor-committee-established-review-nato-bombing-campaign-against-federal#:~:text=Criticism%20of%20the%20NATO%20bombing,deliberately%20or%20recklessly%20attacked%20the.

Infantino, M. and Wang, W., 'Algorithmic Torts: A Prospective Comparative Overview' (2019) 28 Transnational Law and Contemporary Problems 309.

Institute of Medicine, *To Err Is Human: Building a Safer Health System* (National Academies Press 2000).

International Law Association's Study Group on the Conduct of Hostilities in the 21st Century, 'The Conduct of Hostilities and International Humanitarian Law: Challenges of 21st Century Warfare' (2017) 93 International Law Studies 322.

International Military Tribunal at Nuremberg, *Trial of the Major War Criminals before the International Military Tribunal (Proceedings 20 February 1946–7 March 1946)*, vol. 8 (International Military Tribunal at Nuremberg 1947).

Israeli, S., 'Chapter Four of the Wisdom Book of Amenemope', in S. Israelit-Groll (ed.), *Studies in Egyptology*, vol. 1 (Magnes Press 1990).

Jackson, A.E. and Sidoli del Ceno, J., 'Privacy, Participation and the City', in N.M. Davidson and G. Tewari (eds), *Global Perspectives in Urban Law: The Legal Power of Cities* (Routledge 2019).

Jackson, B.W., 'Artificial Intelligence and the Fog of Innovation: A Deep-Dive on Governance and the Liability of Autonomous Systems' (2018) 35 Santa Clara High Technology Law Journal 35.

Jaeger, C.B., 'The Empirical Reasonable Person' (2020) 72 Alabama Law Review 887.

Jansen, N., 'Deliktsrecht: Allgemeines und lex Aquilia', *Handwörterbuch des Europäischen Privatrechts* (Max Planck Institute for Comparative Public Law and International Law 2009). https://hwb-eup2009.mpipriv.de.

Jasanoff, S., *The Ethics of Invention: Technology and the Human Future* (Norton 2016).

Jeutner, V., *Irresolvable Norm Conflicts in International Law: The Concept of a Legal Dilemma* (Oxford University Press 2017).

Jewel, L., 'Does the Reasonable Man Have Obsessive Compulsive Disorder?' (2019) 54 Wake Forest Law Review 1049.

Jodl, A., Teletype, dated 28 October 1944, from Chief of the Operations Staff of the German Armed Forces High Command to Armed Forces Commander in Chief,

Norway Concerning the Evacuation of Northern Norway. Reproduced as Document PS 754 in *United States v Wilhelm List et al.* (Judgment of 19 February 1948), Trials of War Criminals before the Nuernberg Military Tribunals under Control Council Law No. 10, vol. 11 (1950) 836.

Johansen, S.R., *The Military Commander's Necessity: The Law of Armed Conflict and Its Limits* (Cambridge University Press 2019).

Johnson, S., 'The Dignity and Usefulness of Biography (13 October 1750)', *The Rambler*, vol. 2 (J. Payne 1752).

Jones, J.W., *The Law and Legal Theory of the Greeks* (Clarendon 1956).

Jones, W., *An Essay on the Law of Bailments* (Charles Dilly 1781).

Kant, I., 'Beantwortung der Frage: Was ist Aufklärung?' (1784) Berlinische Monatsschrift 481.

Kapnoullas, S. and Clarke, B., 'The Legal Regulation of Comparative Advertising: Old Game, New Rules' (1995) 11 Queensland University of Technology Law Journal 7.

Karenga, M., *Maat, the Moral Ideal in Ancient Egypt: A Study in Classical African Ethics* (Routledge 2004).

Karnow, C.E.A., 'The Application of Traditional Tort Theory to Embodied Machine Intelligence', in R. Calo, A.M. Froomkin and I. Kerr (eds), *Robot Law* (Edward Elgar 2016).

Kaser, M., *Das römische Privatrecht: Erster Abschnitt* (C.H. Beck 1955).

Kaser, M., *Das römische Privatrecht: Zweiter Abschnitt* (C.H. Beck 1975).

Kelley, P.J. and Wendt, L.A., 'What Judges Tell Juries about Negligence: A Review of Pattern Jury Instructions' (2002) 77 Chicago-Kent Law Review 587.

Kelly, G., 'Opie [Née Alderson], Amelia', *Oxford Dictionary of National Biography* (Oxford University Press 2004).

Keltner, D., *The Power Paradox: How We Gain and Lose Influence* (Penguin 2016).

Keltner, D., Gruenfeld, D.H. and Anderson, C., 'Power, Approach, and Inhibition' (2003) 110 Psychological Review 265.

Kemp Allen, C., 'The Judge as Man of the World' (1930) 46 Law Quarterly Review 151.

Kennedy, C., '"Ungovernable Feelings and Passions": Common Sense Philosophy and Mental State Defences in Nineteenth Century Scotland' (2016) 20 Edinburgh Law Review 285.

Kaser, M., 'Declaring Crimes' (2017) 37 Oxford Journal of Legal Studies 741.

Kenny, A., *Freewill and Responsibility* (Routledge 1978).

Kent, C.A., 'Century Club', *Oxford Dictionary of National Biography* (Oxford University Press 2006).

Kierkegaard, S., *Kierkegaard's Writings, vol. 2: The Concept of Irony, with Continual Reference to Socrates/Notes of Schelling's Berlin Lectures* (H.V. Hong and E.H. Hong eds, Princeton University Press 1989).

Klass, G., 'Tailoring ex machina: Perspectives on Personalized Law' (*The University of Chicago Law Review Online*, 9 March 2022). https://lawreviewblog.uchicago.edu/2022/03/09/bp-klass.

Kordi, J.H., 'Personalized Enfranchisement' (*The University of Chicago Law Review Online*, 9 March 2022). https://lawreviewblog.uchicago.edu/2022/03/09/bp-kordi.

Kteily, N.S. and Bruneau, E., 'Darker Demons of Our Nature: The Need to (Re)Focus Attention on Blatant Forms of Dehumanization' (2017) 26 Current Directions in Psychological Science 487.

Kunkel, W., 'Diligentia' (1925) 45 Zeitschrift der Savigny-Stiftung für Rechtsgeschichte: Romanistische Abteilung 266.

Kymlicka, W., Lernestedt, C. and Matravers, M., *Criminal Law and Cultural Diversity* (Oxford University Press 2014).

Lange, H.O. (ed.), *Das Weisheitsbuch des Amenemope aus dem Papyrus 10, 474 des British Museum* (Bianco Luno 1925).

Lau, J., 'Google Maps 101: How AI Helps Predict Traffic and Determine Routes' (Google, 3 September 2020). https://blog.google/products/maps/google-maps-101-how-ai-helps-predict-traffic-and-determine-routes.

Laursen, A., 'NATO, the War over Kosovo, and the ICTY Investigation' (2002) 17 American University International Law Review 765.

Law School Outline Songs, 'Duty of Reasonable Care' (2015). https://soundcloud.com/onel-8/duty-of-reasonable-care.

Leechman, W., 'Preface', in F. Hutcheson, *A System of Moral Philosophy, in Three Books*, vol. 1 (A Millar 1755).

Lemley, M.A. and Casey, B., 'Remedies for Robots' (2019) 86 University of Chicago Law Review 1311.

Lenta, P., 'The Tikoloshe and the Reasonable Man: Transgressing South African Legal Fictions' (2004) 16 Law and Literature 353.

Levin, S. and Wong, J.C., 'Self-Driving Uber Kills Arizona Woman in First Fatal Crash Involving Pedestrian' (*The Guardian*, 19 March 2018).

Lichtheim, M., *Ancient Egyptian Literature, vol. 1: The Old and Middle Kingdoms* (University of California Press 1975).

Lichtheim, M., *Ancient Egyptian Literature, vol. 2: The New Kingdom* (University of California Press 1976).

Lichtheim, M., *Moral Values in Ancient Egypt* (Vandenhoeck & Ruprecht 1997).

Lieblich, E. and Benvenisti, E., 'The Obligation to Exercise Discretion in Warfare: Why Autonomous Weapon Systems Are Unlawful', in N. Bhuta et al. (eds), *Autonomous Weapons Systems: Law, Ethics, Policy* (Cambridge University Press 2016).

Lior, A., 'The AI Accident Network: Artificial Intelligence Liability Meets Network Theory' (2021) 95 Tulane Law Review 1103.

Livingstone, D., *Dr Livingstone's Cambridge Lectures* (W. Monk ed., Deighton, Bell and Co 1858).

Livingstone, D., *Zambezi Expedition of David Livingstone 1858–1863*, vol. 2 (J.P.R. Wallis ed., Chatto & Windus 1956).

Llewellyn, K.N., 'A Realistic Jurisprudence: The Next Step' (1930) 30 Columbia Law Review 431.

Lobban, M., 'Common Law Reasoning and the Foundations of Modern Private Law' (2007) 32 Australian Journal of Legal Philosophy 39.

Lovelace, W.K.-N., *The Agricultural Statistics of France* (Batten 1848).

Luban, D., 'Military Necessity and the Cultures of Military Law' (2013) 26 Leiden Journal of International Law 315.

Malden, H.E., 'Parishes: Clapham', in H.E. Malden (ed.), *A History of the County of Surrey, vol. 4* (Victoria County History 1912).

Malinowska, J.K., 'What Does It Mean to Empathise with a Robot?' (2021) 31 Minds and Machines 361.

Mallison, W.T. and Mallison, S.V., 'The Juridical Status of Irregular Combatants under the International Humanitarian Law of Armed Conflict' (1977) 9 Case Western Reserve Journal of International Law 39.

Man, S.W. and Wai, C.Y., 'Whose Rule of Law? Rethinking Post-Colonial Legal Culture in Hong Kong' (1998) 7 Social & Legal Studies 147.

Manley, G., 'Central England Temperatures: Monthly Means 1659 to 1973' (1974) 100 Quarterly Journal of the Royal Meteorological Society 389.

Marsack, C.C., 'Provocation in Trials for Murder' (1959) Criminal Law Review 697.

Marshall, S.L.A., *Men Against Fire: The Problem of Battle Command in Future War* (Peter Smith 1978).

Martin, R., 'A Feminist View of the Reasonable Man: An Alternative Approach to Liability in Negligence for Personal Injury' (1994) 23 Anglo-American Law Review 334.

Maxwell Fyfe, D., 'Speech by the Lord High Chancellor of Great Britain (1 July 1955)' (1956) Rhodesia and Nyasaland Law Reports ii.

Mayer, J.I., 'Implementing Personalized Negligence Law' (*The University of Chicago Law Review Online*, 9 March 2022). https://lawreviewblog.uchicago.edu/2022/03/09/bp-mayer.

Mayson, S.G., 'But What Is Personalized Law?' (*The University of Chicago Law Review Online*, 9 March 2022). https://lawreviewblog.uchicago.edu/2022/03/09/bp-mayson.

McGinnis, J. and Wasick, S., 'Law's Algorithm' (2015) 66 Florida Law Review 991.

McLaughlin, R., 'The Law of Armed Conflict and International Human Rights Law: Some Paradigmatic Differences and Operational Implications' (2010) 13 Yearbook of International Humanitarian Law 213.

Mellinkoff, D., 'Reasonable Man', in D. Mellinkoff (ed.), *Mellinkoff's Dictionary of American Legal Usage* (Wipf and Stock Publishers 1992).

Mendelssohn, M., 'Ueber die Frage: was heißt aufklären?' (1784) Berlinische Monatsschrift 193.

Merriam, J.J., 'Affirmative Target Identification: Operationalizing the Principle of Distinction for US Warfighters' (2016) 56 Virginia Journal of International Law 83.

Merry, A.F., 'How Does the Law Recognize and Deal with Medical Errors?' (2009) 102 Journal of the Royal Society of Medicine 265.

Miller, A.D. and Perry, R., 'The Reasonable Person' (2012) 87 New York University Law Review 323.

Ministry of Foreign Affairs (Israel), 'The Operation in Gaza: Factual and Legal Aspects' (2009). www.gov.il/en/departments/general/the-operation-in-gaza-factual-and-legal-aspects.

Misselhorn, C., 'Empathy with Inanimate Objects and the Uncanny Valley' (2009) 19 Minds and Machines 345.

Modisane, W.B., *Blame Me on History* (Donker 1986).

Möller, G., 'Das Amtsabzeichen des Oberrichters in der Spätzeit' (1920) 56 Zeitschrift für Ägyptische Sprache und Altertumskunde 67.

Montgomery, T., 'Legal Perspective from the EUCOM Targeting Cell', in A.E. Wall (ed.), *Legal and Ethical Lessons of NATO's Kosovo Campaign*, vol. 78 (Naval War College 2002).

Moore, H.C., *Omnibuses and Cabs: Their Origin and History* (Chapman & Hall 1902).

Moran, M., *Rethinking the Reasonable Person: An Egalitarian Reconstruction of the Objective Standard* (Oxford University Press 2003).

Morenz, S., *Egyptian Religion* (A.E. Keep trans., Cornell University Press 1973).

Moyn, S., 'Empathy in History, Empathizing with Humanity' (2006) 45 History and Theory 397.

Musée des Transports, 'Histoire générale des transports: Stanislas Baudry et les omnibus de Nantes en 1825'. https://amtuir.org/03_htu_generale/htu_1_avant_1870/htu_1.htm#top.

Nader, L., 'Introduction', in L. Nader (ed.), *Ethnography and Comparison in Legal Anthropology* (University of California Press 1969).

Ndungu, N.S., *Key Note Address (Law, Justice and Development Week 2015)* (World Bank 2015). https://thedocs.worldbank.org/en/doc/611001447980399421-0260022015/original/KeynotebyJusticeNjokiNdunguLawJusticeandDevelopmentWeek2015.pdf.

Newton, M.A., 'Modern Military Necessity: The Role and Relevance of Military Lawyers Symposium' (2007) 12 Roger Williams University Law Review 877.

Niebuhr, R., *Moral Man and Immoral Society: A Study in Ethics and Politics* (Charles Scribner's Sons 1932).

Nietzsche, F., *On the Genealogy of Morals* (W. Kaufmann and R.J. Hollingdale trans., Vintage Books 1989).

Noll, G., 'Analogy at War: Proportionality, Equality and the Law of Targeting' (2012) 43 Netherlands Yearbook of International Law 205.

Norrie, A., 'From Criminal Law to Legal Theory: The Mysterious Case of the Reasonable Glue Sniffer' (2002) 65 The Modern Law Review 538.

Nuremberg Trial Day 70 (1946) Sir David Maxwell-Fyfe: Criminal Organizations (1946). www.youtube.com/watch?v=mzJvtj6odwI.

Nussbaum, M.C., 'Poets as Judges: Judicial Rhetoric and the Literary Imagination' (1995) 62 The University of Chicago Law Review 1477.

O'Brien, W.V., *The Yearbook of World Polity* (Praeger 1957).

O'Brien, W.V., 'Law of War, Command Responsibility and Vietnam, The' (1972) 60 Georgetown Law Journal 605.

Office of the Judge Advocate General (Canada), *Joint Doctrine Manual: Law of Armed Conflict at the Tactical and Operational Levels, B-GJ-005-104/FP-021*. www.fichl.org/fileadmin/_migrated/content_uploads/Canadian_LOAC_Manual_2001_English.pdf.

Office of the Prosecutor of the International Criminal Court, *Situation in the Republic of Korea: Article 5 Report* (International Criminal Court 2014). www.icc-cpi.int/sites/default/files/iccdocs/otp/SAS-KOR-Article-5-Public-Report-ENG-05Jun2014.pdf.

Ogorek, R., *Untersuchungen zur Entwicklung der Gefährdungshaftung im 19. Jahrhundert* (Böhlau 1975).

Olásolo, H., *Unlawful Attacks in Combat Situations: From the ICTY's Case Law to the Rome Statute* (Brill Nijhoff 2008).

Opie, A., *Valentine's Eve* (Longman 1816).

Opie, A., *The Quaker, and the Young Man of the World. A Tale of Trials* (Longman 1818).

Opie, A., *The Father and Daughter with Dangers of Coquetry* (K. Shelley and J.B. Pierce eds, Broadview Press 2003).

Opie, A. and Brightwell, C.L., *Memorials of the Life of Amelia Opie: Selected and Arranged from Her Letters, Diaries, and Other Manuscripts* (Fletcher and Alexander 1854).

O'Regan, R.S., 'Ordinary Men and Provocation in Papua and New Guinea' (1972) 21 The International and Comparative Law Quarterly 551.

O'Reilly, H., 'The Trial of the Reasonable Man' (*Trinity College Law Review (TCLR) | Trinity College Dublin*, 22 November 2017). https://trinitycollegelawreview.org/the-trial-of-the-reasonable-man.

Outram, D., *The Enlightenment* (Cambridge University Press 2013).

Oxford English Dictionary Online, s.v. 'Man' (2023). DOI: https://doi.org/10.1093/OED/1034670116.

Oxford English Dictionary Online, s.v. 'Omnibus' (2023). https://doi.org/10.1093/OED/5735743028.

Oz-Salzberger, F., 'Enlightenment, National Enlightenments, and Translation', *The Routledge Companion to Eighteenth Century Philosophy* (Routledge 2017).

Pagallo, U., *The Laws of Robots: Crimes, Contracts, and Torts* (Springer 2013).

Parker, W., 'The Reasonable Person: A Gendered Concept?' (1993) 23 Victoria University of Wellington Law Review 105.

Parks, W.H., 'Command Responsibility For War Crimes' (1973) 62 Military Law Review 1.

Pengilley, W., *Advertising and the Trade Practices Act* (CCH Australia 1981).

Phillips, A., 'When Culture Means Gender: Issues of Cultural Defence in the English Courts' (2003) 66 The Modern Law Review 510.

Picton, M. et al. (eds), *The Crown Court Compendium: Part I (Jury and Trial Management and Summing Up)* (Judicial College 2021).

Piggott, F.T., 'The Reasonable Man at Common Law' (1889) 14 Law Magazine and Law Review 314.

Price, N.W., 'Black-Box Medicine' (2015) 28 Harvard Journal of Law & Technology 419.

Price, T., 'The Meaning of Mang'anja' (1963) 16 The Nyasaland Journal 74.

Prichard, M.J., 'Trespass, Case and the Rule in Williams v. Holland' (1964) 22 The Cambridge Law Journal 234.

Prinz, J., 'Against Empathy' (2011) 49 The Southern Journal of Philosophy 214.

Prosser, W.L., *The Law of Torts* (4th ed., West Publishing 1971).

Protasio, M.R.M., 'The Reasonable Man in the 21st Century' (Tilburg University 2018).

Punch, 'The Voice of the Omnibus' (1855) 28 *Punch* 179.

Quack, J.F., *Die Lehren des Ani: Ein neuägyptischer Weisheitstext in seinem kulturellen Umfeld* (Vandenhoeck & Ruprecht 1994).

Quetelet, A., *A Treatise on Man and the Development of His Faculties* (R. Knox trans., William and Robert Chambers 1842).

Rabin, R.L., 'The Historical Development of the Fault Principle: A Reinterpretation Symposium: Modern Tort Theory' (1980) 15 Georgia Law Review 925.

Radbruch, G., 'Law's Image of the Human' (2020) 40 Oxford Journal of Legal Studies 667.

Ramsey, P., *Love and Society: Essays in the Ethics of Paul Ramsey* (J. Johnson and D. Smith eds, American Academy of Religion 1974).

Raphael, D.D., *The Impartial Spectator: Adam Smith's Moral Philosophy* (Clarendon 2007).

Read, D., *England, 1868-1914: The Age of Urban Democracy* (Longman 1979).

Remarque, E.M., *All Quiet on the Western Front* (A.W. Wheen trans., G.P. Putnam's Sons 1929).

Rendulic, L., *Soldat in stürzenden Reichen* (Damm Verlag 1965).

Reynolds, O.M., Jr, 'The Reasonable Man of Negligence Law: A Health Report on the Odious Creature' (1970) 23 Oklahoma Law Review 410.

Richards, N.M. and Smart, W.D., 'How Should the Law Think about Robots?', in R. Calo, A.M. Froomkin and I. Kerr (eds), *Robot Law* (Edward Elgar 2016).

Robertson, I.H., 'How Power Affects the Brain' (2013) 26 The Psychologist 186.

Robinson, D., *Estrangement and the Somatics of Literature: Tolstoy, Shklovsky, Brecht* (Johns Hopkins University Press 2008).

Ross, A.C., *David Livingstone: Mission and Empire* (Hambledon Continuum 2006).

Runciman, W.B., Merry, A.F. and Tito, F., 'Error, Blame, and the Law in Health Care: An Antipodean Perspective' (2003) 138 Annals of Internal Medicine 974.

Rutherford, I., *Greco-Egyptian Interactions: Literature, Translation, and Culture, 500 BC–AD 300* (Oxford University Press 2016).

Saab, A., 'Emotions and International Law' (2021) 10 ESIL Reflections.

Salib, P.N., 'Complex Algorithmic Law' (*The University of Chicago Law Review Online*, 9 March 2022). https://lawreviewblog.uchicago.edu/2022/03/09/bp-salib.

Saller, R.P., 'Pater Familias, Mater Familias, and the Gendered Semantics of the Roman Household' (1999) 94 Classical Philology 182.

Saltman, M., *The Demise of the Reasonable Man: A Cross-Cultural Study of a Legal Concept* (Transaction Publishers 1991).

Sapir, E., 'The Status of Linguistics as a Science' (1929) 5 Language 207.

Saunders, A., 'Clapham, Please' (n.d.) www.cartoonstock.com/cartoonists/alansaunders.

Schaff, A., *Language and Cognition* (McGraw-Hill 1973).

Scholz, L.H., 'Two Cheers for Cyborgs' (*The University of Chicago Law Review Online*, 9 March 2022). https://lawreviewblog.uchicago.edu/2022/03/09/bp-scholz.

Schottlaender, R., 'Der aristotelische "spoudaios"' (1980) 34 Zeitschrift für philosophische Forschung 385.

Schwartz, E., *Ethik der Griechen* (KF Koehler 1951).

Scott, H., 'The History of Foreseeability' (2019) 72 Current Legal Problems 287.

Seidman, R.B., 'Mens Rea and the Reasonable African: The Pre-Scientific World-View and Mistake of Fact' (1966) 15 The International and Comparative Law Quarterly 1135.

Selbst, A.D., 'Negligence and AI's Human Users' (2020) 100 Boston University Law Review 1315.

Shajobi-Ibikunle, G., 'The Concept of a Reasonable Man in Tort Law: A Need for a Paradigm Shift?' (2018) 2 Kampala International University Law Journal 267.

Shephard, J.B., *Land of the Tikoloshe* (Longmans Green 1955).

Sheppard, B., 'The Reasonableness Machine' (2021) 62 Boston College Law Review 2259.

Shirun-Grumach, I., 'Bemerkungen zu Rhythmus, Form und Inhalt in der Weisheit', in E. Hornung and O. Keel (eds), *Studien zu altägyptischen Lebenslehren* (Vandenhoeck & Ruprecht 1979).

Shoenfelt, E.L., Maue, A.E. and Nelson, J., 'Reasonable Person versus Reasonable Woman: Does It Matter?' (2002) 10 Journal of Gender, Social Policy & the Law 633.

Siedentop, L., *Inventing the Individual: The Origins of Western Liberalism* (Harvard University Press 2014).

Sloane, R.D., 'Puzzles of Proportion and the "Reasonable Military Commander": Reflections on the Law, Ethics, and Geopolitics of Proportionality' (2015) 6 Harvard National Security Journal 299.

Smart, C., *Feminism and the Power of Law* (Routledge 1989).

Smiles, S., *The Life of George Stephenson, Railway Engineer* (John Murray 1859).

Smith, A., *The Theory of Moral Sentiments* (D.D. Raphael and A.L. Macfie eds, Clarendon 1976).

Smith, A., *Lectures on Jurisprudence* (R.L. Meek, D.D. Raphael and P.G. Stein eds, Clarendon 1978).

Smith, A., *The Correspondence of Adam Smith* (E.C. Mossner and I.S. Ross eds, Oxford University Press 1987).

Sobeloff, S.E., 'Insanity and the Criminal Law: From McNaghten to Durham, and Beyond' (1955) 41 American Bar Association Journal 793.

Sørenes, A., 'Tvangsevakuert Som Ti-Åring' *NRK* (Oslo, 26 October 2014).

Stanley, B., 'Anglican Missionary Societies and Agencies in the Nineteenth Century', in R. Strong (ed.), *The Oxford History of Anglicanism, vol. 3: Partisan Anglicanism and its Global Expansion, 1829–c.1914* (Oxford University Press 2017).

Stein, E., *Zum Problem der Einfühlung* (Buchdruckerei des Waisenhauses 1917).

Stephen, L., 'Anonymous Journalism', in A. King and J. Plunkett (eds), *Popular Print Media, 1820-1900*, vol. 2 (Routledge 2004).

Stern, S., 'R v Jones (1703)', in P. Handler, H. Mares and I. Williams (eds), *Landmark Cases in Criminal Law* (Hart 2017).

Stern, S., 'From Clapham to Salina: Locating the Reasonable Man' (2023) Law & Literature 1.

Stopes, C., *The Sphere of 'Man' in Relation to That of 'Woman' in the Constitution* (Fisher Unwin 1907).

Strozzi-Heckler, R., *In Search of the Warrior Spirit: Teaching Awareness Disciplines to the Green Berets* (North Atlantic Books 2003).

Stueber, K., 'Empathy', in E.N. Zalta (ed.), *The Stanford Encyclopedia of Philosophy* (Stanford University 2019). https://plato.stanford.edu/archives/fall2019/entries/empathy.

Stypulkowski, K., *Der bonus pater familias im klassischen Römischen Recht: Soziales Abbild und Rechtsbegriff* (Dr Kovac Verlag 2017).

Sutherland, K., 'Fictional Economies: Adam Smith, Walter Scott and the Nineteenth-Century Novel' (1987) 54 ELH 97.

Suzuki, Y. et al., 'Measuring Empathy for Human and Robot Hand Pain Using Electroencephalography' (2015) 5 Scientific Reports 1.

Sword, M., 'To Err Is Both Human and Non-Human Comments' (2019) 88 UMKC Law Review [i].

Thompson, J., *British Political Culture and the Idea of 'Public Opinion', 1867–1914* (Cambridge University Press 2013).

Thompson, T.J., 'Lake Malawi, I Presume? David Livingstone, Maps and the "Discovery" of Lake Nyassa in 1859' (2013) 66 The Society of Malawi Journal 1.

Thomson, H.C., *Rhodesia and Its Government* (London, Smith, Elder & Co 1898).

Tobia, K.P., 'How People Judge What Is Reasonable' (2018) 70 Alabama Law Review 293.

Tocqueville, A. de, *Journeys to England and Ireland* (J.P. Mayer ed., G. Lawrence and K.P. Mayer trans., Yale University Press 1958).

Tōge, S., 'Little Child', in *Poems of the Atomic Bomb* (K. Thornber trans., University of Chicago 2012).

Traven, D., *Law and Sentiment in International Politics: Ethics, Emotions, and the Evolution of the Laws of War* (Cambridge University Press 2021).

Trench, C.C., *Men Who Ruled Kenya: The Kenya Administration, 1892–1963* (I B Tauris 1993).

Trew, N., 'Dead Letter Law Arising from Strategic Choices: The Difficulty of Achieving Accountability for the Jus in Bello Rules on Proportionality and Precautions in Attack' (University of Exeter 2017). https://ore.exeter.ac.uk/repository/handle/10871/33168?show=full.

Turner, J., *Robot Rules: Regulating Artificial Intelligence* (Springer 2018).

Twining, W.L., 'Introduction' (1973) 17 Journal of African Law 1.

Twining, W.L., 'Normative and Legal Pluralism: A Global Perspective' (2010) 20 Duke Journal of Comparative & International Law 473.

US Nuremberg Tribunal, 'Transcript for NMT7: Hostage Case' (1948). https://nuremberg.law.harvard.edu/transcripts/4-transcript-for-nmt-7-hostage-case?seq=9486&date=1948-01-22.

USAF JAG Department, *Air Force Operations and the Law* (3rd ed., United States Air Force 2014).

Vallar, W.J., 'Can the Reasonable Person Be Religious? Accommodation and the Common Law' (2021) 107 Virginia Law Review 189.

Vitiello, M., 'Defining the Reasonable Person in the Criminal Law: Fighting the Lernean Hydra Symposium: Who Is the Reasonable Person' (2010) 14 Lewis & Clark Law Review 1435.

von Benda-Beckmann, F., *Rechtspluralismus in Malawi: Geschichtliche Entwicklung und heutige Problematik* (Weltforum Verlag 1970).

von Gierke, O., *Der Entwurf eines bürgerlichen Gesetzbuches und das deutsche Recht* (Duncker & Humblot 1889).

von der Groeben, C., 'Criminal Responsibility of German Soldiers in Afghanistan: The Case of Colonel Klein' (2010) 11 German Law Journal 469.

von Humboldt, W., *On Language* (M. Losonsky ed., P. Heath trans., Cambridge University Press 1999).

von Wartburg, W. (ed.), 'Omnis', in *Französisches etymologisches Wörterbuch (Online)* (Mohr 1948).

Wahlberg, L., 'Skäligt Straffansvar För Misstag Inom Medicinsk Vård Och Behandling' (2019) Nordisk socialrättslig tidskrift 115.

Walker, D.M., *The Oxford Companion to Law* (Clarendon 1980).

Wall, A.E. (ed.), 'Discussion: Reasonable Military Commanders and Reasonable Civilians', in *Legal and Ethical Lessons of NATO's Kosovo Campaign*, vol. 78 (Naval War College 2002).

Wall, A.E. (ed.), *Legal and Ethical Lessons of NATO's Kosovo Campaign*, vol. 78 (Naval War College 2002).

Wallis Budge, E.A., *The Teaching of Amenem Apt Son of Kanekht* (Martin Hopkinson 1924).

Watson, A. (ed.), *The Digest of Justinian*, vols 1–4 (University of Pennsylvania Press 1998).

Webb, E., *Eric Voegelin: Philosopher of History* (University of Washington Press 1981).

West, R., 'Jurisprudence and Gender' (1988) 55 The University of Chicago Law Review 1.

Whittemore, L.A., 'Proportionality Decision Making in Targeting: Heuristics, Cognitive Biases, and the Law' (2015) 7 Harvard National Security Journal 577.

Whorf, B.L., 'Science and Linguistics', in J.B. Carroll (ed.), *Language, Thought, and Reality: Selected Writings of Benjamin Lee Whorf* (MIT Press 1956).

Williams, F.D.G., *SLAM: The Influence of S.L.A. Marshall on the United States Army* (S. Canedy ed., Office of the Command Historian, United States Army Training and Doctrine Command 1999).

Williamson, J.G., *Coping with City Growth During the British Industrial Revolution* (Cambridge University Press 2002).

Winfield, P.H., 'The History of Negligence in the Law of Torts' (1926) 42 Law Quarterly Review 184.

Wall, A.E. (ed.), 'The Myth of Absolute Liability' (1926) 42 Law Quarterly Review 37.

Winick, S., 'The Legend of Monsieur Omnès' (*Folklife Today (Library of Congress)*, 12 February 2020). https://blogs.loc.gov/folklife/2020/02/the-legend-of-monsieur-omnes.

Woolf, V., *The Letters of Virginia Woolf*, vol. 6 (1936–41) (N. Nicolson and J. Trautmann eds, Hogarth Press 1980).

WTM, 'Omnibus' (1879) 11 Notes and Queries 455.

Wu, S.S., 'Autonomous Vehicles, Trolley Problems, and the Law' (2020) 22 Ethics and Information Technology 1.

Yates, E., *Land at Last* (2nd ed., Chapman & Hall 1867).

Young, R., 'Sir William Jones and the Translation of Law in India', in M. Wan (ed.), *Reading the Legal Case* (Routledge 2012).

Zekos, G.I., *Economics and Law of Artificial Intelligence: Finance, Economic Impacts, Risk Management and Governance* (Springer 2021).

Zimmermann, R., *The Law of Obligations: Roman Foundations of the Civilian Tradition* (Oxford University Press 1996).

Zweig, S., 'Geschichte als Dichterin', in his *Die schlaflose Welt: Aufsätze und Vorträge aus den Jahren 1909–1941* (K. Beck ed., S Fischer 1983).

Zwiffelhoffer, L., *Die Figur des Durchschnittssmenschen im Verwaltungsrecht* (Mohr Siebeck 2020).

Index